Seventh Heaven

Aston Villa's Victorious '57 Cup Campaign

Forward By
Stan Crowther

Written By
Colin J Abbott

Published By
abz Publications

8 Abbey Close, St Johns, Worcester, WR2 4HR

Colin J Abbott

All rights reserved.
No part of this publication may be reproduced or copied in any manner without the prior permission in writing of the copyholders

A CIP catalogue record for this book is available from the British Library.

ISBN 978-0-9572151-1-5

Printed and bound in Great Britian by
Jellyfish Solutions, Southampton, Hampshire

Contents

	Page
Intro	5
Foreword	11
57 Cup Trail	
Mud glorious mud 3rd round	23
Cloughie bloody useless 4th round	31
Goodbye Bristol City 5th round	37
Pied piper of Burnley 6th round	43
Billy do be a hero semi-final	55
Que sera, sera (whatever will be, will be)	71
The bells are ringing for claret and blue	89
Seventh Heaven	101
The Men Involved	
Eric Houghton	109
1 goalkeeper Nigel 'Nigger' Sims	115
2 right-back Stan 'the wham' Lynn	119
3 left-back Peter 'Elvis' Aldis	121
4 right-half Stan 'Teezy Weezy' Crowther	125
5 centre-half Jimmy 'Laughing Cavalier' Dugdale	129
6 left-half Pat 'seaweed' Saward	133
7 outside-right Les 'smudge' Smith	135
8 inside-right Jackie 'Little General' Sewell	137
9 centre-forward Billy 'Whooping Cough' Myerscough	141
10 inside-left Johnny 'The Blur' Dixon	143
11 outside-right Peter ' Packy' or 'Mac' McParland	149
Derek 'Doc' Pace	153
Billy Moore	157
Recollections and Memories	161
Thanks and Acknowledgments	193
Bibliography	199
Roll of Honour	203

Introduction

The never-ending story

I was born in 1964, seven years after the famous FA Cup triumph which was still relatively fresh in the minds of supporters who had been starved of success for a generation. Those fans could be excused for hanging on to that 4th May 1957 date a little longer.

I grew up in Worcester, an area where Villa support was very prominent at the time. Ours was a staunch claret and blue household and I took my place as a fourth generation fan. My grandfather Fred had witnessed some of Villa's early achievements, the League title win of 1910 and the FA Cup success of 1913 being the ones he recounted to me most often.

He knew Frank Moss senior, a Villa legend who happened to be the publican at the Grosvenor Arms public house in Worcester during the early 1960s (consuming copious amounts of cider was my grandfather's other favourite pastime). It was through him and my father that I was weaned on the names of their favourites - Joe Bache, 'Happy' Harry Hampton, Charlie Wallace, Billy Walker, Frank Barson, Pongo Waring, Eric Houghton; the list was endless. They would then move into the more modern era for my early history lessons. 'Sailor' Brown and Harry Parkes would get a mention; so would Nigel Sims, Peter McParland, Stan 'the Wham'. It was a shock to the system when I discovered Stan had another name – Lynn.

My grandfather died when I was only seven, but it was due to him that I follow Aston Villa. His passing made me long for more knowledge. He could no longer tell me about those players and the trophies from the Villa glory days, so I had to read the books and find the information for myself. It was a joy to do so (it still is) and what's more I was keeping his memory alive.

Writing this book, which is long overdue, has been a bittersweet experience. Digging deep into my memory bank and researching what I couldn't remember has awakened my passion – if that's possible – for this institution of a football club; not that my wife thinks my devotion to Villa has ever waned! The bitter part is that all those years ago as a very small child I would never have dreamt that Nigel, the two Stans, Jimmy, Pat, Les, Jackie, Billy, Johnny and both Peters would remain well into the 21st century as the last Villa representatives responsible for bringing the FA Cup to Villa Park.

I remember the Cup Finals at the close of the 1960s, by which time most households had televisions; there was no longer the need to sit with an ear pressed against the radio, as Stan Crowther had done as a youngster. Everybody wanted to watch the Cup Final – wives, mothers, sisters – everyone. And now it was possible. It was televised overseas too. The FA Cup final was the most famous sporting event in the world and it was on our screens from getting up until going to bed. There was a full day of entertainment relating to the competing sides. You met the players, you met the celebrity fans, you were reminded how the teams got to Wembley and, later, there was even a Cup Final edition of It's a Knockout. It was sheer, non-stop excitement and how I longed for Villa to be involved!

I remember wishing that the claret and blue on the screen for the 1975 FA Cup Final could have been for the leaders – the original wearers of those fine colours, and not one of the followers, West Ham United. The years came and then they went, and still it never happened. We learned to console ourselves; out would come the books, out would come the programmes, all to remember the last time, a lifetime ago...

The Wembley Empire Stadium had hosted many FA Cup Finals prior to the 1957 competition's conclusion, dating back to the famous White Horse final of 1923. But few, if any had carried such importance as this one. Either way the result went, history would be re-written. If Manchester United were to triumph, as the majority of the press and the public thought, then adding the FA Cup to the Division One title would give them the prestigious 'double.' In winning their latest title they had tasted defeat only six times. Who could possibly match this phenomenally talented side that Matt Busby had been busily assembling and fine-tuning since taking on the managers role back in 1945?

United had been First Division champions in back-to-back seasons, so surely it was a mere formality? All United had to do was to turn up on time. This was a team at their zenith, they had the world at their feet; or so everyone thought.

Standing in United's way were a team who had finished the campaign in mid-table mediocrity, certainly not a side to overawe the Reds. Even by goalkeeper Nigel Sims' own admission, "We were good but not great, fit but not fancy." A year earlier, in fact, Villa had only managed to retain top-flight status on the last day of the season, and that was by virtue of goal average!

There's a twist in all good stories, though, and this was no exception. If Villa were victorious, not only would they become the first side to win the trophy for a record seventh time (Blackburn Rovers and Newcastle United had also held aloft the trophy on six occasions) they would also maintain the distinction of being the last side to lift both the Cup and League title in the same campaign, having won the double in 1897. In all the years from the Football League's inauguration of 1888-89 it had only occurred twice, with Preston North End's 'Invincibles' the groundbreakers in that very first season.

Ironically, this wasn't the first time Villa had found themselves in the position of being able to deny the League champions the glory of lifting the FA Cup. On two previous occasions, 1905 against Newcastle United, and again in 1913 versus Sunderland, they had come up against the champions in the FA Cup Final and on both occasions they had been successful,

Aston Villa Football Club had been formed in 1874 and had waited only 13 years to win their first FA Cup Final in 1887. By this time Villa were playing catch up to teams who had already stated their intent in the famous Football Association competition - huge teams from an era when friendlies and Cup matches were the order of the day before the advent of the Football League in 1888. There were the Royal Engineers, Oxford University, Old Etonians, Wanderers, Clapham Rovers and the Old Carthusians, all of whom sadly disappeared without trace and live on only in the record books. The Wanderers, from London, had appeared and been victorious on each of the five occasions they had reached the FA Cup Final during the 1870s. We will never know what they would have gone on to achieve in the modern game had their financial status not declined in the early 1880s to the point where they were dissolved.

Between Villa's maiden victory of 1887 and their sixth Cup triumph of 1920, they had landed the Division One title on six occasions and been runners-up the same number, including the double triumph of 1897. Villa, who had experienced second tier football for the first time in their illustrious history in the late 1930s were still regarded by the football world at large as a huge club because of their outstanding history of successes and their large fan base. It is well documented that such was the dominance of Aston Villa in that golden era that both West Ham and Burnley adopted the Midlanders' claret and blue colours as their own. Both clubs viewed their preferred new choice of colours not only as a means of inspiration but also to intimidate their opposition.

Blackburn Rovers, one of the 12 original members of the Football League had at one time been the leading side, getting their hands on the FA Cup in three consecutive years – 1884, 1885 and 1886.

The Wanderers' initial record of five wins (equalled by Blackburn in 1891) would stand for the next 42 years, broken only when Villa raised the trophy for the sixth time in 1920. Led by captain Andy Ducat, the Midlanders' defeated Huddersfield Town 1-0 after extra-time in the first Cup Final to be staged at Stamford Bridge.

A seventh victory, and the outright record, was now within the Villa's grasp, although it should really have been realised as far back as 1924, when they had been red-hot favourites against a Newcastle United team who had not only finished below them in the table but had also conceded six goals at Villa Park only five days before the Wembley showdown. But the Magpies also managed to delay history being re-written by defying the odds and scoring twice in the last five minutes to defeat Villa 2-0 in the second final to be played at Wembley. The fact that the Geordies were fined £750 by the Football League for resting all 10 outfield players of their Cup side for the League encounter at Villa Park was of little consolation.

It's fair to say that since the advent of the Premier League interest in the FA Cup has waned considerably. Of the 114 clubs that have played in the Football League since 1960, 77 achieved their record attendance figures in FA Cup-ties; now it's only non-League sides who truly profit from the famous competition. Chairman and directors at top clubs are more interested in protecting their investments, teams in the Premier League need to hang on to that status at all cost. They simply cannot afford to be relegated and lose the huge rewards that inclusion in the top flight brings. Championship sides will also forsake the Cup in an age where promotion is the be-all and end-all. If that means sending out the reserves in FA Cup-ties, so be it.

We are lucky at Aston Villa. Our hierarchy want to keep alive the fine Aston Villa Cup-fighting tradition, I should know – I have heard it from the horse's mouth. On Paul Lambert's appointment as team manager, Paul Faulkner the CEO asked of the new arrival, "If there's one thing you do for us in your time here Paul – win us the FA Cup!"

So don't be surprised that under new leadership we move onward and upward and who knows the claret and blue ribbons of the original wearers may one day soon adorn the famous Football Association Challenge Cup and let the sadly departed members of the class of '57 finally rest in peace.

Colin J. Abbott
October 2012

FOREWORD

BY STAN CROWTHER

I have been asked by Colin a good friend of mine if I would write this foreword for his new book 'Seventh Heaven,' Villa's victorious '57 Cup campaign, it's an honour that he thinks so highly of me. I've known him for a number of years and agreed straightaway. He came to me just before he started Nigel Sims' book for information and quotes and when he gave me a copy of the finished book - I was shocked, what a wonderful job he had done on it.

Colin has this notion that I'm unique – because I'm the only person to have legitimately played for two different teams in the same years FA Cup competition. I had played for Villa against Stoke City in two third round matches before I was surprisingly sold to Manchester United in the aftermath of the Munich airport disaster and went on to play cup games for them including the Final itself. I have seen it written down that a fellow team-mate of mine at United – Ernie Taylor, signed from Blackpool as a result of Munich – also shares the distinction of being cup-tied, but he doesn't. Ernie never actually played for Blackpool in the Cup prior to his transfer to Manchester. For that reason he has asked me to also write a bit about my own career, he constantly tells me and my lad Dean that I remain a mystery to a lot of the supporters.

It is a pleasure to put the foreword to such an inspired book. I loved my time at Villa and the Wembley run that has been so well documented in these pages. It evokes special memories of an unforgettable occasion. Seeing the lad's smiling faces again in these pages, lads who all played their hearts out and all played their own vital roles in Villa's record seventh win, will live with me always.

I was born in Bilston, Staffordshire on 3rd September 1935, the youngest of five children, Alf, George, Lilly, Nell and then myself to Joshua and Florence Crowther. I remember my father playing football when I was very young; he had played football for Moxley All Stars. Moxley is the other side of Bilston and they were a good team apparently. I met a guy many years later in Worcester, I was playing for Rugby Town, we'd played the match and were in a pub having a drink. This guy came up to me and told me he used to live in Bilston and that he'd played football with my father and said how good he had been.

It was due to him that I had aspirations to be a footballer; it's all I ever wanted to do. My parents and I never really spoke of my wanting to be a player but I remember listening to one of the first Cup Finals after the war, it was Charlton versus Derby County, a chap called Chris Duffy scored the goal and Charlton won 1-0. Me and my mother were sat listening to it on a radio my brother had bought after the war, I was sat on the floor with my ear next to the radio and my mother was telling me to move away or I would end up deaf. I said, " Mum one day I'll play in that Final." And I did - I got there twice; if my dad had still been around he would have lived on that for the rest of his life. My brothers came down to the Final, George had been a good player in his time but fancied the birds and booze more, Alf always pulled my leg that George was the better player.

My career in football started as a youth where I turned out for Stonefield, I played there for a few years until I signed up for Bilston at around 17 years of age. I broke into the first team about 11 or 12 months later. Bilston had some great players at the time, Lol Pearson, Arthur Wright ex-West Brom, Arthur Swift and Jack Kirkham who had been the Wolves centre-forward before the war. They were a great team, we played in the Birmingham Combination, it was a tremendous League. I remember playing against Burton Albion twice in about a fortnight and Jackie Stamps was playing for the Albion; he had played for England and also for Derby County in the Cup Final. I had two great games against him. After the second game he came up to me and said, "Young man, if you can play like that against me you can play in the First Division." I thought to myself, "that's a nice recommendation."

I played at Bilston for two years, and I was aware that there was interest from some clubs including Aston Villa as scouts had been down watching me for quite a while. Then suddenly, one night as I turned up from work, Bilston's secretary Bert Richards and the Aston Villa manager Eric Houghton were waiting on the doorstep. I said, "I don't know why your here but you'd better come in." Inside Bert introduced me to Mr Houghton again and said, " Stan, this is the manager of Aston Villa and they would like to sign you on." I said, "OK."

It was a lovely situation. I really did love it at Villa, going to work by bus and on the train – doing my training with the lads before catching the train back so far and then the bus home. The guy I was big pals with at the time was Gordon Lee, he lived at Cannock so we'd get the train together, via Perry Barr and Great Barr and we used to finish up at Walsall. "We'd say 'ta ta,' see you tomorrow." He was the last person I believed could be a manager, he was so quiet and never said anything.

The Villa used to send me a card saying where I would be playing on Saturday and whether it was the third team or the Central League. The third team played a lot of their football at Bournville, they had a proper ground there with stands and such so it was strange going and training at the very same place in preparation for a Cup Final only a year later. Villa didn't have their own training ground so we used to train on different football grounds belonging to works, like the HP sauce ground and places like that. Eric was never seen on the training pitch, he did his job on a Saturday. We always went by coach, you'd spend a couple of hours and then come back. It was normally 10 'til 12 and then you were finished for the day. With a lot of time on my hands I spent many hours in the snooker halls, I really enjoyed playing and got very good at it.

We also trained at Villa Park where Billy Moore took charge, he was the best trainer in the world, and you came away from his training sessions absolutely knackered. It was all stamina work, round the edge of the pitch mostly, or up and down the terraces - but all very hard. He had a system where he made you tired, and I mean really tired and then he'd put someone fresh in front of you and he'd say "Go" and you were off again and had to chase them. All stamina, hardly any ballwork, the groundsman didn't like you going on the pitch as you'd bugger it up. We had a little place, a car park beside the Villa Park offices where we played five-a-side matches. Sometimes players would crash into the brick walls and collapse in a heap; you'd expect them not to get back up. There would be as many as 30 players at the training sessions, there was no specific school, the first team trained together with the second and the third team. It was a great club; the happiest time of my life was at the Villa. I remember Jackie Sewell coming shortly after I had joined; he was a very clever player, a valuable member of the team.

After my first season there as a third team player finished I went down to the Villa ground and Billy Moore and Phil Hunt were there. Billy asked me what I was doing there and I told him I was packing it in, "I'm not going to play next year I'm going to get a job and start going back to work." He asked me why and I told him, "You keep playing me inside-forward and I'm not an inside-forward I'm a right-half (wing-half). If you play me out of position I'll stop." Billy said, "I give you my word." And Billy was good as gold, he kept his word, I started the next four games of the new season in the reserves, the Central League, it was called then, and Bill Baxter got injured – his cartilage – and never played again. Eric put me in the first team, that was against Bolton in 1956 and I had an outstanding game. For the rest of the season I was brilliant. I played in my favoured position right through the season and I got picked three times for the U-23 international team, I remember playing against Alex Young and the 'Scots' at Goodison Park. When I left Villa I played for three more clubs and I never, never played right-half again. They played me left-half, that's why I packed it in! I got so fed up with it, what's the point in going out and doing something you don't want to do, if you don't enjoy it? It's ridiculous, because every time I went out to play right-half, I loved it! I had good ball control, a very good passer of the ball and it was great. I think if I'd stayed right-half for the rest of my career I'd have become a very, very good person and a good memory for a lot of people.

In the Final of 1957 most football supporters thought we'd lose 6-0. On the day that Villa team was marvellous. We were absolutely magic against United - they never had a chance. And yet they were all supposed to be better than us. People said I was the best player on the pitch. There was a well known writer in one of the papers, J. L. Manning, he'd been reporting football for years and years and he said it was the best attacking display he'd ever seen and Stanley Rous - Chairman of the FA at the time - he told Eric Houghton "Crowther was the best player on the pitch." Wonderful memories! In the street where I lived they put up bunting and banners everywhere with 'Well done' and 'Welcome home' messages. Frank McGhee used to write for the Daily Mirror, he said United will be up by at least six goals by the end of the game, and we said if Frank McGhee comes into the dressing room at the end of the match, we'll throw him in the bath, but he never came in. He was alright, but he used to favour all the top teams – just to promote himself. He didn't think about the under dogs or anything at all, like we had no feelings at all and he was quite wrong because we never doubted at that time that we would win.

There was no fear at all, throughout the morning, getting up; having breakfast, there was no doubt that we were going to win. Nobody said, "United, we can't beat them." They all said, "We're going to win this afternoon," because that's the sort of guys they were. They were wonderful guys. It was so easy for United, or so everyone said, it wasn't so easy on the pitch though! We had lots of draws on the way to the final, we got great results, but we didn't fear anyone. Luton were a good side in them days, they had Gordon Turner and Bob Morton. Middlesbrough were a decent side and they had a very good inside-forward Lindy Delapenha, I couldn't handle him, I couldn't stop him at all that afternoon. We had Bristol City up here in the fifth round. We were having the team meeting on the Friday, Eric Houghton was reading it out and he came to John Atyeo the City centre-forward who had played for England. Dugdale was sat there, Eric turns to Jimmy and says, "He'll approach you, he'll never go down your right hand side, always down your left.

So we are one up in the match and Atyeo got the ball just inside our half, Dugdale went towards him keeping him on guard, he went past him on his right hand side, Stan Lynn came in, he went down his right hand side, by then he was about 30-yards out and he hit this ball, 'Simsy' never saw it, the ground was really heavy at the time at Villa, really bad, Atyeo hit this ball with his right foot, it went into the top corner, 'Simsy' went up and never got near it. As he came down I was just getting back into the penalty area, 'Nige' says, "Stan," and I said "what." "No right foot!" That was a really funny moment, you had these times in games where the tension was so great and then somebody breaks it and everybody laughs. Burnley were brilliant in them days, we weren't expected to get a result up there, they were a very strong team, unbelievable, Peter Aldis our left-back put through his own goal and Peter 'Mac' got our equaliser. We beat 'em 2-0 at Villa Park in the replay, we played that day in Birmingham's away kit. We didn't like Birmingham at all and they didn't like us very much. I remember once when we had a Cup Final celebration at the Winter Gardens in Birmingham and some of the Birmingham City players turned up – they got chucked out!

The Albion semi-final was probably one of our worst games but we hung in and went to St Andrews for the replay; won by a lovely goal from Bill Myerscough, he headed a great goal, McParland went past Don Howe, good player Don, played for England, 'Mac' crossed the ball to Bill who headed in from the penalty spot on his knees, straight in the corner, Sanders the goalkeeper never had a prayer. Great goal. That sealed his place in the Final, Poor 'Doc' had played all the other rounds and was a good player, he sacrificed a lot for the team, he wasn't the fittest bloke in the world but he used to put himself about a bit on a Saturday afternoon. We all felt sorry for him but 'Doc' took it marvellously, he never complained or anything – he was a really nice bloke. Billy was a lovely guy too, you couldn't fault either of them. 'Doc' used to live at Cannock and he used to pick Billy up and Roy Pritchard and take them to work at Villa. There was no animosity at all.

I met him one day - many years later - where I worked, it was unbelievable because I had no idea at all he was there. The buying manager phoned me up and said to come to his office, he wanted a word with me. I went down and Derek was sitting there, I hadn't seen him for years, I could have fallen down on the floor it must have been 30 years since I'd seen him, I knew 'Doc' was a salesman but I didn't know he did business with my work – Delta. It was a wonderful place to work, the people were marvellous, and when it came time to go home you didn't want to. All my work colleagues knew of my past but I never made any pretence about it, I never told anyone in my life I had been a footballer but they knew somehow.

I went up to Cannock one night to see Derek who was playing darts in the pub. A girl he introduced me to was getting fed up of being ignored because of the darts match. We got talking and she said she was feeling stuffy so I went outside with her. 'Doc' had his van parked and I knew he never locked it. She said, "Shall we go in here?" I replied, "Yeah if you like." We got down in the van and got down to it and suddenly the door opened and 'Doc' said, "My god, I might have known." You know, it still makes me laugh after all these years – it was funny!

I remember playing up in Yorkshire one winter, I don't know if it was Barnsley or Rotherham, somewhere like that. I recall it was bloody freezing though. We came out for the second-half, rubbing our arms to keep warm and blowing into our hands, 'Pacey' who was in the middle of the pitch turned to me and shouted, "Stan," I yelled back, "What's up 'Doc.'" He pointed down at his nicks and shouted back, "I've got a bloody 'hard on!'"

Sometimes I laugh, sometimes I cry, wonderful people and I'll never ever see again and what a shame. I've got the memories, absolutely, at my age that's all you live on and it's really wonderful because I know if I hadn't got the memories of my time in life I'd have been dead a long time ago, so I'm thankful. I often wonder how these players I've known have lived their life, my only concern is that they've had a happy life like I have. I have the memories and no one can take them away from me. I don't have my two Cup Final medals any more; I sold them many years ago to a Manchester businessman. I had been broken into previously, the top drawer had been emptied out all over the floor and a watch I was presented with by the Aston Villa supporters club - for winning the '57 Cup - was taken. My medals were in a different place and they hadn't found them and I realized how lucky I'd been. I'm not materialistic at all and I decided to let them go as the money could be better used for when I pass away without leaving my two children, Kim and Dean in debt.

In my Villa days I used to socialise with Nigel Sims, most weekends when we came back from an away game 'Nige' and me used to go and have a drink at the Tatten Sykes pub in town. The pub owner was called Bill Hancock, a very well known bloke in Wolverhampton, he used to look after us players and we would be sat having a meal after 10 o' clock at night, we would be there until 2am and then we would both walk home, there weren't many cars in those days. It was a job to live never mind buy a car, but footballers have always been portrayed as something extra, something they shouldn't have been, even in those days because they were working class people. They had a working class environment, a working class job so why people should think any different, I don't know. It's incomparable with what today's player's do now and what they earn, it's ridiculous, how can they spend that much money? I bet all the clubs in the Premier League must be in debt and they'll never recover, if they were a fashion industry or a factory they'd be written off.

I turned up at Villa Park one morning for training, afterwards Eric Houghton said, " We're going for a ride me and you and Jack Scamp." He was a big Union negotiator at the time and he was Sir Jack Scamp. We were going up to Manchester; Eric wanted to watch the United match, this was only a week or so after the Munich disaster. We got half way there and Eric said, "I've got a little surprise for you, we haven't just brought you up to watch the match, Manchester United want to sign you on." I said, "Eric I don't want to sign for United, I'm happy where I am, please turn round and take me back home." He replied, "I can't do that I've got tickets and everything." Anyway we got to the Queens Hotel in Piccadilly, Manchester, and we were having dinner and these guys walked over. I knew the one guy, I never saw the other guy before in my life and that was Jimmy Murphy who was acting manager and the other guy with him was Tom Finney. I'd met Tom on a few occasions, played against him and that; we were talking and Tom said, " I wish I was younger Stan and they'd come after me, I'd have signed right away. He had retired by then. It went on and on and in the end I started weakening, the match kicked off at 7.30 pm and it was twenty to seven at the time and I said, "OK, I'll sign for you," so I signed. It was all a mad, mad rush; we were bundled into a Police car and headed to the United ground. We were speeding - the traffic was just a blur - because of the time and we were also driving on the wrong side of the road. A woman came out of a shop and must have looked the wrong way and - BANG - the Police car smacked straight into her. I honestly thought the poor girl would be dead; I said, "Stop the car," to this copper and he said, "I can't stop." "Stop this bloody car will yer!" He stopped the car and we went back to the woman and thankfully she wasn't hurt, she was OK. We asked if she was alright, apologised and said we've got to go. We got to the game at five to seven and I went straight to the dressing room, I'd never met most of the players before because most of them were reserves and I didn't know them. Bill Foulkes, Harry Gregg and Bobby Charlton, I knew. We went out into a very highly charged atmosphere, it was really quite emotional, and beat a very good Sheffield Wednesday side 3-0, this was less than a fortnight after Munich and the Manchester programme from the game famously left the team line-up blank. We stayed the night in the Queens hotel in Piccadilly before coming back down the next day, me Eric and Jack Scamp and that was it - my Villa ending. Very sad, very sad.

My time after Villa certainly wasn't as happy, I always said once I left Villa I wouldn't play football any more and at the time that was a really honest appraisal about the situation and how I felt. Villa fans – the best in the world, you could never run down Villa fans at all, they were wonderful!

I never really got chance to say goodbye to the lads at Villa, some of them said I'd done the wrong thing and I knew that myself, but I had no say in the matter. Manchester was a horrible bloody place, socially it was wonderful, but to live there was horrible, the weather was terrible every day. After I'd been at United a month I thought to myself, I wished I'd never come here, you could understand the situation, the place was abysmal and people were crying all the while. The club put me in digs with Mrs Swinchat and her husband, they were delightful people. One morning I was in my bedroom getting ready to go to training, as I was combing my hair I dropped the brush on the floor. When I went down stairs she was crying and I said, "Oh god, what are you crying for?" She said, "Tommy used to drop the brush on the floor," Tommy Taylor; when he died he was living with the couple. She said that when she had heard the bump it had brought it all back and started her off. They were a lovely couple; if I went out on the night, when I got back there would be a sandwich for me on the table.

Getting to the FA Cup Final of 1958 was a tremendous occasion; Wembley was beloved by everyone in the country. It was fabulous - when you came out of the dressing room at Wembley you walked up a tunnel and you couldn't see the ground or the crowd until you got over the lip of the tunnel and then - it was absolutely awesome, 100,000 people there. I played left-half against Bolton Wanderers, I never played right-half again in the Football League, which was a bit silly really, because once you've made your name in a certain position, you'd think that people would like you to play there. There was an incident in the '58 final too, a chap named Dennis Stevens, a local lad from Dudley, he shot the ball in for Bolton and Harry Gregg, the United 'keeper knocked it up in the air, he turned round facing his own net and Nat Lofthouse came into him and kneed him in the back and the ball went in the net. I used to have a terrific photograph of me grabbing Lofthouse by the shirt as I was saying, "You dirty bugger." Two years running similar incidents happened, the other time was 'Woody' and Mc-Parland, when Wood went off and Blanchflower went in goal and played brilliant – he got man of the match Blanchflower. They used to rave about Duncan Edwards but I played against him a few times and unfortunately he never played well, he had some really bad games against us. He was a big lad and was obviously a very good player because he had a reputation, but when I played against him he looked just an average plodder. Sometimes people and reporters make players, which are not confounded, it happens all the time.

    I had been playing for Manchester United for a few months before Busby came back from Munich. I think he attended the Cup Final. In the close season I was called by United. I was having my tea and the phone went, my wife - at the time - answered it and said, "Stan it's someone from United." I was told to get down the ground as Mr Busby wanted to see me. I made my way down to Old Trafford and was told to go up to his office. I went up and opened the door and sitting there was a bloke I knew by reputation and his photograph – Ted Drake, the old Arsenal player now managing Chelsea. Busby said, "He's come to sign you on." I told him, "I ain't going anywhere! I've just got married and got a baby a few weeks old, Busby replied, "OK, Crowther, you were never my kind of player and at the end of the season your going on the transfer list anyway." I replied, "Thank you very much," and walked out. A few days later we past each other in a corridor, "Your not wanted here Crowther," it was Busby. "Well I might as well leave Manchester then" I mumbled to myself aloud and started walking away. "At least say goodbye," Busby shouted; I stopped, turned around, looked him in the eye and told him exactly what I thought of him. That was the last time I ever saw him.

    I had signed for United against my own will and better judgement; the first time the manager ever spoke to me was to tell me I'm not his kind of player, the second time he bothered to talk to me was to tell me to get lost!

    He was so egotistical about being famous. I had reporters tell me the only reason they put up with him was because they had to keep on his right side. I've never been like that, I was straight down the middle me! I'm a straight guy, I love people I love, I hate people I don't like and I'd never speak to them. I don't know how people can live like that - all this pretence.

I remember playing for Manchester United in the European Cup – it was brilliant, the semi-final against the great AC Milan, we played them at United and won 2-1. When we played them over there, they had an inside-right called Schiaffino, our left-back at the time was Ian Greaves and this bloody winger ran him to death. AC were captained by the Swede Nils Liedholm, who also captained Sweden in the 1958 world cup. We lost 4-0 and that was the end of the dream. If we'd got through we would have played Real Madrid, they had Di Stefano and an outside-left called Gento – never seen anyone so fast in all my life – a great side. It's funny how you remember the great sides, you always remember the forwards and you don't remember the defenders. I can look back over sixty years of watching football and it's been a pleasure. I never believed the talk about myself when I was a player because in those days you didn't. If you knew you were a good player you didn't need anybody else to tell you that.

I still played a lot of snooker and by then was very good. I beat a bloke named Jack Rea, Irish champion at the time. We'd been having a drink and he asked, "Would you like to come back to mine for a drink?" So we went to his and he had a snooker table in one of the rooms. He said, "Can you play, I'll give you 40 start." Fair enough – and I beat him!

Ted Drake knew what was what in football and he saw something in me. I enjoyed myself at Chelsea – it was good. The players were great, I'd played with two or three of them with the England U-23 side 'Greavsie' and Peter Brabrook – a very good player, very fast. I played at Chelsea for a season and a half. I loved London, I wish I could have finished my life there, I'd have been extremely happy. There was always something to do. You could go to museums, theatres, anything. All we had to do - there was a girl at Chelsea, a secretary, you'd say "book me a couple of tickets for this afternoon," and they were done – free!

I left Chelsea in 1961 for Brighton but it didn't work out. Their manager George Curtis was one of these that had to let you know he was in charge. This one afternoon we were getting our kit on to go back out training. One of the young lads had terrible blisters, we had been told to wear these bloody awful rubber soled boots and it was a hot day and they made your feet sweat really bad. I was the captain at the time, so the kids looked to me to sort the problems out. I told Curtis that this young lad couldn't put the boots back on, he could end up crippled for life, "Put them boots on now, do as I say," he shouted. I walked up to him chucked my shirt at him and said, "You'll have to play outside-left," I'd had enough. I got changed and went home. Later that week I discovered I was down to play for the Brighton third team. I went in and told Curtis I knew what his game was and that there was no way I would turn out that weekend. I was called to the ground later that day to appear before the Brighton Board, they didn't let me speak, they had no interest in what I had to say, Curtis had told his side - that was enough, he was the boss. They told me I was finished, I was 27 years-old, they held my registration and wouldn't release me from it, I wasn't going to play for them and I couldn't sign for anyone else. I retired from full-time football.

Everyone thought because you'd been where you had been, you were supposed to do this and that, but you don't want to do that, you got older and you don't want to do that anymore but people expected it because of who you were and what your name was and you couldn't live with it. I know I couldn't live with it, I wanted to get back here and go back to work. Remember there was no money in it in them days, you just got about £2 a week more than working in a factory. If you got £20 a week in the season you got £17 or £18 in the summer and that was your rent money gone.

In them days people used to love football then, now they criticise quite rightly what the players earn- its obscene.

I was very lucky, I played in four cup semi-finals, three U-23 England appearances, two semi-finals in the European Cup and two FA Cup Finals, all in a small amount of time.

Every morning I get up and I look at that team photo of us posing proudly with the FA Cup and I say, "Morning lads," what an honour and a pleasure to have played with them!

The
FA Cup Trail

Mud glorious mud
3rd round

"It's a good job you got that in because I was going to kick you over the line with the ball!" - Stan Lynn

Peter McParland fancied his side could do well, he had said as much back in October, "We were getting a good team together and I thought we could have a good go at the Cup."

FA Cup 3rd Round – If drawn at home, prices of reserved seats to be 7/- (shillings) Trinity Road and 6/- Witton Lane.
Aston Villa Football Club Boardroom minutes, Tuesday 4th December 1956.

In the third round draw made on Monday 10th December 1956, Aston Villa were paired with fellow First Division side Luton Town. The tie scheduled for Saturday 5th January would be played in Bedfordshire at the Hatters' Kenilworth Road ground. Villa being no different from any other club in the land had preferred home advantage.

FA Cup 3rd Round v Luton Town – If a replay is necessary, the Board decided to play on Monday 7th January 1957
Aston Villa Football Club Boardroom minutes, Tuesday 11th December 1956.

Stan Crowther playing in his first full season for the Villa couldn't wait for the match to come round, "It was on my mind all of the time, I wasn't bothered that we were playing an unfancied team in Luton Town, it was an FA Cup-tie and it was glamorous, the magic of the Cup. I would rather it had been at Villa Park – it would have been the icing on the cake, just imagine running out to a packed Villa Park with the Holte End shouting for you."

FA Cup tie v Luton Town – Travel arrangements – The Directors decided to travel by road on 5th January 1957

Aston Villa Football Club Boardroom minutes, Tuesday 18th December 1956.

In the days leading up to the game there was optimism and concern in both camps. Villa had Johnny Dixon, Stan Lynn and Stan Crowther requiring treatment for injuries picked up in the previous week's 0-0 draw at Blackpool, though all three were expected to make the Cup-tie.

To say Stan Crowther was excited about the game was an understatement, "Playing in the league week in and week out determines a teams ability above everything, but to lots of kids following football teams and players alike, the cup was the big one – the one they wanted to win and to have their day at Wembley. I had grown up listening to the FA Cup Final's on the radio and it was the biggest event of the year in the football calendar. I can still recall every Cup win since the war but I can't remember the Champions."

Other good news was the return to light training for both Ken Roberts who had been playing admirably at inside-left prior to breaking his foot, and right-half Bill Baxter who was making a remarkable recovery since his operation for cartilage removal. The club's only concern was that their centre-half Jimmy Dugdale, who had missed the Blackpool match, might have to be covered again by Trevor Birch.

Luton Town's manager Dally Duncan was anxiously waiting to see if his captain and centre-half Sid Owen would be fit to play after injuring his ankle during Luton's visit to Manchester City's Maine Road the previous Saturday. Better news for the Hatters was the probable return of their Eire international right-back Seamus Dunne, who had sat out the previous three games due to shingles. Early indications were that Luton would be able to field their strongest team.

FA Cup tie v Luton Town 5th January – Travel arrangements – The Chairman drew attention to the transport difficulties and it was decided to alter the arrangements. Secretary instructed to book accommodation at the Bridge Hotel, Bedford for Friday 4th January.

Aston Villa Football Club Boardroom minutes, Tuesday 1st January 1957.

The Villa team left Birmingham on the day before the game and broke up their journey by staying in Bedford overnight.

Entry for 4th January, Eric Houghton's personal diary; Stayed at Bridge hotel, Bedford.

Villa manager Eric Houghton publicly stated on the eve of the match that he was somewhat concerned by the state of the Kenilworth Road pitch which his Luton counterpart Duncan described as "a sea of mud."

This was the least of the hosts' worries. Three players, including their influential skipper Owen, had failed late fitness tests. Of the 14 Villa players who left New Street station on the Friday, four were half-backs and no less than seven were forwards, including Billy Myerscough who'd had stitches removed from a head wound the day before. Jimmy Dugdale was pronounced fit from his bout of flu and the Villa were able to put out what was considered their regular side.

Stan Crowther was out of the side when the draw was made, but when Eric recalled him he kept his place, "I hoped I would get to play at Luton. Then knowing I was to be involved in the FA Cup myself was a very exciting prospect – a childhood dream come true."

Peter McParland remembers the game vividly, "It was a very heavy pitch that day, we fully expected a tough game as Luton were a decent side. They played good football, especially at the start of the season, but their pitch used to get really bad with mud and it used to bugger them up a bit. Streten the goalkeeper was an international, as were the two Irish lads Dunne and McNally. Turner was quite a good player too. Owen was their captain but he didn't play.

The line-ups:
Luton Town: Streten, Dunne, McNally, Pearce, Kelly, Shanks, Cullen, Turner, McLeod, Morton, Davies
Aston Villa: Sims, Lynn, Aldis, Crowther, Dugdale, Saward, Smith, Sewell, Pace, Dixon, McParland

Villa adapted slightly better to conditions that the local Luton newspaper described 'as bad as they could get'. It seemed the only possible way that progress would be made was by employing kick and rush tactics, as attempted passes would inevitably settle in the mud. Johnny Dixon's shot from close range was tipped over the bar but could have had the visitors one-up in the first minute. Luton broke next and only a fine save from a leaping Sims, high to the right, prevented Luton from opening the scoring. After the high drama of the opening few minutes the game slowed down turning into a midfield contest, very few passes reaching their intending targets.

Villa earned a corner in the 12th minute. Smith floated the ball over; captain Dixon the quickest to react, headed into the far corner of the net to put his side 1-0 up. "When Johnny put us ahead I thought, this is brilliant. The game had started in a different atmosphere to a League match, more hype and the fans were more vocal," recalled Crowther.

Play was labelled farcical in the Birmingham press, 'the pitch being like a glue-pot except at the four corners.'

Derek Pace, in turning the Luton centre-half, was pulled down and both players sparred up to each other before the referee could assert his authority. Luton then had a valid claim for a penalty when their inside-right Turner was hauled down a few yards inside the box. They were awarded a free kick just outside the area, a decision resented by Hatters fans and players alike. Villa went in at the interval with their slender advantage intact.

Conditions for the Villa defence worsened in the second half; the Oak-Road End, that Luton were now attacking, was known as a trap for the unwary at the best of times. The ball was sticking more than ever. Luton were awarded a penalty just before the hour mark as Stan Crowther handled - and Turner beat Nigel Sims from the spot. Luton, who now looked stronger, were taking the initiative to the visitors.

Within a dozen more minutes their period of pressure paid dividends and the hosts were able to capitalise from a corner. Turner, now provider, curled the ball into the area and Davies managed to steer it beyond the reach of the Villa custodian. Advantage Luton Town.

This setback for the 'Claret & Blue' inspired them to come back with verve and enthusiasm. With the reckless tackles flying in all over the pitch it looked likely that fights would break out at any time. Players were getting brought down all over the park and it wasn't all down to the atrocious state of the playing surface.

Chasing the game, Villa moved their Irish winger McParland into the centre of the pitch with ten minutes remaining. It was a masterstroke from Villa boss Houghton and the reshuffle paid dividends.

"We had a bit of a battle with them, it was 2-1 and we had a corner kick, the ball came across and was in the goalmouth, everybody was in there after it. I was the nearest one to it and because of the mud I dragged it over the line and Stan Lynn was behind me, he said, "It's a good job you got that in because I was going to kick you over the line with the ball," remembers 'Packy' McParland on his equaliser.

McParland had made space for himself and was on hand to calmly drag home the loose ball after Streten, in the Luton goal, had only managed to parry a point blank shot from 'Doc' Pace.

The away side were now in the ascendancy. Luton were fortunate with a few narrow escapes and it was now just a case of hanging on and hoping they could force a replay. McLeod was now the only front player attempting to push forward, while Pearce, making his first appearance of the season in the half-back line, was truly outstanding in Luton's defence.

Two fine efforts by Villa's right-sided attackers Sewell and Smith nearly brought the goals that would have seen their side through without the anxiety of the remaining minutes. Streten kept his team in the tie making several excellent saves late on and as the whistle blew for the end it was the home side that trudged off the ploughed-up pitch breathing the bigger sigh of relief.

Luton Town 2 Aston Villa 2
Dixon,
McParland
half time 0-1, Attendance 20,108

Entry for 5th January, Eric Houghton's personal diary; Cup-tie at Luton, drew 2-2 on TV. Trained 10am, inspected pitch – very muddy.

Arrangements by the Villa Board had been made in early December in the case of a Villa Park replay being necessary. The players trooped off knowing that they would be locking horns again less than 48 hours later, at 2.00pm on on Monday 7th January.

Derek Pace, Stan Lynn and Peter McParland reported to Villa Park on Sunday for treatment, but in no instance were the injuries sufficiently serious for any of them to be ruled out.

Luton travelled to the Midlands on the day of the match but broke their journey by lunching at Coventry. It was here that the decision was taken that skipper Sid Owen and fellow defenders Bud Aherne and Ray Smith would be unable to take their places in the starting line up. Both teams would field the same XI that started the Kenilworth Road tie.

A crowd of only 28,536 turned out for the replay. After their flirtation with relegation the previous year, expectations weren't particularly high among the 'Claret & Blue' faithful and the Villa Board couldn't really have expected anything different.

Compared with the sticky pitch on Saturday the Villa Park playing surface was considered far easier going, though still heavy, as Mr Jobling from Morecambe, the same referee from the first tie, got the game started.

Villa had lost the toss, so Pace kicked off for the hosts and started in motion an immediate promising raid. A delightful pass from the wing from the Villa captain Dixon set up McParland who luckily for the Hatters slightly misjudged the flight of the ball - a scoring opportunity lost.

Luton soon retaliated and it was clear this was going to be a stern rough-tough test of a tie between two very hard-playing sides, with Villa providing the football and Luton adding some desperate tackling which the Birmingham-based press described as 'beyond the pale.'

There was very little between the two sides but the home crowd were soon calling for a penalty. Winger Les Smith, who had cleverly hooked the ball over McNally, turned well but then found himself tackled and grounded.

A piece of McParland brilliance saw him beat three defenders before cracking a blistering shot while under pressure from Kelly. The ball fizzed past the upright, grazing it as it went. Smith then flashed in a shot which hit a Luton player on the arm and bounded clear with Streten in the Hatters' goal beaten.

A Derek Pace corner was headed fractionally wide by McParland, while another flag-kick headed by the same player landed on top of the net. It was a mystery how Villa went in at the half-time break having failed to cash in on their superiority, numerous chances having been missed.

The game resumed with the visitors looking the stronger but when Luton Town bore down on the Villa custodian, the Villa wing-halves and defenders were too much for their opponents' wingers and mopped up sufficiently. Regardless, Luton would still have had to outwit Nigel Sims, a giant of a keeper in both physique and stature.

Finally Villa, raiding as a pack yet again, managed to break the deadlock on the hour mark, their persistence and determination coming up trumps with the goal the crowd had been so patiently waiting for.

Kelly and McNally went in for the same ball and in the confusion Pace nipped in to gain possession and centred for Dixon. Running at top speed, the skipper met the ball perfectly with his head to send it rocketing past the Luton custodian who was wrongly placed and had no chance.

Luton, who at this time were enjoying slightly more play than they had in the first period now looked resigned to defeat. They had conceded first in a game that looked likely to be won by a single goal. Villa repeatedly tried to make the game safe and hope completely deserted Luton when Villa's skipper scored his and Villa's second of the afternoon.

Streten parried a goalbound Smith shot but Jackie Sewell collected the loose ball and instinctively crossed it inside where Dixon blasted in from close range to make it 2-0 to Villa and leave Luton down and seemingly out.

Sims was called on right at the death, denying Luton's outside-right Turner by diving full length to save at the foot of the post. But for the Town defence it had been a difficult match, with the ball continually coming back at them.

Aston Villa 2 Luton Town 0 half-time 0-0
Dixon 2
half-time 0-0 , Attendance 28,536

Entry for 7th January, Eric Houghton's personal diary; Cup-tie replay won 2-0. Syd D and Frank S came.

McNally had played impressively and knew he had been in a game, even though he had been unable to curb completely a winger in Villa's Leslie Smith, who had taken knock after knock for the cause and had still came back for more. Streten had been far busier than Sims in the other goal making several excellent saves.

"It wasn't an easy draw - it was a case of we have to go there and give it a go, no one thought about playing defensively, you rode your luck and went forward trying to win the game all the time. We got away with a draw and took them back to Villa Park where we took them easily in the replay. Villa were on top from the very start and we were never in any danger and rolled them over." – Peter McParland

The draw for the fourth round had been made prior to kick off and when asked what Villa manager Eric Houghton thought about being paired away to Middlesbrough or Charlton, he replied, "I think it's about time we were drawn at home! Except for last season's third round game against Hull City, Villa haven't had a home tie since I came back to Villa Park in 1953.

"I don't think the fourth round will be as difficult as the draw we had for the third round this time. Neither Middlesbrough nor Charlton are as hard a side to beat as Luton, though if we do get through to the fourth round I don't mind really who we meet.

"We've beaten Charlton twice already this season, so perhaps Middlesbrough at Ayresome Park might be the tougher proposition. But I still think it's about time we had a home match. Let's get over the first hurdle before we start theorising our prospects."

Charlton managed to claim a 1-1 draw at Ayresome Park and in the replay at The Valley it was Middlesbrough who progressed 3-2 to meet Villa at home in the fourth round.

Receipts v Luton Town FA Cup replay Jan 7th £3,852, 6/-
Aston Villa Football Club Boardroom minutes, Tuesday 15th January 1957.

Cloughie – bloody useless!

4th round

"I think it was our best performance of the entire Cup run, we played really well that day because they had 'Cloughie' at the time getting goals – Jimmy gave him one kick all afternoon and he scored from it." -

Peter McParland

FA Cup – 4th Round v Middlesbrough, – Date of replay in necessary, Monday 28th January. Prices of reserved seats 7/- Trinity Rd and 6/- Witton Lane
Aston Villa Football Club Boardroom 'minutes,' Tuesday 15th January 1957

In preparation for the forthcoming cup-tie Peter McParland and his team-mates would train in their new - less than familiar - Villa shirts. "We had a practise match in the week before the game; it was the first time we had worn blue shirts - Manchester City's colours. Billy Moore's side wore the blue shirts, Derek Pace had to play in the reserves in the practise match even though he was in the first team fo Saturday. Billy was playing for us, all the boys were amazed that he did this. We let the game go for a time then we would hold the ball and Billy would come looking for it; we'd wait until he was marked and then give it to him. Trevor Birch was the lad who was picking him up, Trevor knew when to come in and take the ball off him. We were just having a bit of fun with him."

Team v Middlesbrough FA Cup – 4th Round, away January 26th Sims, Lynn, Aldis, Crowther, Dugdale, Saward, Smith, Sewell, Pace, Dixon, McParland
Aston Villa Football Club Boardroom 'minutes,' Tuesday 22nd January 1957

On the eve of the fourth round tie between Middlesbrough and Villa, the home side were forced into a change when their 19-year-old right-winger Billy Day broke down during a fitness trial. Jamaican Lindy Delapenha stepped into the breech. Peter McParland remembers Boro's late inclusion as being a decent player, before the end of the day, Stan Crowther would begrudgingly agree.

Villa, meanwhile, were certain to be back to full strength after their custodian Nigel Sims and winger Peter McParland had been declared fit and restored back to the first team squad after coming through training sessions, having sat out the 3-0 defeat by Spurs the previous weekend. Both men were included in the party that travelled up to the North East on the Friday and stayed overnight in Saltburn. The visitors fielded the same side as the one that disposed of Luton in round three and cup fever was starting to take hold in the West Midlands. Aware that Villa, Blues, Wolves and Albion could all reach the last 16 if they won their respective ties, the Birmingham Mail bought out a special cup edition.

Entry for 25th January, Eric Houghton's personal diary; Stayed Zetland hotel, Saltburn. Rain and mild.

The team line-ups:
Middlesbrough: Taylor, Barnard, Stonehouse, Harris, Robinson, Dicks, Delapenha, Scott, Clough, Fitzsimons, Burbeck
Aston Villa: Sims, Lynn, Aldis, Crowther, Dugdale, Saward, Smith, Sewell, Pace, Dixon, McParland

Eric Houghton, giving the lads his team talk in the dressing room prior to kick-off, pointed to the Villa centre-half and said, "Jimmy, this Clough lad, he's good with his left, he's good with his right, but apart from that he's bloody useless." There was a loud bang from the rear of the dressing room. Keeper Nigel Sims, who wasn't a small lad, had laughed so hard that he had fallen off the bench! Eric's remark may well have been tongue-in-cheek; Cloughie wasn't just good - he was phenomenal. He scored 251 goals in 274 matches – what more could be added?

Despite heavy overnight rain the pitch was described as being 'perfect condition for football.' The sun shining brightly was more reminiscent of a September day than late January.

But the day didn't start too smoothly for the visitors. Due to severe stomach pains captain Johnny Dixon spent a sleepless Friday night and was kept in bed by orders of the club doctor until two hours before the team bus left for the ground.

Due to a clash of colours, Middlesbrough were forced to abandon their normal red jerseys, turning out in white shirts and black nicks, while Villa wore light blue tops. When warming up before kick-off, Nigel Sims had a few words of wisdom for his defence, "Keep 'Cloughie' quiet lads and we know we are in with a shout." A crowd of 42,396 had gathered for the match and there were groans from all corners of Ayresome Park when Villa's skipper Dixon won the toss.

The visitors launched immediately into their task, breaking down the right wing. A superb pass from Les Smith found Peter McParland but the Irish outside-left hesitated and Boro's Barnard was able to whip the ball away.
Back came the home side, Fitzsimons raced through but badly misplaced his shot. From a corner kick Middlesbrough's Brian Clough headed straight into Sims' grateful hands before Villa drove forward again, through clever link up play between Pace and Smith. Unfortunately no other player had ventured far enough up field to accept the centre-forward's cross.

Jimmy Dugdale was well aware of the Clough threat and four times in quick succession he robbed the striker of service. Middlesbrough piled on tremendous pressure and were rewarded when they broke the deadlock in the 27th minute. A Fitzsimons header was pushed away by Sims after smart work from Delaphena and Burbeck, and Clough was able to shake off the attentions of his marker to rifle the ball home.

Villa's wing-backs began to get a hold on the game and six minutes before the interval Pat Saward pushed well up the field before swinging over an inch-perfect centre for 'Doc' Pace to get his head on to the ball and pull the score level at 1-1.

Derek had scored his first FA Cup goal and it was a crucial one. As the Villa News & Record observed, 'It was a superbly taken goal and a vital one for it whipped up a Villa side which, playing against a strong wind, appeared to be flagging.'

The visitors' joy was short lived because a mere four minutes later Boro had regained the advantage – and what a soft goal to concede. The home side's wing-half Harris totally surprised the unsighted Sims by unleashing an optimistic 20-yard drive which went through the heavily congested area before nestling in the bottom corner of the net. Boro went in at half-time deservedly leading 2-1 through very well-taken goals brought about by their ability to move the ball quickly, in spite of the fact Villa's defence and particularly Dugdale, had been magnificent.

As the second half unfolded, though, it was obvious very early on that Boro's strength and stamina had somehow deserted them. Their formation was all at sea now and the visitors started to exert pressure which led to a second equaliser.

Middlesbrough's inside-right Scott, attempting not to concede a throw-in, cleared downfield in full-back fashion. Saward collected the poor clearance and pushed the ball to Dixon, who was within striking distance of the opposition goal. The skipper laid an inch-perfect pass for winger Smith, who taking it in his stride, struck the ball firmly past the hapless Peter Taylor. Villa had levelled the tie and it was now one-way traffic, Taylor being the far busier stopper.

According to the North-East based Northern Echo newspaper, the home crowd were getting restless, screaming for their players to 'Give it to the Golden Boy, Clough.' Dicks, while trying to clear under pressure, attempted to head the ball over his own bar, but he had underestimated the speed of the cross and was grateful to see his 'keeper Taylor avert the danger at the second attempt.

The picture of the game now, was one of Villa's superior skill and stamina and this was highlighted perfectly when the ever-alert Dixon ran into space to collect an intelligently headed flick on from Pace - after clever work from Saward - and put his side into the lead. It seemed that the longer the game went on, the more Villa strengthened their grip. Middlesbrough rallied in the last 10 minutes as they had in the first half, but with the now harassed Sims saving twice from Scott and then punching away a Brian Clough goalbound drive, the Villans' defence held out resolutely until the final whistle.

Middlesborough 2 Aston Villa 3 half-time 2-1
Pace
Smith
Dixon
half-time 2-1, Attendance 42,396

Entry for 26th January, Eric Houghton's personal diary; Cup-tie at Middlesbrough won 3-2

Finally, Aston Villa had won a cup-tie at the first time of asking, the last time this had been achieved having been against Rotherham four years earlier. Middlesbrough had thrown away any chance of winning by moving back immediately after the half-time break to defend their slender lead and allow the visitors to take the game to them, which is exactly what the encouraged Aston Villa side did.

Delapenha had been a constant thorn for Villa's blonde wing-half Crowther, "He ran me in circles nearly the entire game. By the time I had learnt his tricks the match was over, but we had done enough."

Pat Saward, who was improving with every game, touched his peak in this tie. 'From his passes stemmed all three Villa goals' reported the Birmingham Mail. Derek Pace agreed. "That was my first goal in the cup and what a smashing centre from Pat Saward," he said. Les Smith was also pleased about his contribution. "I shouted for the ball and saw the goal, took a bang, and there it was, in the net. When that went in I knew we were as good as there." But keeper Nigel Sims was not so pleased. "That Harris goal was a real fluke," he said. "There was a crowd of players in front of me so I moved over to the right to get sight of the ball. How it came through all those players I don't know, but I didn't see it until it went past me." Smiling Villa boss, Eric Houghton stated that Villa had deserved to win and he'd wished that the people who had been calling his side dirty had been at the game. Villa had played some excellent football and made it to the last 16.

The excitement carried on as the Villa party emerged on to the platform at Middlesbrough train station to return back to New Street station. Hundreds of wildly excited Villa fans formed a back-slapping, hand-shaking avenue through which the Villa players had to fight to get to their train. Captain Johnny Dixon was 'hoisted aloft' and chaired along to his compartment.

The Villa outside-left, 'Packy' McParland would later class this performance as the Villa's best of the whole 1957 Cup campaign. The two second-half goals from Pace and Dixon, had secured them a place in Monday's live midday radio draw for the next round. That draw would see Villa finally gain home advantage. They would face Second Division outfit Bristol City at Villa Park.

W Moore (Trainer) The chairman had an interview with Moore and gave an assurance we expected him to remain with us next season. Moore stated his desire to progress in the game and gave notice that he would leave at the end of the season. The Chairman advised Moore the club would not oppose his decision
Aston Villa Football Club Boardroom 'minutes,' Tuesday 29th January 1957

Portsmouth FC – Our League match on 16th February postponed on account of FA Cup-tie – Suggested new date Monday 18th February at Villa Park if cup-tie is completed
Aston Villa Football Club Boardroom 'minutes,' Tuesday 29th January 1957

FA Cup - 5th Round v Bristol City at Villa Park 16th February. Prices of seating accommodation, 8/6d & 6/-. Date of replay to be mutually agreed upon
Aston Villa Football Club Boardroom 'minutes,' Tuesday 29th January 1957

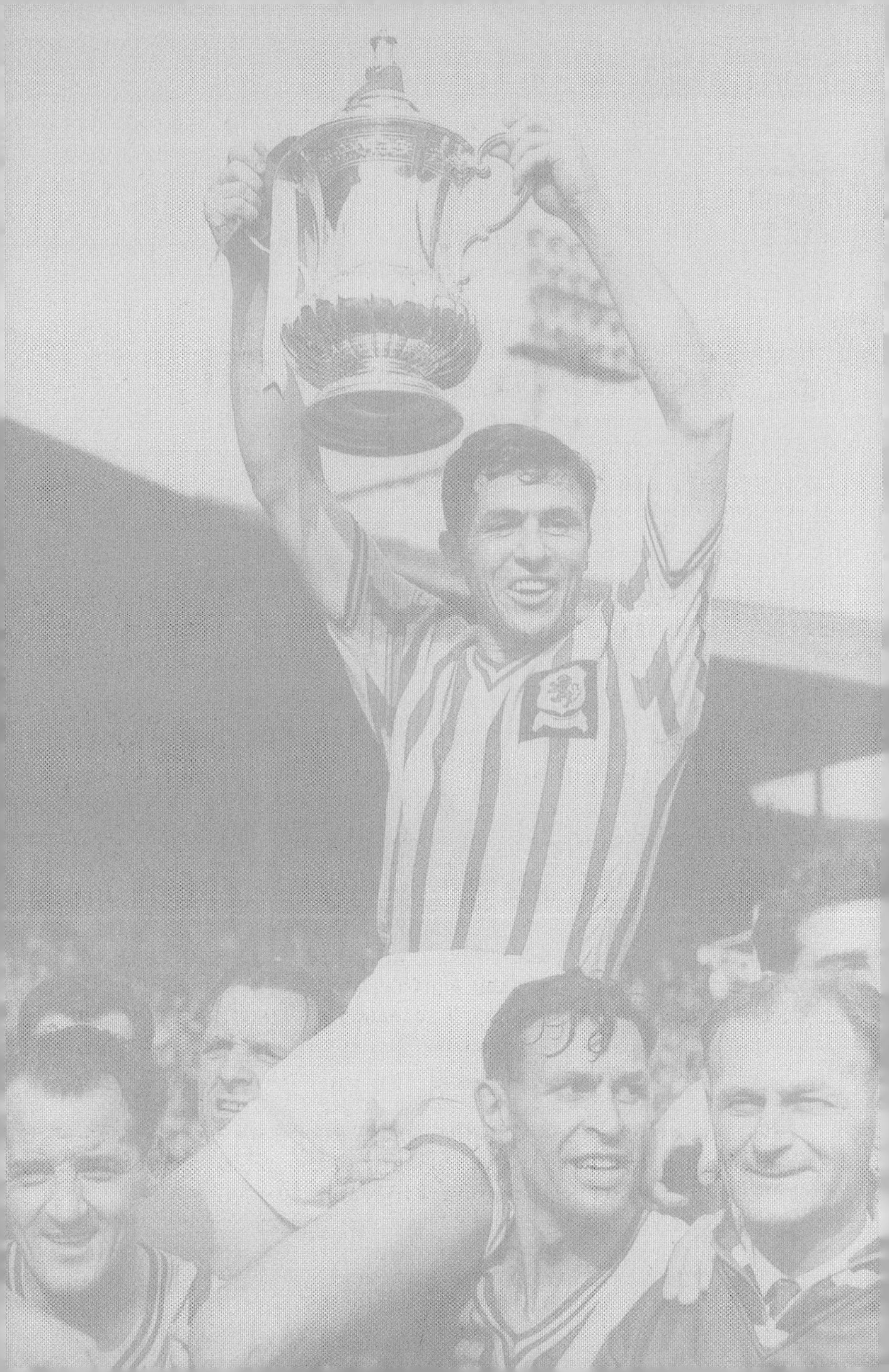

Goodbye Bristol City
5th round

"The atmosphere in Villa Park was unlike anything I had ever experienced. The noise was like thunder and the hairs on my neck stood up – I will never forget it." – Stan Crowther

With Villa having home advantage in this famous competition for only the second time during Eric Houghton's tenure, and the team looking for a place in the last eight at the expense of a Second Division side, it was expected that supporters would turn out in large numbers.

Bristol City had progressed to this stage after convincing wins against Rotherham United (4-1) and non-League Rhyl (3-0). They may have been playing their football in the second flight, but the visit to the Midlands held no fears for them. They knew they were always in with a chance if they could supply their England international centre-forward John Atyeo. He had scored a brace in both previous rounds of the FA Cup, had bagged three against Sheffield United a month earlier and had already found the net on 19 occasions in the current campaign. Atyeo was raring to go, to pit his wits against top class defenders.

FA Cup - 5th Round v Bristol City – At the request of Bristol City Secretary, have agreed to date of replay, if necessary, as Wednesday 20th February

Aston Villa Football Club Boardroom minutes, Tuesday 12th February 1957.

Portsmouth F.C – If FA Cup-tie completed on 16th February. Portsmouth agreed to play our postponed League match with them at Villa Park on Monday 18th February.

Aston Villa Football Club Boardroom minutes, Tuesday 12th February 1957.

FA Cup 6th Round – Arrangements if necessary – The Directors decide to have an 'all ticket' match if drawn at home. Prices of seating accommodation 10/6d & 8/- and ordinary League match prices for standing enclosures and ground.

Aston Villa Football Club Boardroom minutes, Tuesday 12th February 1957

Two days before the match, the hosts' only doubt was whether Derek Pace would be fit after sitting out Villa's two recent league matches, Roy Chapman having deputised. Eric Houghton told the press it would depend on Pace coming through a severe test, stating that the striker required "heavy ball work." Thursday's training geared for Saturday's Cup-tie consisted of ball work at Ellisons Sports ground, laps around Villa Park and gym work. Bristol City manager Pat Beasley had no concerns. His centre-half Ernie Peacock was declared fit to play after missing two matches but would have to wear heavy strapping on his left thigh, so City would field the same side that had defeated Rhyl 3-0 in the fourth round.

The Robins made the relatively short journey up the A38 on the eve of the match and the Bristol contingent including 13 players stayed overnight in Droitwich before leaving at mid-day on the Saturday to make the short trip to Aston. Derek Pace was declared fit on Friday after coming through a stern test without reaction.

"They were a good Second Division team, they were a hard working side and they had a big inside-left called John Atyeo. The funny thing was Jimmy Eason used to go and watch the teams before we played them in the cup and he came back with a report about him. On the Friday morning, he said, "Atyeo, his right foot is a dummy and the left is the danger," he made that report at the team meeting," McParland recalled.

Not only would Aston Villa be fielding the same side that had got them to this stage, they would also be turning out in the same light blue shirts they had worn at Ayresome Park. Their famous claret and blue jerseys would clash with Bristol City's red shirts, so in accordance with FA Cup regulations, both teams would change. Bristol appeared in white shirts and black shorts.

The weather hadn't been kind in the week leading up to the game with rain falling for most of that period, leaving the Villa ground staff rather anxious as the middle of the park was particularly sodden. Fortunately no rain fell on the morning of the game, which helped a little, but it was still far from conducive to good football, despite a good layer of sand down the middle. One newspaper reporter likened the playing surface to an 'uncooked Christmas pudding.'

With the high expectancy of a larger than average crowd, Villa urged their supporters to get to the ground early and stated that the turnstiles would open at 12.30 pm. The club weren't disappointed; fans made sure they weren't going to miss out and turned up in their droves. A crowd of 63,099, including a substantial following from the

West Country – believed to be in the region of 10,000 – poured into Villa Park. It was the largest attendance at the venue since Villa played Wolverhampton Wanderers over the festive period of 1949.

The team line-ups:
Aston Villa: Sims, Lynn, Aldis, Crowther, Dugdale, Saward, Smith, Sewell, Pace, Dixon, McParland
Bristol City: Anderson, Bailey, Thresher, White, Peacock, Burden, Hinshelwood, Williams, Atyeo, Ethbridge, Watkins

Dixon won the toss and Villa started the game at lightning speed. Bristol's centre-half conceded a first minute corner but the home side were unable to capitalise, Doc Pace heading just over Bob Anderson's bar. In the early periods of the game it appeared that City were suffering from big occasion nerves. Villa moved the ball quickly across the Villa Park pitch and the Bristol defence looked vulnerable under pressure. In one raid the hosts nearly opened the scoring when captain Johnny Dixon shot just a couple of yards wide. Villa maintained the pressure on a City rearguard who were grateful to their veteran centre-half Ernie Peacock for getting in the way of a goal bound stinging shot from Villa outside-right Les Smith. Crowther got on to the end of the resulting corner but shot well wide.

Cheers rang out when the Villa trainer was called to administer treatment to referee Williams after he injured his lower back. When the game resumed the visitors were not without their chances; in an attacking spell, Atyeo, beat Villa's centre-half Jimmy Dugdale and played the ball out to winger Hinshelwood, who should have made better of his shot that dropped only inches over the bar. "Jimmy was being given a sterner test by John Atyeo than he got most Saturdays in Division One," recalled Nigel Sims.

A great spell by the hosts saw them denied three times in quick succession. City's goal, it seemed, led a charmed life, with the tenacious wing-half White being called upon to make several clearances. Watkins, meanwhile, squandered a good chance for the visitors, curling his shot out of the reach of Villa custodian Sims, but just over the bar.

The pitch was now cutting up badly, especially in the goalmouths. An attempted clearance by the City defence fell straight to the prowling 'Doc' Pace, who snatched at his chance when he should have taken more time, the shot being rather tame and directly into the hands of a relieved Anderson.

But the deadlock was broken in the 36th minute when, during a lightning raid, Pace was able to connect with a superbly executed Jackie Sewell pass into the goalmouth and neatly steer it beyond City 'keeper Anderson. City's defenders appealed in vain for offside but the lineman's flag remained resolutely by his side and the goal stood. It immediately prompted renditions of a newly aired ditty to ring out around the Villa Park terracing:

> **It's a long way to get to Wembley,**
> **It's a long way to go,**
> **It's a long way to get to Wembley,**
> **But we'll get there I know!**
> **Goodbye Bristol City**
> **Goodbye Middlesbrough**
> **It's a long way to get to Wembley,**
> **But we'll get there I know!**

Sewell was close to getting his name on the score-sheet when his 25-yard drive was too high for the City stopper. Unfortunately it wouldn't drop in time and sailed over the crossbar and out of harm's way. Just before half-time, Villa were unlucky not to double their advantage. McParland made a brilliant run through the middle of the park beating both Peacock and White but his goal bound shot was steered round the post for a corner by the covering Bailey. The teams trudged off through the mud for the interval break, with Villa holding a slender 1-0 lead.

With the speed of Peter 'Mac' and Leslie Smith on the flanks, it was a mystery why the Villa continually raided through the centre where conditions were described as 'exceedingly gluey.' Villa should have scored only two minutes after the break, after smart work from Dixon and McParland had put Sewell into a scoring position, but the inside-forwards failure to shoot first time meant he was robbed of the ball by Burden. In spite of this close call, it was the visitors who seized the initiative, their approach being far more direct than Villa's.

This sustained pressure led to striker Atyeo scoring the City equaliser with a goal described in the press as 'out of this world.' Latching onto a Peacock through ball, Atyeo swerved past Stan Lynn and Jimmy Dugdale before ploughing through the mud and unleashing a rising right-foot shot that rocketed high into the far corner of the net. The Bristol contingent lifted the roof, their golden boy Atyeo, had done it again.

Packy McParland laughed as he recalled the moment City levelled the tie, "Atyeo turned inside Jimmy and whacked one straight into the top corner with his right foot. Jimmy Eason came in with that one and he never lived it down. We used to say to him the following Saturday's in the dressing room, "What about the dummy right foot?"

Villa were now spurred into action, moving far more effectively; winger Smith raced through, only to have White take the ball off his toe, and captain Johnny Dixon headed marginally over from a Smith corner.

In the 72nd minute Villa got their noses in front for the second time. Neat work between the Villa's left-sided attackers resulted in a very low cross centred into the goalmouth, Sewell threw himself forward and his head barely a foot from the ground connected perfectly to send the ball beyond Anderson and into the net.

Jackie had told Peter before the game that as long as he got the crosses whipped in, he would get on the end of them, "He nearly beat me with the one that resulted in the winner; It's the only time I can recall heading a ball when it's been on the deck."

"I got a run down the left wing and crossed the ball which was about three inches off the ground and Jackie Sewell headed it – his nose must have been trailing the deck! - Peter McParland

City were unable to get the ball forward in support of their talismanic striker and with Villa appearing tireless, it looked more likely that the game would run down to a home victory. The visitors' task was made even more difficult when the heavily-strapped Peacock pulled a muscle in his 'good' right leg and had to go off.

Bristol managed to thwart Villa from finding the net yet again when both Pace and Dixon were denied late chances before the referee signalled the end of the contest.

Aston Villa 2 Bristol City 1
Pace
Sewell
half-time 1-0, Attendance 63,099

Entry for 16th February, Eric Houghton's personal diary; Bristol City FA Cup 5th round, won 2-1 - hard match.

As the players left the field the huge crowd gave both teams a great ovation. Villa were safely through to the quarter-finals. "The noise had been constant for the entire match and what a reception we got at the final whistle. I hadn't experienced anything like it in my life, I was smiling to myself and shaking my head in disbelief. It made you wonder - could the fans make any more noise if we won them the bloody Cup?" Said a smiling, reminiscing Stan Crowther.

"Given luck, we should have had a draw," manager Pat Beasley told waiting reporters, to which Eric Houghton responded that his side had been the stronger in the muddy conditions.
Even so, the Villa boss conceded that his team had been fortunate in the build-up to the first goal when Jackie Sewell appeared to have strayed offside before pulling the ball back for Pace. Eric also declared, "If John Atyeo had been up against any other centre-half than Jimmy Dugdale he would have scored a hatful."

"The Bristol lads were playing the big stadium and they were loving it, they were playing their hearts out and giving us a right going over and we were lucky not to be a goal down by half-time. They really got at us and they had the crowd behind them.

Playing in the atmosphere was terrific - for them as well - and they were taking advantage of all that. We got a grip in the second-half. That game was an outstanding example of the little team coming and getting into the atmosphere of Villa Park, a big, big crowd and having us on the run, but we got out of it in the end. It was a tough game - Bristol," McParland said.

Receipts v Bristol City FA Cup - 5th Round, Feb 16th - £9,352   14/6.
Aston Villa Football Club Boardroom minutes, Tuesday 19th February 1957.

The pied piper of Burnley

6th round

The season had begun well for Villa wing-half Bill Baxter, who had started the first nine matches of the campaign. Then injury struck, and although Baxter made two attempted comebacks, it was to no avail. His time in a Villa shirt had come to an end – or had it?

Come Saturday 2nd March and the ever committed Bill Baxter once again appeared in the famous claret and blue jersey of Aston Villa – albeit wrapped around his neck! He cut a fine figure, resplendent in a top hat, complete with rattle; Bill played the lead role in an impromptu performance of the pied piper. His followers? A substantial percentage of Villa's claret and blue army!

The setting wasn't under the glare of stage lights; this was the cobbled sidestreets of the small Lancashire town of Burnley - en route to the ground ahead of the FA Cup quarter-final. On arriving at Turf Moor, though Baxter discovered that the doorman hadn't read the script - he refused Bill entry, not believing he was a Villa player! It took the intervention of his teammates to convince the Burnley official otherwise.

That wasn't the only novel occurrence ahead of the Burnley v Villa game. The sixth round draw was made live on television – the first time this had ever occurred. Previously it had broadcast on BBC radio at midday on the Monday following the weekend ties.

Of the eight teams left in the competition, four were Midlands based sides, three from the West-Midlands, Aston Villa, West Bromwich Albion and Birmingham City plus Second Division outfit Nottingham Forest, who would gain promotion at the end of the season under the guidance of Villa legend Billy Walker. Arsenal were the lone capital representatives, with Manchester United, Burnley and the wild card of the pack Bournemouth & Boscombe Athletic making up the quarter-final contestants.

The inclusion of Division Three South side Bournemouth certainly added spice to the proceedings. They had negotiated the first three rounds against similar level opposition before travelling to Molineux and beating a Wolves team who were sitting fourth in the First Division.

In the fifth round the Cherries were drawn at home to Tottenham Hotspur, who were second only to leaders Manchester United in the top flight, so all the talk in the build-up was the footballing lesson that Spurs planned on giving the South Coast rascals a day they would never forget.

Spurs did indeed give their lowly opponents a day never to be forgotten, although it was quite the reverse of what was expected. Bournemouth, who harried and chased all afternoon, never gave Spurs a minute on the ball, and played Jimmy Anderson's team off the Dean Court pitch, finishing 3-1 winners. Luckily for Villa, it was never an option that they might also end up with egg on their faces, with Bournemouth drawn at home to Matt Busby's Manchester United.

With only two balls remaining in the hat it was simple mathematics that Villa would meet Burnley. It just remained to be seen who would be drawn out first. Villa came out second, which meant they had the one draw they had desperately wanted to avoid – a trip to Turf Moor, where Burnley were unbeaten. Villa wins were certainly thin on their ground, too. A solitary draw from their last 11 visits was all they could offer, their last win in that corner of Lancashire having come when Villa were plying their trade in the second flight during the late 1930s. Peter McParland, who was eating his lunch at the time of the cup draw, nearly choked when he heard the news! The following day when the players turned in for training, all talk was about the draw and the bogey that needed to be laid to rest. But there was an optimistic atmosphere; everyone was as keen as mustard and couldn't wait for the first Saturday in March.

"Well if we don't beat 'em now we'll have to do 'em in the final" remembered Stan Crowther.

Rearranged dates of F L fixtures – Cardiff City, home, if FA Cup-tie is completed on 2nd March, match to be played on Wednesday 6th March. If a draw on 2nd March - on Wednesday 13th March. Sunderland, home, Secretary instructed to try and arrange between April 6 & 13. Aston Villa Football Club Boardroom minutes, Tuesday 19th February 1957.

FA Cup - 6th Round v Burnley – Date of replay 6th March and prices of tickets for seating accommodation are 8/6d & 6/-. Team manager to ascertain if players desire to travel overnight for cup-tie on 2nd March .Aston Villa Football Club Boardroom minutes, Tuesday 19th February 1957. Directors meeting No 24.

Peter McParland's recollection of the draw, "On the Monday the draw for the sixth round of the Cup was made during the 6 o' clock news and was shown on television. During the day the lads (players) were chatting with each other about all the teams that were left in the Cup, there were eight teams left, we said we'll play anybody, anywhere, but we don't want Burnley away, because they were a bogey side - Villa hadn't won there in a long while. There were two teams left in the hat at the end of the draw, I was watching it having my tea in the digs and the two teams were Burnley and Villa. I make a bit of a joke with some – I swallowed a whole sausage when they called out Burnley."

"They were a tough team to play against – Burnley, up there. Nobody liked to go there actually, a lot of players would say 'jeez.' It's a right drive, you have to get to Manchester then you drive over the tops and down dale and into Burnley. You know you're going to have a right tough old afternoon, chasing round after them."

The Football Challenge Cup Semi-Final – Request for Villa Park for one of the Semi-Finals or replay. The Chjairman [sic] had instructed Secretary to inform the Football Association we would be delighted to place our ground at their disposal.
Aston Villa Football Club Boardroom minutes, Tuesday 26th February 1957.

"The Football Association - French Cup Winners v. FA Cup Winner - Invitation received from The Football Association that if we were winners of the FA Cup to play this match on Sunday 26th May 1957 under floodlights. The Board decided to accept invitation but would definitely not play under floodlights
Aston Villa Football Club Boardroom minutes, Tuesday 26th February 1957.

Team v Burnley FA Cup - 6th Round a, March 23rd[sic], selected from; Sims, Lynn, Aldis, Crowther, Dugdale, Saward, Smith, Sewell, Pace, Myerscough, Dixon, McParland. To accompany Chapman, Birch. Team manager's request for 12 players to witness Cup-tie at Burnley 23 rd March.
Aston Villa Football Club Boardroom 'minutes,' Tuesday 26th February 1957.

On the Thursday prior to the game it was unsure whether Derek Pace would lead the Villa attack. All Villa boss Eric Houghton would say was that Pace "didn't train today - he had treatment, while the other lads did track and gym work." 'Doc' had previously strained a groin and although he had been drafted in to play in the previous round against Bristol City, he hadn't featured in any of the three league matches since the 1-1 draw at home to Leeds United on 2nd February when he had scored the equaliser. Everyone else was fit apart from Ken Roberts (knee) and Ray Hogg, who had received a nasty cut above the eye in a reserve match against Huddersfield Town and had required stitches.

Before the Villa party travelled north to stay overnight in Blackpool on the eve of the match it was declared Pace was fit and the team would remain the same that had negotiated all four previous cup games. As a precaution, the Villa management included two forwards Roy Chapman and Billy Myerscough among the three travelling reserves, the versatile Trevor Birch making up the trio.

On the morning of the game, a Birmingham reporter known as 'Citizen' gave Villa very little chance. He wrote that "only if Villa show some of the fight they are capable of, can they force a draw," adding that having Pace back in the side enhanced their chances slightly. "Derek Pace is not a great footballer, but has tremendous energy," he observed. "He's almost too industrious!" Citizen also acknowledged Villa's strength in defence but then said they lacked the cohesion and finish that Burnley possessed in attack.

The team were followed to Lancashire by an estimated 10,000 of their claret & blue army, the majority travelling by rail with the Aston Villa Supporters Club, leaving Witton very early on the Saturday morning aboard 10 special coaches. The Villa contingent swelled the Turf Moor gate to 49,346, Burnley's biggest crowd of the season. This had been anticipated by the local police force, which had drafted in extra sergeants and constables from the neighbouring Rochdale force and mounted Police from the Lancashire County Constabulary.

Nigel Sims thought the Villa had taken a wrong turn somewhere along the way, "The sun was shining when we got to Burnley, it had never done this before. It nearly always chucked it down or at best was grey and dull and our results weren't much better. It did make me think – perhaps we were due a result."

Stan Crowther wasn't too impressed with the venue or the location, "Where the hell were we going? After leaving Manchester – what seemed like hours ago - there was nothing but hills, more hills and sheep. It was really bleak, moors for miles and we were in the middle of nowhere. It didn't feel like we were off to play a match, more like a mystery trip and we'd got lost. Burnley wasn't the biggest of places but by kick-off the old ground - and it was old, believe you me - was bloody full. Where had everyone come from – the place was absolutely packed. 'Simsy had said on the way it would be raining, I wish I had put a bet on with him, it was the only time he was ever wrong."

As in the previous rounds, Villa donned their light blue shirts because a clash of colours meant both they and Burnley had to wear alternatives. As the lads started getting changed for the match, Stan Crowther remembers manager Eric Houghton run through his observations of the opponents, citing the Burnley inside-right, Jimmy McIlroy as their main threat, "He might wear the No 8 jersey but he will pop up all over the place, pulling you out of position Peter (Aldis) and Jimmy (Dugdale). Make sure he is closely watched."

The Burnley winger Brian Pilkington also came in for special mention. Nigel Sims recalls "We were even more determined to get a result when we discovered that Burnley had organised a party for that same evening, by way of celebrating the fact they would reach the semi-final. We thought it was bloody cheeky to be honest, not to mention disrespectful. It was their downfall; it served to inspire us even more!"

The team line-ups:
Burnley: Blacklaw, Angus, Winton, Seith, Adamson, Miller, Newlands, McIlroy, Lawson, Cheesebrough, Pilkington
Aston Villa: Sims, Lynn, Aldis, Crowther, Dugdale, Saward, Smith, Sewell, Pace, Dixon, McParland

Even though Villa skipper Johnny Dixon won the toss, the Villa defence were on the back foot almost immediately, clearing a free-kick taken by Burnley wing-half Seith after only 10 seconds. It was all Burnley in the opening skirmishes and when Ian Lawson was presented with a scoring opportunity from five yards out it took the experience of both Aldis, who took the ball off Lawson's foot and then Pat Saward, to complete the clearance. Again the hosts broke forward and Albert Cheesebrough's wonderful 30-yard crossfield pass was picked up by Pilkington who smartly rounded Stan Lynn, only to see his centre cleared from a Villa area packed with defenders.

The visitors' first real effort didn't arrive until the 13th minute, Les Smith hugging the touchline before delivering a perfect cross for 'Packy' McParland. From an acute angle the Villa man headed towards the goal where Doug Winton (who would sign for the Villa January 1959) was relieved to scramble the ball to safety. This was the closest either side had come to breaking the deadlock at that stage. McIlroy and Newlands then combined to set up Lawson, only for the youngster to shoot just wide but it was Villa's Peter Aldis who was first on the scoresheet. Not that the full-back was in the mood to celebrate.

Peter's only previous goal had been back in August 1952; a 35-yard header against Sunderland, but this one was at the wrong end. Cheesebrough had walked through the Villa defence and just when it appeared he had over-run the ball he cut it back from beside the post. It eluded the attention of 'keeper Sims, and Aldis, who was backtracking to cover the menace of Lawson, could do nothing as the ball hit him and ran into the empty net.

This setback for the visitors, according to the local Burnley Express, just made the Villa temper hotter! 'The Villa side showed the unsuspecting Turf Moor public that they were prepared to blast their way into the next round and employ tactics that were a revelation to the more sedate Burnley supporters who were not used to the same bludgeoning methods.'

Immediately after his own-goal, Aldis was called upon to chase back from the half-way line and with a sigh of relief from everyone of claret and blue persuasion, was able to slam the ball off Lawson's toe. Lawson came out of that challenge with a limp, and seconds later, after a tussle with Derek Pace; Jimmy Adamson was left writhing in agony in the penalty area. Players and trainers crowded round but after a short time the battle commenced.

Villa now had the bit between their teeth and wing-half Pat Saward moved up field to unleash a 20-yarder, which looked every inch a goal until Burnley's young keeper Adam Blacklaw reached to fingertip the ball over the bar for a corner. Jackie Sewell was also frustrated by the 18-year-old 'keeper. His shot cannoned off a defender's leg and was almost across the line before the youngster clawed it away.

A goalmouth scramble in the dying seconds of the first half was described in the Burnley press as 'a disgraceful fist-raising maul,' and the visitors were deemed to be the villains. A scrum of 10 players piled up in the Burnley penalty area after Blacklaw had been knocked over by two Villa forwards as he plucked a corner kick cleanly out of the air. Immediately it was fists-up by his colleagues as the referee stepped in and calmed things down by awarding the home side a free kick.

"We had a big support up with us that day in Burnley, a big crowd came up with us. It was a typical hard game – it was actually a nice spring day – and they got the lead 1-0 and we battled on to half-time to hold on to them," recalls McParland.

Nigel Sims remembered the atmosphere in the changing room during the interval. "We couldn't put two passes together," he said. "It was dire, and we were just not in it at all for the first 45 minutes. But we were confident enough in the dressing room and thought we could get something out of the game. We knew Burnley should have been out of sight at half-time and the fact they weren't only gave us hope."

For all it was the hosts who had created and missed by far the better chances in the first half, Burnley's best period of the game was straight after the interval, Villa's defence looked far from being impregnable and Burnley should have put the tie beyond doubt when Lawson, McIlroy and Pilkington all missed chances from favourable positions. Pilkington's drive hit the foot of the post before the ball was scrambled away; Lawson saw an easy chance go begging, his effort going wide of the far post when it would have been easier to hit the target; and wing-half Miller, with a great burst down the left side, was left rueing his spurned chance. One newspaper report observed that his enthusiasm was far greater than his accuracy! After a shaky restart Villa started to regroup and assert some authority, another reporter claiming that they 'fought like tigers.' Burnley, who were starting to feel the pace, were inviting fast tackles and received them, some being harder than they had bargained for.

Then Villa's relentless pressure finally paid off. Late in the game Leslie Smith controlled a throw-in, deceived Winton and had McIlroy in knots, before cutting inside and sending over an inch-perfect cross which 'Packy' McParland raced onto and headed past Blacklaw. A move that he and Leslie Smith had been practising in training had paid dividends; Villa lived to fight another day.

The Burnley Express claimed, 'the home side still had chances to prevent a journey to Villa Park, including a beautifully-worked trick free-kick, only for Pilkington to head Newland's centre over the crossbar.' The Birmingham papers stated that Villa 'had the urgency the Cup demands.'
Neither side could fashion a winner so the tie was to be resumed at Villa Park the following Wednesday afternoon.

Burnley 1 Aston Villa 1
McParland
half-time 1-0, Attendance 49,346

Burnley forward Jimmy McIlroy offered the following account of the match, "Against the Villa, we took an early lead and without playing really well, held it until a few minutes from the end of the game. Then the most dangerous man in soccer at converting the pass to the far-post - Peter McParland - popped up to head the equaliser from his favourite position. But there should never have been a replay, in the first 10 minutes or so I squared two passes across the face of the goal, both taken by Ian Lawson in his stride. From very close range, Ian side-footed the ball wide each time."

Not to be overlooked, McParland also put forward his thoughts, "It was the same in the second-half for a time and then we came into the game a wee bit more and Leslie Smith made a good run down the right and he hit a cracking cross over about 20 minutes to go and I 'Macced' it; it flew into the back of the net, I had got between two players to head it. Blacklaw never had a chance with my header; I managed to hit the ball perfectly. After that it was a bit of a battle as well to hold on, which we did and we were able to get them back to Villa Park."

As a result of the Turf Moor battle Jimmy Adamson, Ian Lawson, Albert Cheesebrough and Brian Pilkington were all casualties, while Villa also had players hurt in the bruising encounter. Les Smith received a kick on the thigh and Jimmy Dugdale, a black eye for his efforts, while Peter McParland, Stan Lynn and Derek Pace were also slightly injured. All of the problems were seen as no more than superficial, though, and the Midlanders were fully expected to name the same side for the replay.

On Monday 4th March, when the semi-final draw was made, there were still seven teams in contention, Bournemouth & Boscombe Athletic being the only definite casualties after losing 2-1 at home to the Busby Babes. Birmingham City had been held at home by Billy Walker's Forest and other local side; Albion had drawn 2-2 at The Hawthorns against Arsenal. The semi-final pairings were:

Manchester United v Birmingham City/Nottingham Forest.
Aston Villa/Burnley v West Bromwich Albion/Arsenal.

On hearing the draw Aston Villa manager Eric Houghton was asked by the press for his thoughts. "I have had a feeling for a long time that this year's Final will be between Villa and Birmingham," he replied. "Now I am more convinced than ever. But first we have to concentrate on Wednesday's replay with Burnley. If we can get through that all right – and I think we shall – I see no reason why we should not win the semi-final with Albion or Arsenal. Yes, we have a good chance of reaching Wembley. There's a fine club spirit among the Villa players. They are all triers and fighters."

The following day Burnley's newly-wed wing-half Brian Miller was informed that he would have to play out of position at centre-half in place of Jimmy Adamson who was ruled out of the replay due to damaged knee ligaments, his usual left-half slot being taken by Les Shannon, though team selection would be deferred until just before kick-off.

The visitors' party of 15 players, including reserves Alan Shackleton and Angus Alexander, made their way to Leamington Spa where they stayed overnight before resuming the journey to Birmingham on the day of the game. Eric Houghton, meanwhile, went to Highbury to catch the Arsenal v West Bromwich Albion replay in order to cast his eye over Villa's potential 'semi' opponents.

Alan Brown the Burnley boss had suggested to his Villa counterpart that they should toss a coin to decide the colours of the kit for the replay as they had before the Turf Moor tie. Villa lost this time and in order not to clash with Burnley's dark shirt and shorts, they borrowed local rivals Birmingham City's red away jerseys, one local paper observing that Villa would take to the field in the national colours of the Welsh. Villa remained unchanged while Burnley had to make three changes to the side that drew at Turf Moor.

With Albion safely negotiating their replay at Highbury with a 2-1 victory, the Football Association remained tight-lipped on the venue for the second semi-final, though an official did tell reporters, "Authority to make the choice has been vested in the secretary, Sir Stanley Rous and the chairman and one or two members of the committee. They will confer after the Villa Park game today. Of course, we have one or two grounds in mind, but at the moment it's 'no names, no pack drill'."

The Birmingham Mail drew their own conclusion, 'It remains anyone's guess; if Villa meet Albion, St Andrews or Molineux would seem ideal choices. If Burnley confound the prophets, then one of the Manchester or Liverpool grounds seems indicated.' It was an inspired piece; both grounds would see semi-final action.

The team line-ups:
Aston Villa: Sims, Lynn, Aldis, Crowther, Dugdale, Saward, Smith, Sewell, Pace, Dixon, McParland
Burnley: Blacklaw, Angus, Winton, Seith, Miller, Shannon, Newlands, McIlroy, Shackleton, Cheesebrough, Pilkington

Burnley started the match far more brightly than the hosts, which was quite a shock for the travelling support. They had witnessed eight straight league and cup defeats for their team at this famous old Midlands ground and it was for this very reason that many thought they had burnt their bridges by not getting the required result at home. But Burnley's early play was described in the Lancashire Express & News as 'a revelation,' and 'their best Villa Park display for years.' Gone was the hesitancy; breaks down both wings saw Shackleton in scoring positions with only Villa custodian Sims to beat. Sims and full-back Lynn were credited with being responsible for keeping Villa in the tie. Jimmy Dugdale, in showing Burnley how to defend, had received a black eye in the first tie and now he completed the pair in a heading clash with debutant centre-forward Alan Shackleton! Despite his two bruisers, though, Dugdale was once again a rock in the home defence.

Following more pressure from the visitors, Cheesebrough's spanking drive had 'goal' written all over it, until Sims, diving down to save right-handed with a panther-like plunge, managed to keep out what was described as the best shot of the match.

Going into the replay, Villa had the second tightest defence in the League and Burnley soon realised why. The only problem for the Villa forward line was they were up against the meanest defence – Burnley had conceded two less than the men from Aston. But they were without their hugely experienced centre-half Jimmy Adamson and missed his calm direction and marshalling of the defence, not to mention his cunning distribution.

After Burnley's fruitless 10-minute spell of dominance, Villa's powerful, uncomplicated style of play came to the fore; they took the shortest route to goal with the least number of necessary passes. This tactic started to take its toll on Burnley, with Villa ploughing relentlessly through the mud, whereas Burnley's young side, being more slightly built, tried to fashion the game through the wings and not the heavy porridge-pot centre. The home side were now well in command and increasing the tempo of their attacks, with Peter McParland, Jackie Sewell and Derek Pace all going close.

Villa made the breakthrough in the 18th minute. Industrious right-winger Les Smith, who was left unmarked from a Stan Lynn throw-in, chipped the ball over Shannon and waltzed around Winton before unleashing a fierce shot that Burnley stopper Blacklaw couldn't hold. The ball spilled from his grasp, and as he struggled to reach it in the mud, Villa captain Dixon slid in to poke the ball into the net. First blood to Aston Villa, the roar from the 46,531 crowd evoked all that pre-war Villa glory as they worked towards their 15th semi-final.

Young Shackleton troubled the Villa defence with seven minutes remaining of the first half, his header beating Nigel Sims but headed off the line by the ever-dependable Stan 'the wham' Lynn. How many times over the years had Stan got the Villa out of jail? Out of gratitude a relived Sims lifted Lynn up into the air in a bear-like hug! The start of the second half saw referee Mr Topliss appear in a white cricket shirt, his black jersey having caused confusion because it was not dissimilar from Burnley's dark blue kit. Eric Houghton claimed, "My players said his gear was clashing with Burnley's Oxford-blue rig. I asked the referee if he would like to make himself less like a Burnley player!"

Burnley were fortunate not to concede a penalty when a defender clearly handled with the ref unsighted. In another home attack, Smith crossed hard for Sewell, whose 30-yard volley flashed just wide.

But a second Villa goal looked increasingly imminent and the decisive strike arrived with 20 minutes left on the clock. Burnley's Irish international McIlroy was plotting and probing in the Villa area when Dugdale, aware of the danger, cleared the ball upfield to Smith, who pushed the ball to his wing partner Sewell.

The inside-forward – fighting harder than ever before in his career – played it straight back to Smith who in turn stroked the ball to Dixon. The skipper hit a sweeping pass to the left wing where McParland surged forward beyond the marking full-back and hit a crisp shot over the onrushing Blacklaw as the goalkeeper dived despairingly at his feet. From then on there was no doubt about the outcome because the uphill task faced by Burnley was simply too great.

The game was now being totally controlled by the home side, Villa thoroughly deserving the position they had created for themselves. The outcome was certainly fair, a just reward for the yeoman half-back work of Crowther, Dugdale and Saward, the enthusiasm of Smith, McParland and Pace, the sprightly fancy of Sewell and the untarnished skill of Dixon.

Aston Villa 2 Burnley 0
Dixon
McParland
half-time 1-0, Attendance 46,531

Villa's McParland was Burnley's nemesis, he had scored in both games, "To Burnley it was like us going to them, and they didn't like coming to Villa Park they had a job to win at ours because we always beat them - a reversal of it all. We 'done' them 2-0. The conditions were bad, at Villa Park something had happened under the turf and it didn't take the rain well; I think the soil went rotten, it had to be dug up the next close season. We were very fit and Billy Moore had us in good condition all the time so we were always able to work our way through it so that was a good grounding."

An hour after the game Villa Park was split by a blinding controversy – are these Villa strong men a little too tough or the victims of a smear campaign?

One newspaper reported that Villa's football 'won't win any beauty contests, but on the evidence of the Cup replay, their non-stop slog through the mud, it will take a fighting team to keep them from Wembley.'

Another paper claimed, 'Bang goes the vision of a soccer sweet Wembley Final. Burnley were perhaps the only side remaining, fit to match the finer arts with kingly Manchester United. The smooth fineries of Burnley's babes being ruthlessly cut down by Villa,'

A scout from another club said angrily, "Villa's tackling was an insult to every team that tries to play football. They dare not use these tactics if they got to Wembley." But one reporter came to the team's defence, writing 'Let me say it firmly, Villa did not bulldoze Alan Brown's boys out of the cup, Villa systematically overran Burnley.'

And proud Villa boss Houghton said, "How dare they criticise my lads after today. They were hard, but we had to play it hard against a fast, clever team like Burnley."

Another paper stated, 'Villa went relentlessly into the job of winning. They were faster than Burnley, always challenging for the loose ball first. They were harder than Burnley, tackling solidly and jolting their opponents out of their composure. And most of all, they had the killer punch - where matches are won and lost - in the goalmouth.'

Many Burnley fans labelled the Villa players a dirty and tough bunch after the final whistle. "Sour grapes, if you ask me" Villa stopper Nigel Sims remembered, "After all, we had just dumped their team out of the Cup. Stan Lynn even got an anonymous, vicious letter with a Burnley postmark."

Sims had picked up Johnny Dixon during the excitement. The skipper told his keeper, "Put me down Nigel and get on with the game. My 13 and a half stone is too much for you to be carrying around!"

Last word to the scorer of Villa's second goal, 'Packy' McParland, "It was the best worked-for goal I have seen since I joined Villa."

McParland wore the No 11 shirt that belonged to Alex Govan, Birmingham City's pint sized outside-left. He informed reporters after the game that every time he bent down the shirt rolled up his back like a window blind!

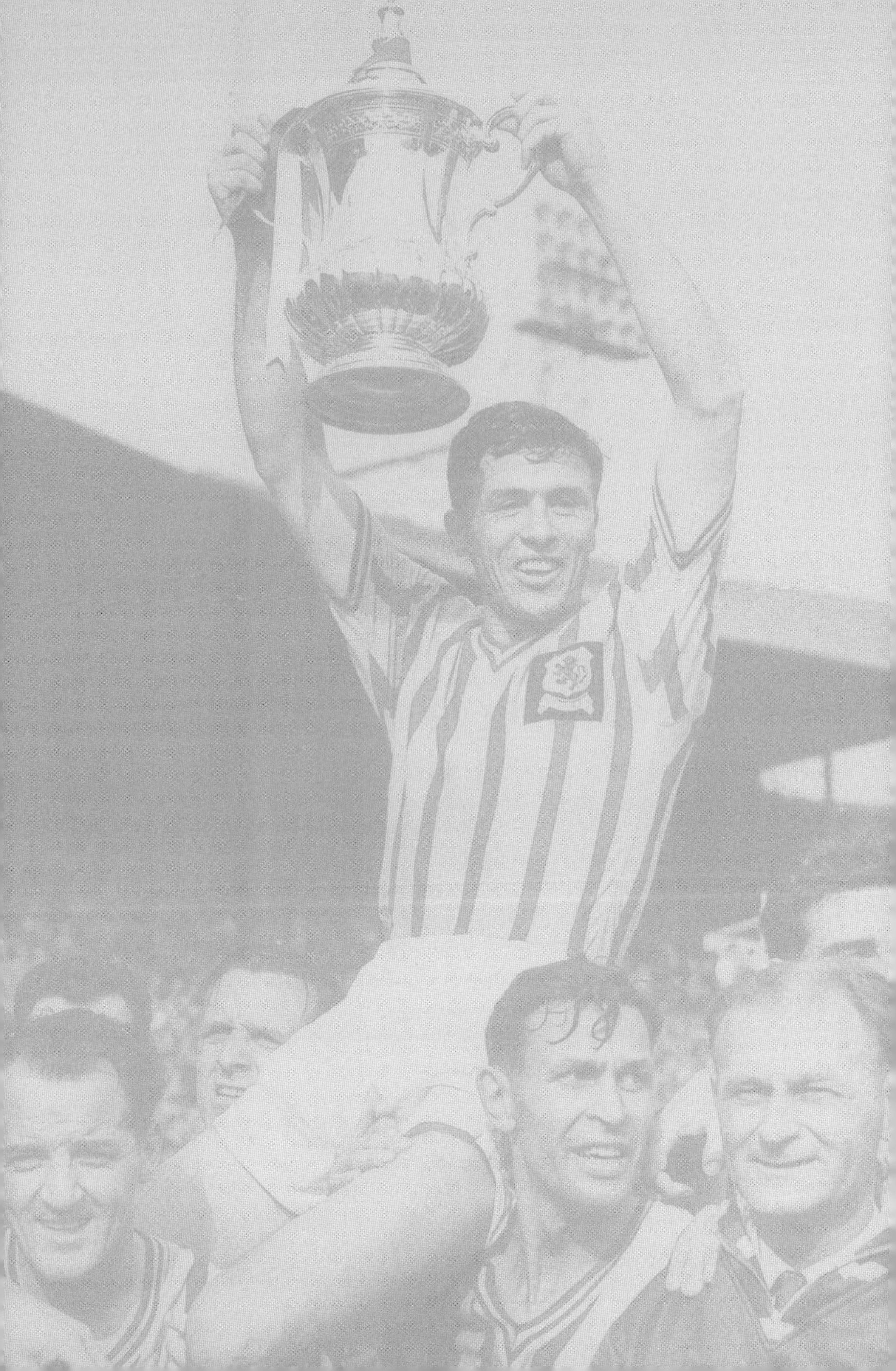

Billy - do be a hero!
semi-final

Villa had made it to their 15th FA Cup semi-final – and their first since before the Second World War, when they had been a Second Division side. It was a record shared, strangely enough, with their opponents West Bromwich Albion. The Baggies had won nine of their previous 14 semis whereas Villa had been successful on eight occasions. Whatever happened, the West Midlands would boast at least one finalist and perhaps if Birmingham City could 'up' their game against the mighty Manchester United in the other semi-final, the area would provide both finalists. The last time this occurred had been in 1931 when Albion had defeated Blues. The venue for the all-Midlands tie was to be the locally-based Wolverhampton Wanderers ground, Molineux.

Burnley F.C - League, a. providing FA Cup Semi-Final completed, re arranged date – Tuesday 26th March 1957
Aston Villa Football Club Boardroom minutes, Wednesday 13th March 1957.

"Evening Despatch" – Request for permission for a photograph of Aston Villa, Birmingham City & W.B. Albion, players & officials to be taken at Villa Park on Monday 18th March to mark the occasion of three Midlands Clubs appearing in the FA Cup Semi-finals. – The board decided to agree to this request.
Aston Villa Football Club Boardroom minutes, Wednesday 13th March 1957.

The Evening Despatch photo-call of Villa, Albion and Blues was arranged to take place on the bowling green at Villa Park and was intended for the local 'rags' only, the nationals weren't wanted in attendance for this all Midlands affair. Somehow the news was leaked and a few spies with cameras were hiding in the vegetation with one even managing to get a lofty viewpoint from high in the Trinity Road stand. As all three teams players and officials posed and the local press were about to snap the occasion for posterity, the unwanted photographers were discovered and cleared away from the scene before the locals got their desired shots.

Special training – If FA Cup Semi-Final completed on 23rd March, player's to have a few days at Blackpool
Aston Villa Football Club Boardroom minutes, Wednesday 13th March 1957.

As Villa had progressed in the Cup not only had the players started believing something special could happen – and supporters clearly felt the same. Attendances had jumped from 28,536 for the third round replay against Luton Town to a whopping 63,099 for the fifth-round tie against Bristol City.

Sadly, more and more space in newspapers' sports sections had been devoted to Villa's tactics in reaching the last four of the competition. The further the Villa progressed, the more intense it had become, every incident getting dragged up and scrutinized. It seemed everybody had an opinion; accusations and counter accusations were fired backwards and forwards, filling more space than the actual match reports.

Villa legend Albert Evans, the sole survivor of Villa's double winning side of 1897 and now 81, proudly predicted "Villa to win the Cup," adding "I like the present Villa team's first-time tackling and their showing as ninety-minute fighters who never acknowledge defeat."

Jimmy Hogan, another claret & blue legend, was also right behind the team, backing them to not only beat West Brom but to go on and lift the Cup, even if they had to face Manchester United. Hogan was an individual whose reasoning commanded the utmost respect – he was the manager who had led Villa back from their wilderness years of Second Division football in the late 1930s to their rightful place back in the top flight, and was hugely respected throughout the football world.

"Villa have been trained into England's fittest team," said Hogan. "And to win the Cup, playing match after match and all of them getting harder and harder, you have to be fit. They have proved it by the way they have out-stayed their opponents in the rounds up to the semi-final. They have come from behind time after time. What's more they have proved their ability to produce their best away from home and, remember, the semi-final and final are away games.

"They went to Luton on a sticky pitch, they were losing 2-1, they fought back made a draw and won the replay at home. At Middlesbrough, they were losing 2-1 and proved their superb fitness by a great fighting display in the second half to win that tie. They then went to Burnley, which was a tremendous test to set them; it became worse when they were behind as a result of an own goal, even that didn't upset them. They came from behind again and again and forced a draw. Then we saw them beat Burnley here (Villa Park) to get into the semi-final. They have a wonderful team spirit, as good as any Villa team ever had, and this Bill Moore is a hard trainer and a good one. His boys have responded so well that there'll never be any doubts about their ability to stick it out to the end."

It was announced by the club that their badge (lion rampant over the motto 'Prepared') would be worn on the shirts for the Albion cup game. This was, in fact, the first time the Villa badge had adorned the famous claret & blue jersey. A very brief history lesson – for the first four years of Villa's formation they had played in stripes, as it seems everyone else did. As the Villa had aspirations they decided to go with a self-colour and from 1878 chose black tops. These were sombre and to add a little relief it was decided to wear the club crest on the shirt, as it had appeared on club notepaper.

Due to Villa's Scottish connection, most notably George Ramsey and William McGregor this crest happened to be a rampant Scottish lion. The ones to adorn the shirts were dinner plate sized red lions (facing to the right) and were sewn on by none other than William McGregor's sister. These paled with washing and replacements were sent for from Scotland. These were added and taken off prior to the jerseys being washed; they only appeared until February 1881. The next time a badge was used on the shirts was the season of 1886/87 the year the Villa won the FA Cup for the first time and were known as the 'chocolate and blues' due to the colours of the striped jerseys they played in, this badge was the Birmingham 'coat of arms' of the time and would last only one season. The famous claret & blue colours came into effect in the second half of the year 1887, and would remain, albeit without a badge until the Albion match 70 years later!

No special training was supplemented for the Cup-tie. "Just routine, with probably a little golf on Wednesday," declared Eric Houghton.

Ex-Villa star Dickie Dorsett - who had made just shy of 300 first team appearances in the claret & blue and was now coach to the Villa third team in the Birmingham and District League - put the first team players through their paces in a few sprinting sessions at the Ellisons ground in Witton in the days leading up to the Molineux clash.

In the build-up to the big day, Eric Houghton, announced on the Wednesday that he would sit on the Pace-Myerscough centre-forward dilemma and would not announce his semi-final side until Friday at the earliest, though he added that the centre-forward post was the only vacancy to be filled now that Stan Crowther would be back in the side against West Brom. "No doubt about him; he's fit and in full training" added Houghton "Stan could have played against Arsenal last Saturday if it had come to push, but his foot was just a bit sore and it was better to rest him."

Crowther had come in relatively early in the season due to an injury to Bill Baxter, he knew Baxter's misfortune had been his good luck. "I was a desperate man when I was left out of the Highbury game, what if Eric fancied Trevor Birch and he took my place in the semi's, he had performed bloody well against Arsenal. Vic Crowe had come back against Manchester a few months ago, was he fit again? I thought we had a good chance at getting to Wembley, I had dreamed of this as a kid and I didn't want to miss out if we got there."

Only a fully-fit Pace would get the position of leader of Villa's attack against Albion. Houghton explained, "We shall finish our training programme tomorrow (Thursday). On Friday morning we shall probably have a sprint or two and then we shall see whether Pace is ready to come into the team. That doesn't mean he will go in automatically. Billy Myerscough has played very well since we moved him to centre-forward and I have got to make up my mind whether Derek can do any better."

Pace had played in all six previous Cup-ties, scoring against both Middlesbrough and Bristol City. An article in the Birmingham Mail mentioned how Pace would offer nuisance value to the Villa. 'Albion play short passes out of their danger area,' it observed, 'and they can be harassed by such a player as Pace who persistently chases the ball.'

Pace had played with Villa's reserve team at Liverpool the previous Saturday, coming through without any reaction from the groin strain which had been troubling him.

On the eve of the big day details were published in the Birmingham Mail for re-play arrangements, if required. St Andrews – home of neighbouring Birmingham City – was the chosen venue, with game scheduled for the following Thursday at 2.30pm. In the same day's edition the West Bromwich Albion side for the big game was listed. Albion's Maurice Setters, it was reported, would stand down from the Baggies' half-back line. The team announced reverted to the old half-back line of Dudley, Kennedy and Barlow. With no other changes they would field the side that had drawn at home to Arsenal in the sixth round tie, in which Kennedy was injured.

Seven of their team had appeared in their FA Cup triumph of 1954, as had Jimmy Dugdale who was now playing in claret and blue. Jim Sanders would be making his 350th appearance for the Albion. Villa meanwhile named a squad of 12 players to travel to Wolverhampton; "It is highly probable that Myerscough will be the centre-forward – I would say it is almost a hundred to one chance – but it is not definite yet," Houghton told reporter 'Citizen.'

On the morning of the match the Birmingham Mail declared 'The great Villa centre-forward mystery is over.' Billy Myerscough had received the nod and would lead the Villa attack, so both teams were at full strength. Traffic was heavy and Villa's team bus had a police escort all the way through Wolverhampton, arriving at Molineux only 50 minutes before kick-off. Before boarding, Villa boss Houghton had sent a telegram to his Birmingham counterpart, City manager Arthur Turner, who was in Sheffield for the other semi-final It said, "Hope we meet at Wembley."

The team line-ups:
Aston Villa: Sims, Lynn, Aldis, Crowther, Dugdale, Saward, Smith, Sewell, Myerscough, Dixon, McParland
West Bromwich Albion: Sanders, Howe, Millard, Dudley, Kennedy, Barlow, Griffin, Whitehouse, Allen, Kevan, Horobin

The Molineux ground had been packed well before the teams arrived with the crowd entertained for the hour before kick-off by a Royal Air Force band. Albion were first to take the field, captain Ray Barlow carrying a good luck charm, a small horseshoe from a wedding cake which had been given to him from the father of the bride whose fashionable wedding had been in progress at the hotel where the Baggies had taken their pre-match lunch.

Villa who had been allocated the home dressing room emerged soon after. Johnny Dixon tossed the coin and lost the call, so Villa kicked off with the wind at their backs in the first half. Almost immediately Les Smith had the chance to set Villa on their first attack but was unable to control the ball. Villa threatened from a throw in, Myerscough looking particularly lively but Barlow realised the danger and stepped in to pass back to Albion keeper Sanders.

West Brom broke forward, a slide rule pass from Derek Kevan setting up Griffin, whose cross was cleared by wing-half Saward. Again Albion attacked, a Ronnie Allen scorcher from the right being only partially blocked by Peter Aldis before it was properly cleared. Brian Whitehouse was on it in a flash, swivelling and unleashing a low angled drive past Nigel Sims. One-nil to the Baggies.

Villa, renowned for refusing to concede defeat after being behind in the early stages, quickly challenged the West Brom defence with Billy Myerscough - playing in his first cup-tie – firing a yard wide.

Albion, with Roy Horobin combining with Allen, threatened near the bye-line but full-back Stan Lynn ultimately outwitted the pair of them, blocking their chance to cross. Villa's attacks were less frequent than the Baggies at this stage and each one fizzled out when Barlow was on hand with his uncanny interceptions and superb tackling. West Brom were having by far the lion's share of the possession, their supremacy stemming from the strength of their wing-halves. As a result Jackie Sewell, who was having a bit of an off day, saw many passes go astray.

The conditions that afternoon in a sunny Wolverhampton didn't help the claret and blues. They had slogged all winter up and down heavy muddy pitches, the ball soaking up water like sponges. With stamina and strength the key, Villa were conditioned for such adversities. That day, though, the pitch was good, the weather fine and the ball light.

A determined attack ended with Villa's Irish outside-left Peter McParland crashing in a shot that Sanders did well to hold. Villa went close when Stan Crowther put in a centre; Barlow could only glance it skywards, Sanders was able to get a fist on it as it hit the underside of the bar and came crashing back down. Kennedy, standing on the goal line gratefully cleared it. The Villa spirit was evident but the Albion defence was very experienced.

With the clock running down and seven minutes remaining of the first half Villa skipper Dixon put in a truly fine centre. Packy McParland, running full tilt, connected ever so sweetly with his head and the ball rocketed past the helpless Sanders. Villa should have been overrun, yet now they were back in it.

Yet the cries from the 20,000-strong claret & blue army had hardly died down when Albion broke forward and launched an all-out attack to regain the lead. A speculative through ball from Millard went straight through Pat Saward's legs and the ball fell kindly to Whitehouse, who turned in an instant shot and beat Sims from close.

Saward was visibly annoyed with himself, beating the ground in despair; all it had required was a 'hoof into row Z,' but the ball had bounced unkindly and clean through his legs. With no time left to salvage the half and with the cheers of the Baggies crowd still resounding throughout Molineux, Villa along with the Albion trooped off the pitch, the men from Aston trailed 2-1 at the interval.

Straight from the restart West Brom moved forward hoping to consolidate their position. Only the intervention of the ever-alert Villa centre-half Jimmy Dugdale who quashed Griffin's attempt to centre the ball at the expense of a throw-in kept his side in the tie. Don Howe received the throw-in but mis-hit the ball and enabled Saward to make a clearance.

Villa offered their defence brief respite when winger Les Smith took on the Albion back line, beating Millard only to see Barlow block his way. From the resulting corner Kennedy was able to clear the danger by heading upfield. The Baggies were now getting in their stride, Horobin and Allen combining cleverly with the latter sending Derek Kevan through.

With 18 minutes of the second period played, the Villa manager called for Peter 'Mac' to move inside with Myerscough shifting wide to run the left-wing; only time would tell if this was a masterstroke or mistake. A masterly tackle by Barlow thwarted a Villa thrust down the right flank but his uncharacteristically poor pass gave the initiative straight back. Unfortunately Dixon's header caused Sanders no trouble. Villa now had a little more possession but carried neither the craft nor the finish to punish their opponents. With only 10 minutes remaining it looked all over for Villa. Ronnie Allen tricked his way through the Villa rearguard past three defenders and strode into the penalty area. He only had to pull the trigger and Albion would surely have been going back to the Empire Stadium for their second Cup Final in three years. Allen fired and the ball was hit firm and true, looking every inch a goal. But Nigel Sims hurled his huge physique upwards, and with his fingertips he managed to push the ball over the bar.

Sims, so long denied a chance to shine at Molineux during his time with Wolves, had shown his true worth at every opportunity. He had already saved from Kevan and Allen attempts and had shown he was no shrinking violet time and again as he plunged down into a surging mass of bodies to seize the ball when all seemed lost for the claret & blue cause.

The Albion fans buried their heads in disbelief. That would certainly have put the game to bed. West Brom had been the better side for almost the whole game, being more composed, organised and dangerous every time they pushed forward. Villa had only given brief glimpses of their best form, three corners in a brief spell all being too tame to cause concern.

Yet again Villa were on the back foot – until Stan Lynn thumped a long clearance down the left flank. Billy Myerscough, who had hardly been involved in the game, was first to the loose ball, running with it and neatly turning his marker Howe. With Baggies keeper Sanders off his line, Myerscough floated a delicate cross into the centre – and Albion's surprised defence were powerless to stop the rapidly-advancing McParland from reaching and then connecting with the ball first and hitting it firmly. Only centre-half Kennedy on the goal-line offered any resistance but it eluded his desperate attempt at handling it before nestling in the corner of the net.

With only four minutes left Villa had equalised, and what followed on the North Bank where the Villa fans were congregated was mass euphoria. The Albion fans couldn't believe their rotten luck; never again would they have a better chance to put one over their local rivals, because they had been streets ahead for the majority of the game.

Not long after 'Packy' had got his side back into the tie a chance opened up for him to possibly bag the winner, "Just after the equaliser I got the ball on the half-way line in the middle of the centre-circle. I controlled the pass and I had Ray Barlow and Joe Kennedy in front of me. I said to myself 'I'm going to take them, I'm going to run them through; but because I was sort of recovering from scoring the equaliser, I was battling for wind and at that particular time I couldn't raise enough steam to get through. Looking at it I fancied my chances, I just didn't have enough power to get them; had I rested for a few minutes and picked the same ball up I would have been able to skin the both of them but I couldn't do it to maybe get the winner."

But how many times had Villa's never-say-die attitude prevented them from going out of the competition? Just when they had seemed doomed to fail they had pulled it out of the bag yet again. Surely it was fate? The name Aston Villa must already be written on the famous trophy!

West Bromwich Albion 2 Aston Villa 2
McParland 2
half-time 2-1, Attendance 55,549

The Villa saviour with a brace of goals – Peter McParland, "That was a bit of a battle over at Molineux, they scored and we had to battle back each time, actually Pat Saward made a couple of mistakes for their goals – he mistrapped one and got caught in possession with the bounce and Brian Whitehouse knocked both of them in the back of the net. One nil and then we got back to one all, and then he did it again and we had another fight on our hands. I got the equaliser four minutes from time."

"It was a very hard game and Albion were off to a good start with that early goal," said Eric Houghton. "But my lads fought back well after being twice behind – as they always do. We can play much better than this."

Skipper Johnny Dixon was only too well aware that his side had got out of jail, insisting, "We were put off by the sudden change from swamps we've been playing on lately, to this bone-hard bumpy pitch. We all felt that by going in hard for the ball we should be beaten by the bounce. We won't make the same mistake next time; we won't be as bad as that again."

As news filtered down form Sheffield, the teams were aware that Birmingham City had lost 2-0 in their semi-final encounter with Manchester United at Hillsborough. There was to be no all-Midland final, and Matt Busby and Co would have to wait until Thursday at the earliest before they would know their Wembley opponents.

Focus quickly shifted from what had gone to what was coming. Tickets went on sale at Villa Park, The Hawthorns and the replay venue St Andrews on the Sunday morning, with many fans queuing at Villa Park from early Saturday evening.

In Monday's Birmingham Post it was reported that no players had sustained serious injuries and all who had played at Molineux would be available for the replay. No Villa players had reported to Villa Park for treatment, though Albion had a few players carrying minor knocks. Millard had bruised his knee and thigh, both Allen and Horobin had knocks to their knees and Kevan had received a cut below the eye from a Jackie Sewell elbow. But this wasn't sufficient to need stitches and all four players were expected to take their places in the Albion line-up.

One of the Post reporters, meanwhile, was of the opinion that Villa would be better suited in the replay to switching Myerscough and McParland and playing the latter down the middle, as Albion had been more threatened once the claret & blue had made the tactical move mid way through the second half.

An appeal went out to supporters of West Brom through the local press when it was brought to light that someone in The Hawthorns ticket office had been removing the ticket on the wrong perforation, which would mean difficulty gaining admission to St Andrews. A return trip to the Baggies' office for the purchaser to collect the correct piece was the advice the paper was giving.

Team v W.B. Albion – FA Cup Semi-Final replay at St Andrews, 28th March; Sims, Lynn, Aldis, Crowther, Dugdale, Saward, Smith, Sewell, Myerscough, Dixon, McParland – Pace to accompany

Aston Villa Football Club Boardroom minutes, Tuesday 26th March 1957.

On Wednesday, Houghton finished off the replay preparations with a team talk behind closed doors. A few minutes previously he had informed the waiting press that his Villa side would be unchanged from that which had played at Wolverhampton. He had already said after the game he knew his boys could play better than they had at Molineux. Now he added "We know that tomorrow is the big test. I've picked the same team because of that. There was no need for panic changes and I've given Bill Myerscough the centre-forward position again because I was quite satisfied with what he did at Molineux."

The Villa side went through a few loosening-up exercises before finishing their training schedule with a game of football in the car park. At the same time a few miles away at The Hawthorns, Albion manager Vic Buckingham announced, "We will be unchanged."

The Baggies were extremely fortunate to have their centre-forward Ronnie Allen available for selection. He had been called for jury duty at West Bromwich Quarter Sessions, due to take place on the Thursday, the day of the game. "He applied for exemption and because of the special circumstances we released him." Mr Day, the West Brom town clerk, told the Evening Despatch.

A few of Stan Crowther's mates weren't as lucky as Ronnie Allen. They were told they couldn't be excused from work for the game, "It didn't stop three of them downing tools to come and watch us, they were told not to bother showing back up. They didn't, they went next door and got jobs the day after – they were good lads."

The gates at St Andrew's opened at mid-day with the majority of the spectators inside the ground well before the scheduled 2.30pm kick-off. A Royal Air Force marching band entertained the huge numbers, just as they had the previous Saturday, adding an air of importance to the occasion.   Manchester United manager Matt Busby was also present, hoping to gain valuable insight on his team's cup-final opponents.

The team line-ups:
Aston Villa: Sims, Lynn, Aldis, Crowther, Dugdale, Saward, Smith, Sewell, Myerscough, Dixon, McParland
West Bromwich Albion: Sanders, Howe, Millard, Dudley, Kennedy, Barlow, Griffin, Whitehouse, Allen, Kevan, Horobin

Before kick-off, Middlesbrough-based referee Mr Howley called the two captains to the centre circle. Ray Barlow won the toss and Villa defended the Railway End in the first half. Poor control from Kevan and then Griffin offered Villa their first break but Myerscough couldn't advance beyond Millard. Albion then hit on the counter-attack but play stopped when the flag went up as Allen had strayed into an offside position. Before play resumed a photographer's plate, which had been left in the centre of the pitch, was quickly removed.

Villa were the first to threaten, a quick move between Crowther and Sewell setting Dixon on his way The Villa skipper hit it first time, hard and true, but the advancing Albion keeper was able to turn it around the post. From Smith's flag-kick, Myerscough got power behind his header but not accuracy and the ball whistled past the wrong side of the upright for a goal-kick to the Baggies.

Early nerves were evident in both sides, resulting in some scrappy football. But Nigel Sims had no such problem, the Villa keeper taking the ball off the head of Derek Kevan, who had chased Don Howe's speculative long clearance.

Pat Saward had determination written all over his face, he wouldn't be guilty of gifting any goals to the opposition this time around. Play was end-to-end, corners coming thick and fast. Kennedy conceded from a Stan Crowther centre only for Jimmy Dugdale to do likewise at the other end moments later, although the attacks lacked penetration. The game had just entered the 17th minute when – BANG – more controversy! No doubt this would set the Villa detractors in motion yet again. Ronnie Allen and Jimmy Dugdale challenged in the air for possession and there was a sickening collision of heads as both players fell to the turf. There was no malice or viciousness from either player; in fact off the field the two were best of mates. Unfortunately, only Dugdale made signs of movement, Allen lay totally still. The trainers rushed across to the unconscious centre-forward and carried him off to the sideline where, with the help of the club physiotherapist, they worked on him furiously for seven frantic minutes. He was gradually helped to his feet and assisted the short distance to the bench where he sat down, although he was visibly badly hurt. To the crowd's astonishment, though, Allen then stood up and went back onto the pitch! He looked around in a daze for a few moments and wandered back off again to be taken promptly to the dressing room.

Villa obviously wanted to make the extra man count and pushed relentlessly at the Albion defence. Ray Barlow rallied his defence; he was doing the work of two men now. But Villa couldn't take advantage and it was their opponents, despite their handicap, who continued to impress. Barlow now, pushing up every time the Baggies attacked had two scorching drives. Sims was able to push the first over the bar, the second he was able to hold.

At the other end, McParland found himself in space to shoot but snapped at his shot and watched his effort go high and wide. The Irishman had another chance when he saw Sanders out of position but Kennedy, cleaning up at the back, was able to head

The class of 1920. Villa's last FA Cup win.

Preparing for Luton tie.

Dixon scores against Hatters

Dixon makes it 3-2 at Ayresome Park.

Doc Pace partially obscured nets Villa's opener

SEWELL...LOOKING WORTH EVERY PENNY

Jackie Sewell's diving header secures Villa's winner

Peter Aldis runs the ball into his own net

Mac plants the ball in the correct net to level the score

Pace goes close while Winton can only watch.

Captain Dixon sets Villa on their way 1-0

Johnny's goal from another angle

Grounded McParland seals the victory.

For locals only, Villa, Albion and Blues all reach the last four

Off to Molineux we go

With Villa trailing 1-0 Stan Lynn clears off the line to keep Villa's hopes alive.

Former Villa star Leslie Smith shows off the semi-final shirt complete with badge.

McParland nets his second

Molineux action

Peter McParland celebrating his first goal

Billy Myerscough celebrates after laying on Villa's last-ditch equaliser.

Johnny Dixon leads the team out at St Andrew's

Billy on his knees - praying it goes in.

Albion's defence appear at sixes and sevens as obscured Myerscough nets only goal.

Get him off! Now we might be in with a shout.

Aston Villa Win Their Way to Wembley

Here is his friend Mr. Billy Ward (left) handing over the key to ...
on are Les Smith and Stan Lynn.

JIMMY AND MRS. DUGDALE.

Jimmy Dugdale and wife stepping out at the Tower Ballroom

Surely we'll never sell all these handbooks.

Aston Villa proudly show off their Wembley '57 kit.

"Howay gaffer, the blue shirt matches my eyes," says Bill Moore

My ball, training at Bournville.

Eric Houghton watches over events at Bournville.

The Wembley attack aired at Bournville, L to R, Smith, Sewell, Myerscough, Dixon and McParland.

Training at Ellisons, it's not as dangerous as Bournville.

Ouch, Jimmy Dugdale inspects his ankle.

Villa fan Ron Hibbs (kneeling behind small lad) and friend Clifford Orp at New Street station

Villa legend Frank Moss, FA Cup winner in 1920.

Thumbs up for the Villa.

17 single fares to Snow Hill station please driver.

A relaxed and confident team arrive in London

Myerscough, Dugdale, Lynn, Saward and Smith take a closer look at Wembley's pitch.

Albert Evans, sole survivor from Villa's 'double' winning side of 1897, off to Wembley

Checking if the Queen will have a good view of the match.

Wembley bound, John Russell.    Moore checking the studs with Dugdale and McParland.

L to R, Smith, Saward, Sewell and Crowther flick through the programme.

How can you lose in these?

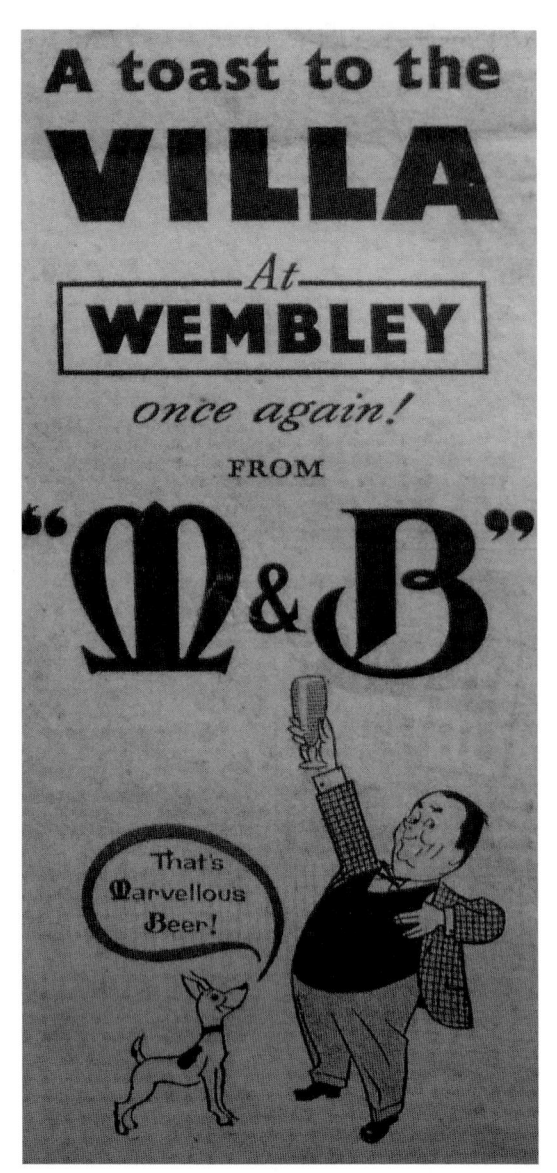

Newspaper ad.

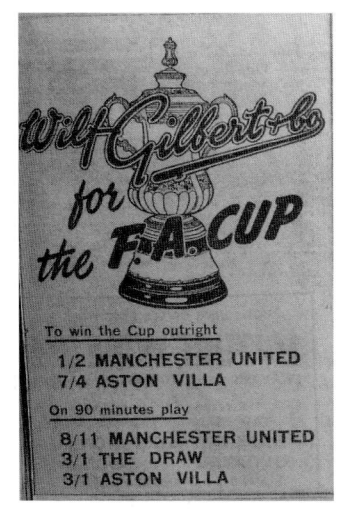

Fancy a flutter?

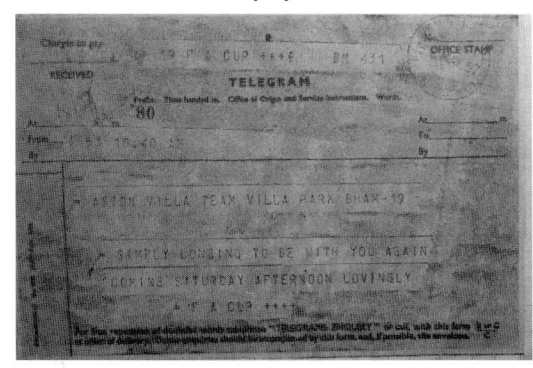

Telegram from the FA Cup.

away the danger. Kennedy was then spoken to by the referee for pulling down McParland after the Villa forward had outpaced Barlow and Dudley.

With the clock running down towards half-time a Jackie Sewell lob dropped near the right-hand goalpost. The bounce of the ball beat West Brom's full-back Howe, enabling McParland to nip in and clip the ball back into the centre of the goalmouth. Billy Myerscough - who three weeks earlier had been plying his trade in the Villa's reserve side – reached it fractionally before the advancing Jim Sanders could catch hold of it. Myerscough who was by this time on his knees, watched the ball hit the net for his first senior goal – and what a game in which to achieve it! Villa had taken the lead in the semi-final tie for the first time in nearly 130 minutes of football.

Straight away, Albion broke forward with their new 'main man' Barlow, who hit a belter from the edge of the penalty area which caught out Sims and hit the foot of the post before rebounding to Kevan. Thankfully the Albion man was only able to shoot wide from the acute angle in the last action of a yet another controversial first half.

As the teams left the field Peter looked up as he heard his name called, "We'd had this battle in the first half and I remember going in at half-time and there was two fellows on the roof of the stand. One shouted down 'Hey Peter get the ball up the field, can't we get the ball up? Don't be playing at the back. We'd got a goal early on – Billy Myerscough – I was able to flick a ball onto Billy's head and he was down on his knees and headed it in. After that we sort of dropped off and let them have a go at us, we were trying to hold on to what we had."

During the interval a hunched Ronnie Allen sat in the dressing room with a blanket over his shoulders. Albion chairman Major Wilson Keys delivered the verdict, "It is severe concussion. He is out for the rest of the game."

The Villa team and 10-man Albion took their place on the field for the second half and the game resumed. With only four minutes gone, there was disbelief all around St Andrew's when Allen came back and took up position on the pitch, even though he was so groggy he lined up facing the wrong way. Credit to him, he stayed on for the remainder of the game but although he got in an occasional shot he was never going to dictate like the Baggies supporters knew he could.

Peter McParland had a chance to put the game beyond Albion's reach following clever work between the Villa scorer Myerscough and their captain, Dixon. It was left for the Irish attacker to pick his spot from only six yards out, but he somehow contrived to miscue and watched in horror as the ball missed its intended target.

West Brom's first shot of the half, from Horobin, was well off target and didn't trouble Sims. Allen, though still dazed wandered about in the inside-left position, hitting a first time shot from a Griffin centre only for his effort to sail harmlessly over the bar. To be fair, Albion's handicap wouldn't have been noticed had Derek Kevan, who had been called up for England duty against Scotland the following week, accepted the easy opportunities that had came his way. The most glaring miss was not really Derek's fault. Just after the hour mark the Baggies were sent on their way by an intelligent Allen through ball which evaded Dugdale and was placed squarely in front of the advancing Kevan.

With the Villa defence wide open, Kevan's shot was firm and accurate and was wide of the outstretched Sims. But with the ball sailing beyond the floored Villa stopper and seemingly into the net, it hit the retreating Villa full-back Stan Lynn - who was running towards his goal with his back facing the play – square on his heel and deflected from its obvious path and round the post, out for a flag kick. How lucky could Villa get?

The Villans' attempts on goal were getting fewer and further between, and with Albion's urgency and dominance to get the ball up to the other end it severely restricted the Villa attack and piled pressure at the same time on the claret and blue defence. Sims watched in despair as centre-half Kennedy's header beat him "There wasn't anything I could do but watch the ball rolling and bouncing along the length of the crossbar, almost in slow motion" recalled the keeper. "It could have gone anywhere."

Peter McParland remembers the incident vividly also, "The second half again was a bit of a battle. I found myself back in the penalty area and there was a corner kick in the game. The ball was headed up and it got on the crossbar and bounced 2 or 3 times and Nigel Sims gave it a thump and banged it away for a corner. Stan Lynn was under the bar near Nigel, he said, 'Look 'Packy' get up there near the half way line, we are going to hammer it up to you; you go now.' I couldn't get a one on one with the goalkeeper; he came out once to kick it when I was after him. I occupied the defenders at the back then, they were afraid of a breakaway."

Villa's defence were hemmed inside their own area for long periods but they never buckled; they tackled, turned and twisted – anything to keep the 'Baggies' at bay. And Albion were certainly going for it, throwing everybody forward. In another attack Ray Barlow beat Sims to the ball only to watch his header sail over the bar. Crowther tackled Whitehouse in the nick of time; time which, for the Villa, seemed to have stopped. But they had nearly run the clock down. One minute remained - a miniscule, insignificant amount of time but still long enough for West Brom to force three corners.

To the Villa fans, that minute felt like an hour. Hands covered faces, nails were bitten to the quick and many supporters hurriedly said prayers, particularly when Kevan, totally absorbed, met one corner with a powerful header. On any other day the ball would have be buried in the net, but it wasn't his day, the ball thundering against the cross bar before being scrambled to safety.

Time had finally, finally passed, and the referee's whistle was instantly drowned out by the rapturous cheers of the masses of the claret and blue army.

Aston Villa 1 West Bromwich Albion 0
Myerscough
half-time 1-0, Attendance 58,067

Peter McParland recounts in his autobiography 'Going for Goal,' walking off the pitch and an Albion fan hissing at him, "You lucky lot!"

Villa had done it; they had defied the critics, the conditions and the opponents placed before them yet again. Next stop was Wembley Stadium. How ironic it was that Villa, the last side to have successfully claimed the League and Cup double – a record that had stood now for an astonishing 60 years – should now stand in the way of Manchester United, the recently-crowned League champions in their quest for the 'modern miracle!'

The Villa players couldn't contain their delight. "We were lucky that day, we all went back to Villa Park after the game and celebrated in true style," smiled 'keeper Nigel Sims.

Jimmy Dugdale said about the first-half incident with Ronnie Allen, "It was one of those cases where you have to go for the ball and our heads simply collided. I feel terrible." To which Allen magnanimously replied, "My collision with Jimmy Dugdale was an accident. I've no complaints at all."

Goal scorer Billy Myerscough making only his seventh first team appearance for the Villa, beamed when he was interviewed, "The goal was my first for the club – and it has put us in the Final. It's marvellous!"

Eric Houghton commented, "We would have preferred to have won against 11 fit men. Our fitness played a big part – it was a tribute to our trainer Billy Moore. There have been cleverer sides at Villa Park but none have been in better condition or played better as a team than the present one. We shall go into the final quietly confident. After all, we drew at Old Trafford three weeks ago."

Sadly, the manager revealed that he had received many threatening and vindictive letters over his decision to drop Derek Pace in preference to Billy Myerscough – and there was more vitriol to follow.

A few days after the game Jimmy Dugdale received a 'poison pen' letter, the writer expressing his disgust at what Jimmy had done to Allen, 'A nicer player than Allen never stepped on a field. This incident has killed my love for football,' the letter continued. Jimmy was getting used to receiving such garbage he had also been the recipient of something similar after the Burnley quarter-final.

Aston Villa Shareholders Association re FA Cup Final tickets – After discussion, the Board decided that in view of each shareholder being able to obtain a ticket if application was made, it was not the intention to make a 'Block' allocation this year as in previous years

Aston Villa Football Club Boardroom minutes, Tuesday 2nd April 1957.

FA Cup Final 1957 – Preliminary arrangements were discussed. The dinner and hotel accommodation left in the hands of the Chairman
Aston Villa Football Club Boardroom minutes, Tuesday 2nd April 1957.

Arising out of the minutes the Chairman informed Mr J Broughton, the Board had decided not to make a 'Block' allocation of FA Cup Final tickets to the Shareholders Association this season. Mr Broughton agreed with action taken
Aston Villa Football Club Boardroom minutes, Tuesday 9th April 1957.

Irish FA – World Cup – Request for P McParland, if selected, on 25th April in Rome and 1st May in Belfast – The Board decided not to release McParland for either match
Aston Villa Football Club Boardroom minutes, Tuesday 9th April 1957.

With a date in a Wembley Cup Final only 37 days away, Villa amazingly still had over a quarter of their League matches to be played. As their involvement in the cup had progressed – with replays adding to the fixture congestion - it had meant that no less than 11 games were still to be played and the football authorities were adamant that the backlog would be cleared prior to the Wembley date of Saturday 4th. There would be no leeway.

Eric Houghton gave his lads a team talk to remember prior to the first league game – against Preston North End - after the semi-final victory. "Now lads," he told them, "don't become too wrapped up with thoughts of Wembley and not getting injured. It's when you ease off that you are more likely to get caught!"

The schedule was heavy going at the start of April, with just a few days between some fixtures and then a block of three games in only six days. Houghton decided enough was enough; he had to rest some of the first team. Villa already had enough points on the board to guarantee safety, unlike the previous season when they had been constantly looking over their shoulders. The old adage that winning games inspires confidence was certainly correct. Since Villa had kicked off their cup campaign at Kenilworth Road back in January they had tasted defeat in only two League games.

Trained by the iron-willed Billy Moore, they were renowned for their strength and stamina, those characteristics being more prevalent on heavy pitches or late into games when opponents would visibly flag. But this punishing schedule was too much even for them. In the seventh fixture of the outstanding 11, Villa travelled to Turf Moor where Burnley remained unbeaten. It was unlikely that Villa would emerge from the game with both points and unscathed, given that feelings were still running high in Burnley following the physical quarter-final clash between the clubs.

Sensibly, the Villa management took the decision to play mostly reserves in order to restrict the likelihood of injuries to key players. Of the regular line-up, only Jimmy Dugdale, Pat Saward, Jackie Sewell and Peter McParland took to the field in Lancashire although Villa certainly weren't disgraced, going down 2-1 with 'Doc' Pace doing his chances of a Wembley place no harm by scoring the visitors' goal.

An article in the following morning's Birmingham Mail (Tuesday 16th April) revealed that the game at Burnley could cost Villa £400 as well as a two-point deduction. The article said the game should have been played on a Saturday, when Burnley would have expected a gate of 22,000; the previous night's encounter had been attended by 18,000, and the difference in revenue to Burnley was £400. This was the amount of compensation they were seeking from their visitors.

By playing so many reserves, Houghton feared he might upset the Football League but the close result was definitely favourable for the club; it also showed him that the reserves were nearing the real thing. There was no mention anywhere after the initial Mail article regarding a two-point deduction and, as the final league table testifies, was never enforced.

Villa had four more League fixtures to fulfil – in a period of only eight days. Fielding the Wembley XI for the first two matches against Newcastle United and Wolverhampton Wanderers, they took maximum points, lifting them up to ninth in the table. With a few minor tweaks in the line-ups for the remaining games, Villa lost both, but by then the looming Final was fixed very firmly in the players' thoughts. They finished the season in a commendable 10th position but more importantly they had wrapped up their campaign with no injury worries – no thanks to the Football League!

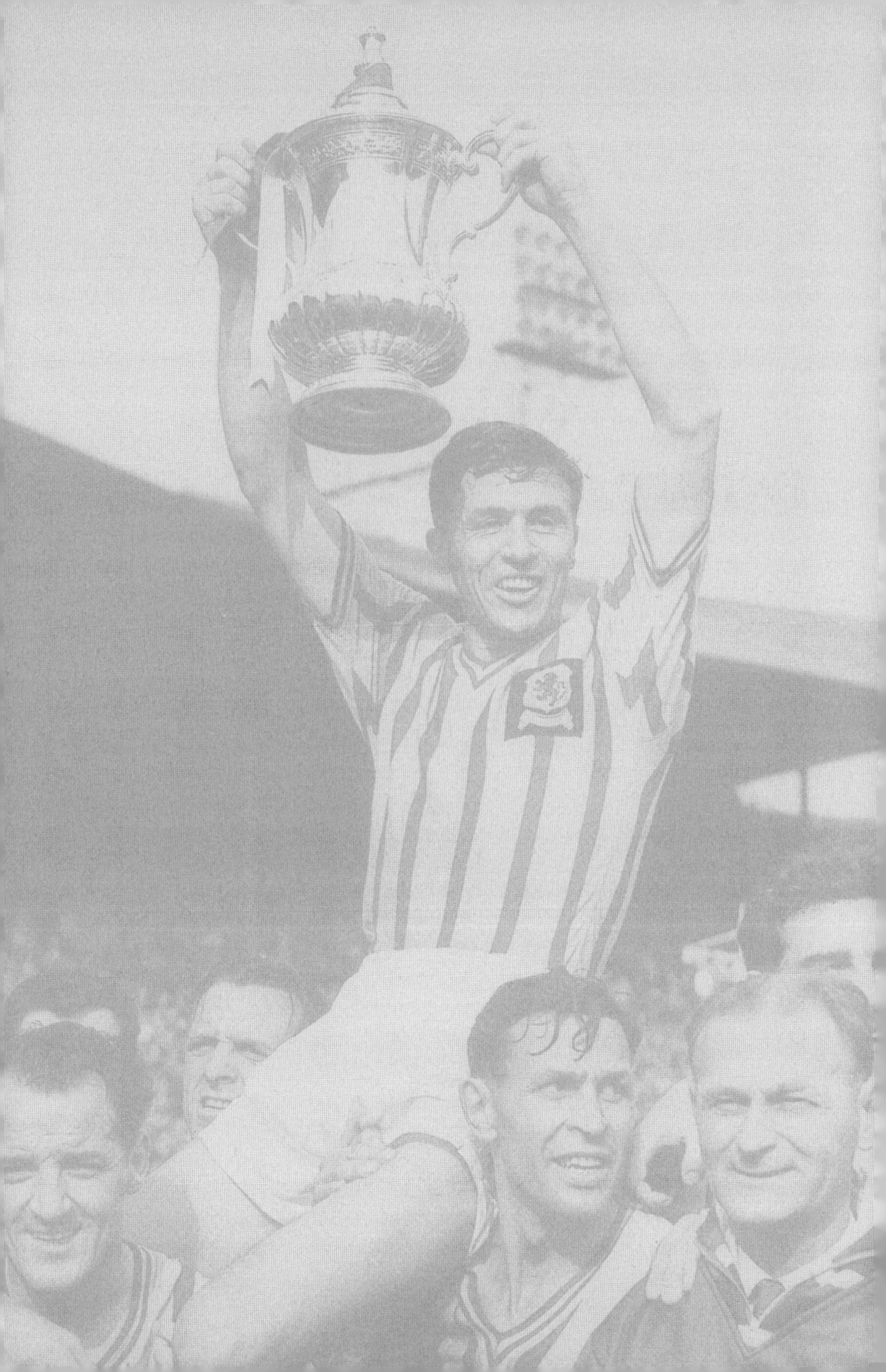

Que sera, sera (whatever will be, will be)
Final preparation

After the semi-final victory against Albion, a meeting was arranged by centre-half Jimmy Dugdale in the Villa Park boot room with Eric Houghton and Billy Moore. It was hoped that the players might capitalise on the fact they had reached the Final and make themselves a few quid from the achievement! The club's hierarchy readily agreed to this request an each player was given a specific job. Captain Johnny Dixon negotiated a free raincoat for every player from Swallow Raincoats. Jackie Sewell and Jimmy Dugdale were asked to organise a dance to be held at the Tower Ballroom in Edgbaston; some of the other players were in charge of boot sponsorship, a boot manufacturer putting £150 into the players' kitty. ASTON VILLA 'PREPARED' was released - a handbook of Villa players, 1956-57. It went on sale for 1/6d (7.5p) and fans could buy copies directly from the Villa players at specially organised signing events. The biggest money-spinner for the players' kitty was the club's generous offer of 1,000 Cup Final tickets to be sold, with all proceeds to go to the team.

In accordance with a Football Association ruling, Villa and Manchester United were required to drop their respective famous colours of claret & blue and red. Eric Houghton and Matt Busby had a meeting regarding the subject on the evening of 15th April at Turf Moor, when Villa were in Lancashire to play their re-arranged match against Burnley. The Manchester club opted for their all-white strip with red piping on the jerseys' collar and cuffs, a red stripe down the shorts and red turnovers on the socks. Villa had only recently had their lion crest adorn their shirts, now they would have to go back to the manufacturers of their football jerseys – Bukta, based in Stockport.

Houghton had given it considerable consideration before settling on the idea of stripes. It was while he had been thumbing through a book on the history of Aston Villa that he had noted that the Villa's first victorious FA Cup-winning side of 1887 had played in striped jerseys, albeit chocolate and blue. If stripes had been good enough then, he concluded, they were good enough now.

The kit suppliers didn't disappoint, coming up with two superb designs, a claret shirt with blue striping and a light blue alternative with claret stripes. The latter design was chosen. Bukta also gave Villa the choice of having five one-inch thick or eight half-inch claret stripes across the front, the former receiving the vote (though in reality it was actually six one-inch stripes down the front of the jersey). Eric Houghton wanted the new kits with V-necks, short sleeved and as light as a knitting machine could make them. Banking on the usual cricket weather on Cup Final day, he also wanted them available in time for training prior to Wembley showpiece. His reasoning was that with the shirt being entirely new to his players, he wanted to make certain that everyone was thoroughly accustomed to playing in it and "recognising a team-mate in the split second of a glance up the field."

Busby's side had already clinched the League title with three games to spare. Villa had no more distractions apart from what were, to all intents and purposes, meaningless remaining League fixtures, and were counting down the calendar to their date with destiny in the capital. United, though, were still involved in European competition and still had to face Spanish giants Real Madrid in the second leg of the European Cup semi-final only 10 days before the Wembley showdown. United had lost the first leg 3-1 at the Santiago Bernabeu Stadium, so Real came over to England knowing they had a two-goal cushion. At Old Trafford on April 24th they pulled off a 2-2 draw to win the semi-final tie 5-3 on aggregate. The chance of Manchester United landing the treble had gone.

BBC Television – Request to take films for television on 27th April for reproduction at 10.30pm – Granted, providing necessary permission given by the Football League
Aston Villa Football Club Boardroom minutes, Wednesday 24th April 1957.

Press of Birmingham Dinner – Providing Aston Villa win the FA Cup Final, invitation extended to Directors, Officials and Players to attend Dinner on 10th May. – Invitation accepted & Secretary instructed to forward suggested names.
Aston Villa Football Club Boardroom minutes, Wednesday 24th April 1957.

On Wednesday evening all eyes were on the Tower Ballroom in Edgbaston, where the motto was 'Go Gay' for the meet-the-supporters dance that the Villa players had organised. The fans turned out in huge numbers to meet and dance the night away with their idols. Peter Aldis certainly didn't disappoint, giving his hamstrings a bit of a workout at the same time, high kicking along with the ladies in a claret & blue version of the hokey-cokey!

"One of the lads suggested that we take along our players 'Prepared' handbook, as we might be able to sell a few copies," remembered Nigel Sims. "It was staggering how many fans had come simply to collect our signatures, rather than to dance. I bet I signed hundreds of those books that night, though it was all for a good cause. God knows what they fetch nowadays with all those signatures I probably couldn't afford one!"

Nigel spent the remainder of the night selling Cup Final tickets for the players' pool. Signs were prominently positioned to respectfully remind patrons not to bop, jive or creep, though rock 'n roll was permitted. The enjoyable event rolled on for four hours. "As tough as any match," was trainer Billy Moore's verdict, who for once allowed his instructions to be ignored as he jokingly ordered Jimmy Dugdale, "Get outside and run round the reservoir twice."

Jackie Sewell agreed to a series of interviews by one of the local papers. The questions and answers sessions had begun after Villa had progressed at the expense of Burnley in the quarter-finals. They concluded a week before the Final, prior to the Villa's last League game of the season, at home to Luton Town. The football journalist set the ball rolling by asking the Villa's inside-right if the team had improved since the semi-final; Jackie said they had, they then went on to analyse the improvement.

REPORTER: "Are Aston Villa through to the semi-final of the FA Cup because they are the current masters of mud?"

JACKIE SEWELL: "The mud has had an influence, but let's be clear. We have not got there only because of the mud. We have not just slogged our way to the semi-final. We have played good football, too, when we have been able to. From the start of the season we have trained to be super fit; there is no fitter team than Villa. That has brought us through when conditions have been terrible – that and the fact that we have played straight-forward football that wins matches in the mud. If all grounds had been good I still think we should have got through, although it might have been more of a struggle. Conditions at Middlesbrough and Burnley were good. The Middlesbrough pitch was the best I have played on this year – and we played our best football in the Cup."

REPORTER: "When I have seen you play, physical strength and power seem to have been the major factor. Is this so?"

JACKIE SEWELL: "That's probably because you have only seen us on heavy grounds in the Cup when physical fitness has been the deciding factor. It was certainly true against Bristol City, who gave us our hardest match. But we won in the end because we stayed the distance better than they did. We are nearly all big fellows and when big men are super-fit they are bound to look physically dominant, particularly in the tackle. You have to be able to tackle well and win the ball often to do any good in the Cup."

REPORTER: "I suppose it is because of so much tackling that it is said you stop other people playing football?"

JACKIE SEWELL: "And so we do – because we keep on taking the ball from them by good, honest tackling. And the less your opponents see of the ball the less football they can play. That means your side must have more of the ball but they must be able to do something with it to make progress. Out of this I think you can find the maxim for Cup success – first and foremost you must have the power and determination to get the ball and then make a show when you have got it. If you are a hard side with a fair amount of football then you can go all the way. It does not apply so much in the League because there is less tackling."

REPORTER: "You talk of strength and hardness in the tackle. Hasn't that led to the suggestion that you are a robust strong-arm side?

JACKIE SEWELL: "I can't deny that strongly enough. The lads have been riled by these suggestions from people who don't understand what they are saying. Certainly we go in hard and we go in quickly, and when a strong man knocks a little fellow off the ball it may look rough, but it is a long way from being anything like dirty. I dismiss it as a lot of silly talk. When it is 50-50 between two players in a tackle often the weaker player loses balance and goes down. You can't play if you can't get the ball, and we don't mean to lose sight of that. But to say we get it by rough tactics is ridiculous. I regard crude, wild tackling as rough play and you don't see it from Villa. My idea of rough play is the man who comes in with his foot up – and there is certainly none of that. We have backs and halves who go in quickly and hard but they are football-minded. If they weren't, we forwards would have a bad time – but we are enjoying ourselves.

Because I think a lot of tackling gets misinterpreted these days I want to say this; opponents cannot expect to hold the ball and bring it to us or try and drag it past us in the sludge and expect to get away with it. That gives us the chance to go in and we go in hard with the one and only intention of playing the ball. The player about to be tackled tries to flick the ball away. Sometimes, a split-second after the ball has gone, the tackler, following through with the pace of his tackle, is carried into the opponent. I agree it is a foul but it cannot be regarded as dirty because the intention was to play the ball."

REPORTER: "It is difficult to identify a clear-cut method in Villa's attacking play. Do you work to a basic plan?"

JACKIE SEWELL: "If you mean anything as clear as, say, the Revie Plan then the answer is 'No' because we have tried to avoid a stereotyped way of playing. But we do work to a basic method. During the season we have developed the straight-forward ball, getting away more and more from the short square-passing. We want the ball played from behind as quickly and straight into the attack, and we aim to get the wingers into position to enable them to cross as fast as they can into the penalty area to our men going forward with defenders still running back into position. We believe in one pass of 25 yards rather than two of ten yards. The longer the pass the greater the chance of error, but the more effective it is when it clicks. We have analysed the things that each of us can do best. We have assessed ourselves as a team and we concentrate on a method that enables each man to do what he can most easily do, most often."

REPORTER: They said you were a team without a chance when you reached the final. Since then your record of five wins, two draws and three defeats, and with reserves in nearly every game, has made people take notice. The greatest improvement has been in attack, with 19 goals for and 11 against in those 10 games. Have you developed a new attacking method since the semi-final?

JACKIE SEWELL: I told you we weren't going to let Wembley worry us and it hasn't. In fact, it has been very much the other way. There is nothing new in our forward play. We have had a pattern of going-on all season, but it has not been evident because of two things. It is a variable system and therefore not so marked as some. We don't rely on one man to do one job. We work a moving centre-forward, but that doesn't mean only one other man, say Johnny Dixon, can go through the middle. The score-sheet shows how the wingers – who have scored more goals than any Villa wing pair since before the war – and Dixon and myself have come through as spearheads. Secondly, we are developing it more and more now, repeating the moves more often and the very fact it is coming on so well at this time is just what we wanted.

REPORTER: So you feel that not only have you retained your edge for Wembley, but you will go there as a more effective attacking side?

SEWELL: I do indeed. I think we've come a long way since the semi-final. We're not accustomed to dry conditions and we have reached such a peak of confidence that we are trying things more often than are needed to make the attack pattern click. I, particularly, can feel the difference. From my point of view it is easier to play. The idea of how we want to play has 'bedded' in as it were. Men want the ball and are easier to find because they know better what to do. I can look up now and see a man going, straight away. That is the difference.

REPORTER: In the semi-final the team seemed to be tense and your football suffered as a result. Isn't it possible that the Final atmosphere will have the similar effect?

SEWELL: I believe we have now established our attacking play to the extent that it will not be lost in the Final. It failed us to some extent in the semi-final, it is true, but only because it was not such a confirmed part of the side as it is now. And another thing, we're not playing relaxed football in the sense that we are taking it easy. The football looks relaxed because we are playing it now in the way we want to. The physical effort is very much there, but it is being applied differently. AND I STILL BELIEVE WE ARE GOING TO WIN!

REPORTER: "I have never seen a team bound for the Cup Final play with such determination after the semi-final as Villa have done. How do you manage to put Wembley out of your mind?"

JACKIE SEWELL: "In one sense it is very much in our minds. Not a day goes by when we are not concerned with such things a s personal appearances, advertising or our souvenir booklet. But it is true that for 90 minutes in every game we forget Wembley. We are proud of what we have achieved this season. We've built up a record – one defeat in the last 17 games is part of it – and a big reputation. We don't want to lose face if we can help it. We have enough pride in ourselves not to allow people to toy with us and make us look silly. That would happen soon enough if we didn't try. Another thing; in 12 months we have known the difference between winning and losing runs. We know what winning, or at least not losing, does to a team's confidence, and the different atmosphere it creates in the dressing-room. We want to stay happy and full of confidence. There is no better way of ensuring that than by winning matches."

REPORTER: "Apparently that does not apply only to the Cup Final team. You beat Birmingham with five reserves in your side. How about that?"

JACKIE SEWELL: "I'm quite sure it is a case of a new confidence having gone right through the club. The reserves are very conscious that we have reached the Final. They are determined not to let the club down."

REPORTER: "Your efforts since the semi-final have surprised many people, particularly as you were safe in the table. What do you say to that?"

JACKIE SEWELL: "Being safe was not good enough for us. We believe we are as good as Manchester United, and the nearer we can finish to them in the League the better. Then people can't say, 'Here's United on top and Villa below halfway; what a difference!' We'll be a lot nearer to united by Wembley time."

REPORTER: "The worry of getting injured plagues so many teams on the way to Wembley. There seems little suggestion by Villa that players are concerned about getting hurt. What is your answer to this?"

JACKIE SEWELL: "Before our first League game after the semi-final the boss called us together and reminded us that players having reached the Final often think too much about Wembley, and become obsessed with the idea of not getting hurt. 'It is when you start easing off and trying to avoid injury that you are most likely to get hurt,' he said. 'Now you're there, go out and enjoy your football and try to forgot Wembley.' We appreciated the point because we knew he was right, and we tried to follow his advice."

REPORTER: "Isn't it surprising that you should have all weighed in 100% with no exceptions?"

JACKIE SEWELL: "The very fact we have is typical of the great spirit at Villa Park. We are essentially a team with no individuals dominating the rest. In spite of playing matches every two days, as we have done recently, everyone has wanted to play. In fact, players with minor knocks have been forced to rest. Johnny Dixon, Les Smith and myself all had knocks after the Cardiff game. It was suggested that we should rest for the next match. None of us wanted to stand down, and in the end the boss had to make the decision. We have not played 'picnic' games since the semi-final, either. Four of the five matches have been against teams who have had particularly good reasons for wanting to win. We have failed only once – at Cardiff – and after that game we were disgusted with ourselves for losing because we knew we had tried to be exhibitionists. We thought Cardiff would be too easy after we had beaten them 4-1 a week before at Villa Park."

On Saturday 27th April, before an adoring Villa Park crowd, Villa prepared to wrap up the campaign. They faced a Luton Town side who were only four points behind them in the League. Many were surprised to see Villa field such a strong side with the Final only a week away. Nine players who would star in the Wembley showdown the following weekend took the field against the Hatters. Crowther and McParland, the two missing players had to sit it out due to knocks. Villa boss Houghton had stated his intent in the previous evening's papers. "I am sticking to the policy decided after the semi-final," he said. "We don't start thinking about Wembley until after the last match of the season. That means playing a full side when I can. There is another point about playing our Wembley side; it will provide them with a good work-out which will probably mean we shall cut out a practice match next week. We shall be training at Villa Park as usual right up to Friday morning and we shall travel on Friday afternoon, as we did for the ties at Luton, Middlesbrough and Burnley. You see, we are trying to treat the match as just another cup-tie."

The team's League commitments were concluded satisfactorily, despite a 3-1 reversal at home to Luton, because they had suffered no serious injuries to their likely Wembley XI. Nigel Sims suffered a kick below the knee during the game and played the second half with his knee heavily strapped. He had received treatment after the game and was content that it was just bruising. "I shall be training with the lads," he added confidently.

The club could now focus fully on how to defeat Manchester United, recently-crowned First Division champions and now 90 minutes away from a probable double. Only Preston and Villa had ever achieved the feat and Villa remained the last team to accomplish it when they won the League title and FA Cup in 1897. Their record had certainly stood the test of time – six decades! And a claret and blue win would not only deny United the double, it would also set Villa apart; an outright record of seven FA Cup triumphs.

Villa made no special Cup training arrangements in the build up to the Final, their regular weekly practice games being carried out with grim intensity under the watchful eye of disciplinarian Billy Moore. This was balanced by the cheerful persona of the dressing room, the light-hearted golf outings, the feelgood factor and the steely determination that was evident in the spirit that enveloped the first team players.

"We were all the best of friends, we really were," said Nigel Sims. "And in Billy Moore, we had a trainer that we would have run through brick walls for, if he'd asked us." Villa's preparation for the Wembley showdown was no different from the earlier rounds and they used local works sports grounds, Ellisons ground in Witton being favourable for the sprinting sessions.

Team V Manchester United FA Cup Final May 4 :- Sims, Lynn, Aldis, Crowther, Dugdale, Saward, Smith, Sewell, Myerscough, Dixon, McParland.

Aston Villa Football Club Boardroom minutes, Monday 29th April 1957.

It was surprising to see the team line-up appear in the minutes nearly a week prior to the match taking place, even though the book was restricted to a very select few. Eric Houghton was described in the papers of the time as being highly superstitious, he refused to reveal the side until the Friday, that's how he had done it in each previous round – team announcement on Friday – and it had worked. It was also written that Eric would wear his lucky heavy Abercrombie overcoat on the day of the Final regardless of what the weather had in store.

On Tuesday 30th April, Moore put the players through their hardest day's training since the semi-final victory, warning United that it was going to be a tough Final. "The lads won't be holding anything back," he said. "We won't go out there trying to play pretty-pretty football just because we are in a Cup Final. We shall be playing the type of game which has taken us there. My lads will be going in for the ball hard and clean. There will be nothing vicious. They are not taught tactics which are likely to cripple an opponent, but they are taught how to go in hard and make sure of getting possession. My ideal is the man who knows how to go for the ball when he hasn't got it. Recently we may not seem to have been tackling so hard, but that doesn't mean we are trying to discover some new style for the Final.

"When we were tackling harder we were playing on pitches inches deep in mud when the ball keeps low. The last few games have been on bone hard grounds when the ball has bounced high – and then you can't go into tackles. At Wembley the turf is so good that it will keep the ball at the ideal height for us to go in and get it – and we shall. We shall hold nothing back, just because it is an occasion."

Tuesday's Daily Mirror reported that 'Villa have training sessions arranged for both morning and afternoon and from now on they will wear their new claret & blue striped Final jerseys for each training period.'

In the days leading up to Wembley it had been decided long in advance that, if permission were granted, training would place at the Cadbury works ground based in the Birmingham area of Bournville because the pitch was very similar to that of the Wembley playing surface. "It was widely known that the Bournville pitch was the envy of some League sides, it was like a tennis court," Villa keeper Nigel Sims recalled. Permission was granted and on Wednesday 1st May the Cadbury workers were among the first to see Villa's new, specially commissioned Cup Final shirts as they were aired for the first time.

It was a sentimental return for left-back Peter Aldis. Not only had he worked as a chocolate mould polisher in the dominant red-brick factory that overshadowed the pitch, he had played at the ground on many occasions as a 15-year-old for the Bournville youth team. Later on in the day he sipped tea with the men he had worked alongside before he had made it as a professional footballer.

According to Sims, "After a 40 minute first team versus reserves game on the Bournville pitch, our trainer Bill Moore was worried that there were a few too many bumps on the surface and a player could go over on his ankle." Between Eric Houghton, Billy Moore and Dickie Dorsett, who was also along to help with the training, it was decided to end it prematurely. The entire session had lasted only 70 minutes.

Peter McParland also remembers the Bournville session, "Somebody had said when we got to Wembley that the Bournville pitch was just like Wembley's pitch and we went up there and it was full of ruts and ridges. One of the lads stumbled a wee bit and Billy Moore stopped the game. The pitch was terrible. The press were all there watching and made a big thing of it."

On the Thursday morning, one of the local Birmingham papers ran the headline **VILLA CUT PRACTICE MATCH AFTER SCARE.** The report went on to say how Jimmy Dugdale had limped out of a tackle with Vic Crowe and it was only after sitting down and rubbing his sore ankle that he realised it would be all right. Then Les Smith and Trevor Birch clashed heads as they went for an aerial ball. Smith went down as though pole-axed. Eric Houghton who was also participating in the game, looked on in shock and said his blood had run cold. Smith, thankfully, was soon up with nothing more than a headache.

Custodian Sims, meanwhile, had to receive infra-red treatment for a severely bruised thigh after making numerous saves, because the pitch was well grassed but the ground extremely hard. The plug was pulled on training in the shadows of Bournville's vast chocolate factory; it had been short and not so sweet!

Derek Pace, who had played centre-forward for the reserves was interviewed by an observing reporter, he said he had realised for some time that he wouldn't feature in the Final. "I felt after we had won the semi-final that the same team would go through to Wembley, barring injuries," he said. "It has been a disappointment, naturally, but it is better to know rather than to go on hoping and then have the disappointment coming as a surprise."

Following their business as usual routine, the Villa players enjoyed a round of golf at the Walmley course, there was a tremendous rivalry between McParland, Sewell, Lynn and Smith on the links. The only omission from the group was Nigel Sims, he had received a bump on his knee last Saturday and as he was no golfer it was decided that he would have treatment for it today. His no-show prompted a response from trainer Moore, "That's no scare, Nigel is 100% fit, had he been a golfer he would have been here today."

Legendary wing-wizard Stanley Matthews was tipping Villa to lift the Cup, "Villa have struck wonderful form at the right time. They are strong in defence, tough in the tackle and their forwards have been getting goals – which gives super confidence to any team. This game may depend on Wembley nerves. I have played in three Cup Finals and I know what a severe nervous strain it can be. Manchester United, however seem to have the knack of taking every big match as an ordinary game of football, but Villa should not be jittery either. Many of them are experienced players, and the knowledge that they are the Wembley underdogs may give them an added incentive to win. As a Northerner I hope Manchester United can bring the Cup back up North – but I've a hunch that Villa will end the sequence and win for the seventh time in their history."

For one Houghton, the Final couldn't arrive quickly enough – not Eric, the manager, but his long-suffering wife Muriel. Ever since Villa had booked their date at Wembley, Mrs Houghton had been up until 3.00am most days, answering shoals of letters addressed to her husband from fans pleading for help obtaining Wembley tickets. As well as dashing off letters, she was taking phone calls at the couple's Sutton Coldfield home from 8 o' clock in the morning until after midnight. "When this is over there'll be a lovely dozy fortnight in Looe," was how she consoled herself.

With the serious Cup training now at an end Eric Houghton breathing a sigh of relief said, "Thank goodness that's over," as the team trailed off Ellison's recreation ground at Witton. He had witnessed both Jackie Sewell and Stan Crowther have close-calls. Thursday's training had been intense; moves were practised with wingers made to cross pinball centres for the inside men to drill into the net. All five forwards took turns with shots, testing Sims with only seconds between each shot. The ground was bone hard and it was noticeable how infrequently Nigel dived down, "The knee is a bit sore, but it will be alright for Saturday." As if to prove a point, Nigel Sims then went on to kick the ball repeatedly over the half-way line, with either foot. A five-a-side match concluded the day's business.

Eric Houghton attended the Football Writers Association annual dinner on the Thursday evening. He could have taken the easy option and remained overnight in London and met up with his team the following day, but Eric chose to travel back to the

Midlands. He took the midnight train from Euston back to Birmingham and, accompanied by sports journalist Peter Morris, an ardent Villa supporter, arrived back in the early hours.

During the journey the reporter asked Houghton what he thought of the negative newspaper reports that gave the Villa no chance in the Final. Houghton responded in his quiet unassuming way, "You know, we've got Manchester United worried more than they have us. They are expected to win, we are not. So what have we to lose?"

On the eve of the big day, Wembley Stadium's head groundsman Percy Young rose early and busied himself putting the final touches to the famous turf, including whitewashing the penalty spots. This was the 21st time he had carried out such arrangements for the Cup Final and for the past year he had kept the velvety carpet in aristocratic condition. "Tomorrow the eyes of the world will be watching," he said. Mr Young slept at the stadium on the Friday night, enabling him to be up and ready at 6.00am to walk the hallowed turf, remove any weeds and sort out any imperfections.

Entry for 3rd May, Eric Houghton's personal diary; Training, left Birmingham 12 noon by train. Stayed at Brent bridge hotel.

On the eve of the Cup Final before turning up at Villa Park, captain Johnny Dixon called in at the vicarage attached to Aston Church, he wanted to ask a favour of his good friend Canon Warman. "If Aston Villa win the Cup tomorrow, would you ring the church bells for the team?" Canon Warman told Dixon he would gladly do it, they had been close friends for a long time, Johnny sang in the church choir and helped where he could, he would often take the collection plate round and due to his appearing in the church there were always flocks of women all wanting to make a fuss of him.

After Villa won the Wembley match Canon Warman kept his word, he rang the church bells – The bells are ringing for claret and blue, the bells are ringing for claret and blue.

After a very short workout of mainly stretching and limbering exercises in the morning at their famous old ground in the shadows of Aston Hall, Villa's players took the short bus journey from Villa Park to Snow Hill train station to catch their London-bound train. Manager Eric Houghton had his lucky hat and coat on. He had worn the green trilby hat and heavy Abercrombie overcoat at every Cup-tie, and creature of habit Eric will wear them tomorrow at Wembley, "Even if it is boiling hot."

Eager autograph hunters besieged them and none was left disappointed. Station inspector Mr Taylor broadcast over the loudspeaker system a message from the station staff, wishing the team every success at Wembley and expressing the hope that they return with the Cup; Stan Crowther recalled how they broke open a pack of cards to while away some journey time.

As the Villa train pulled into London a compartment full of smiles and thumbs up all round confronted the waiting press on the platform. The atmosphere was relaxed and the players oozed confidence, as did a very proud Villa boss. The press boys scrambled and jostled for the big stories and interviews and none was left wanting as Eric and his boys gleefully answered all that was thrown in their direction.

"I have been in soccer for 30 years, and have played in two Wembley internationals, but the proudest moment of my career will come tomorrow when I take Aston Villa on to the field as their manager," Eric told reporters. "I know that for seven years I was at Notts County, but ever since I joined Villa as a 16-year-old, claret and blue has run in my veins. And can you wonder? In those early years of mine the great names of this great club, such as Jack Devey and Howard (Spencer), became implanted in my mind and I knew I was part and parcel of a great tradition."

"Of course things have not gone well at Villa Park since the war, but even so the legend of Aston Villa remains. That is why I have received good luck messages from Australia, New Zealand, South Africa, Canada, Denmark and scores of other more remote spots. I must tell you about the message from Denmark. It goes back to 1934 when Villa reached the semi-final. A gentleman from Denmark wrote to me then asking for the players' autographs, and I obliged. I didn't hear from him again until we were through to the final this year. Now he is 80 years of age and wishing us luck at Wembley. This surely means that the name of Aston Villa, despite all the setbacks, still means a very great deal."

"In the last few weeks I have had further proof of this in my travels up and down the country. As I said, Villa have had their troubles of recent years. There has had to be rebuilding in all sorts of directions and not least in the matter of morale and club loyalty. And it is here that I point to the major reason for our long awaited return to Wembley. In all departments there has been 100 per cent effort; there has been a wonderful, steady pull together."

"I don't like to think of any single person in saying how it has come about. We are a club; everyone has done his job well – and I like to think that 'we' have done it, in the plural. But a special word to the players. We can all play our parts off the field, but it is the players who really count. They are the men who achieve the results, and they have put simply everything into this truly wonderful effort. They are not pampered, they are men that know what is expected of them and I am quite sure they have given their best because they are playing for Aston Villa."

"And let me pay tribute to the younger players. Those who have come into the first team have never let us down, and I am happy to think, thanks to our youth policy, that there are others still to come who can also join us in our present pride. Now for tomorrow, if Villa win the Cup for the first time in 37 years, I know there will be tremendous jubilation – and that's how I hope it will be. But I'll say this; providing the boys give of their best, as they have done so far, then win, lose or draw, we at Villa Park will be proud of them."

After the boss had said his piece, captain Johnny Dixon and then his warriors were all set the same poser, "What was their most memorable moment of the Cup campaign?"

Johnny Dixon: "Our supporters have been a tremendous help, not only in the later stages of this exciting Cup run, but in the early rounds when most people thought we hadn't a chance. The season's greatest moment for me was when the fans chaired me across the platform at Middlesbrough station after our victory. We knew then that we had to get to Wembley if only for the sake of our supporters. Now our aim is to bring the Cup back to Villa Park."

Nigel Sims: "A lot of people have said my goalkeeping has been the biggest single factor in Villa's improvement. This is nonsense! I believe that I play behind one of the greatest defensive triangles in the country – and it is these three men who have made me look good. I always kid Stan Lynn that he is the best goalkeeper on the books. But he always replies that I am the best right-back! My big moment of the Cup run? Well, the moment which gave me most pleasure was when I saved from Ray Barlow at St Andrews – I've never been so relieved after a save in all my life.

Stan Lynn: "I'm proud to have been part of this Aston Villa side which has fought through to Wembley – but let's not forget the magnificent support which has helped us along. Never shall I forget the moment when the fans started singing Tipperary at Turf Moor. It made us all realise how much it meant to those people who have stuck to us while Villa have been having a bad time since the war. The singing gave us new heart when Burnley where in front, and Peter McParland's great equaliser was the sweetest thing I have ever seen."

Peter Aldis: "Can you imagine my feelings when I accidentally deflected the ball into my own net at Burnley? I thought I had thrown away all my years of striving for Villa with that one mistake. But when McParland headed in that equaliser, everything I possessed would have been his for the asking. My high moment? There isn't just one. To play in a Villa side that fights and plays as one, as we have done this season, has been one long round of pleasure."

Stan Crowther: "It seems impossible now to think that just a few weeks ago I asked Mr Houghton to drop me because I felt so down-hearted. How glad I am now that the boss kept faith in me and refused. It's a pretty bewildering thing to travel from Bilston to Wembley in less than two years, but the more experienced players have helped tremendously to bring me along."

Jimmy Dugdale: "To go to Wembley for the first time with Albion seemed too good to be true. But I just can't describe my feelings to be going there again with a club like Villa. I suppose I am at a slight advantage over the other lads, having been there before, and I hope to help them out in the dressing room before the match. I think perhaps the moment which stands out most in my mind about our Cup run is when Billy

Myerscough scored our goal at St Andrew's. I knew then that Villa were bound for Wembley."

Pat Saward: "My greatest hero is fellow Irishman Peter McParland. And of course, everyone must know why? He was the one who made up for my mistakes in the semi-final at Molineux by scoring two equalisers. When I let that ball bounce through my legs for Whitehouse to score, I thought for sure that I had spoiled everything. Thank goodness Peter came along and saved my life. Here's to the luck of the Irish'!"

Leslie Smith: "Why will Villa trot out onto the famous Wembley pitch tomorrow afternoon after being on the floor last season? Because of the great club pride at Villa Park! My biggest moment came when I cracked the ball towards the far post at Burnley for McParland to run in and equalise. It was one of the greatest headed goals I have ever seen."

Jackie Sewell: "It might seem strange to say that being within a hair's breadth of being relegated has resulted in Villa getting to Wembley, but I feel that that is exactly what has happened. At the end of last season we learned to fight for every ball, and to struggle for 90 minutes of every game."

Billy Myerscough: "When I first played centre-forward for Villa against Manchester United at Old Trafford I never dreamed that in a few weeks I would be leading Villa against the famous Busby Babes at Wembley. It is playing alongside better players which has helped my own play to improve. I suppose it natural that the moment that stands out in my mind was when I saw my header flash into the net at St Andrews. But perhaps an even bigger relief was when the final whistle went – and I knew we were Wembley-bound."

Peter McParland: I'm the guy who has been lucky enough to score my goals when they have been most needed – but the one which has a special place in my memory was the Burnley equaliser. We went to Turf Moor very much the underdogs. Hardly anyone gave us a chance. And it certainly looked that way until Les Smith cracked the ball over for me to equalise."

Where Villa had rolled into London in buoyant mood and displayed a willingness to talk with the press, an entirely different picture was painted by the News Chronicle reporter on Manchester United's arrival in the capital. From leaving the train to boarding their coach there was no signing autographs, no posing for pictures and no conversation, while small boys were reported to have been brushed aside by the players. When Matt Busby allowed four press photographers on board the coach, United captain Roger Byrne leapt to his feet and shouted "Get out, we've had enough. Get off the coach." When Busby asked what was wrong a club official said the players were a little nervous! As the coach pulled out of Euston station, Byrne knelt on the floor, away from the prying lenses. United, with an average age of just 22, were the youngest-ever Cup-finalists – and it looked like they might just be the most nervous, too. Had the bookmakers been aware of United's bizarre behaviour they would surely have slashed the odds on the Red Devils to win. Villa were quoted as 11-4 outsiders by many bookies. They were regarded by many people as whipping boys and were supposedly heading for Wembley's severest Cup Final defeat.

The Villa team had a brief visit to the stadium to get a general feel for the place. Billy Moore, not one to miss an opportunity, soon had Jimmy Dugdale and Peter McParland pitch-side with their shoes off, trying on various football boots and checking on the suitability of nylon or leather studs. The players also popped up to the royal box - where they posed for pictures and got an idea what view the Queen would have of the game. Their chosen base for the weekend was the Brent Bridge Hotel, situated in North London. It was an ideal location, just five miles from Wembley.

"The favourite hotel for the clubs was Hendon Hall but Manchester United were staying there so we had Brent Bridge, it was a nice hotel all the same and nice and quiet, we had no problems, it was all kept under wraps where we were staying to prevent people coming round and bothering us" recalled McParland

The Villa players were free to do whatever they wanted on the evening, with the manager's blessing. Houghton's philosophy was that "if they haven't got the sense to look after themselves at such a crucial time then they shouldn't be playing for Aston Villa."

The Villa players and some club officials spent the early evening in the Hendon cinema; where by chance they bumped into the Manchester contingent that had decided to go to the same picture house as they were also staying in the area at the Hendon Hall Hotel. Peter McParland thinks they watched either a Humphrey Bogart or a James Cagney movie. Accompanying the Villa members was a rookie reporter from the Sports Argus who had earlier in the season been assigned the task of covering their Cup run. The job had gone to the youngster, as Villa weren't expected to progress too far. So all the way from Luton to Wembley he went, travelling home by charabanc, train and then charabanc. During this time Eric Houghton had taken the young reporter under his wing, acting as a kindly, helpful Uncle figure. The reporter remembered the night of the cinema trip. "Eric called the players together for a team talk and instructed them on how to conduct themselves on Cup Final eve. I found out shortly afterwards that he had told them he was going to the cinema and that anyone who wanted to go was welcome, those who didn't fancy it could stay behind. Apparently the only rules were, no boozing and not too late to bed." When the players emerged from the meeting the rookie asked Jimmy Dugdale what instructions they had been given. Jimmy replied, "If we want to play in the Final we must be careful how we cross the road!"

Later in the evening as the Villa party made their way back to the hotel after watching the film, a mischievous Eric Houghton surrounded by many of his players, crammed into a phone box and called their hotel pretending to be a newspaper reporter, he claimed to be Harry Ditton of the News of the World and conducted a telephone interview with Villa trainer Billy Moore. Billy answered all that was asked of him and went on to say the team had been to the stadium earlier in the day to try the various different studs. The players were all struggling from bursting out laughing and giving the game away. Stan Crowther saw firsthand Billy's response when they arrived back at the hotel, " He went bloody mad, effing and blinding, not many people got one over on the canny Geordie!" After the film some of the lads got taxis back to the hotel and Peter recalls, how some of the lads including himself and Eric Houghton were stood for ages, waiting for another one to come along.

They desperately wanted to win the Cup at the first attempt, rather than having to go through the process all over again in a replay arranged for the following Thursday night at Everton's Goodison Park if required.

A huge percentage of the 25,000 Villa fans made their way down to London for the Final travelled on Friday evening, many supporters going straight to the train station after leaving work. All London-bound trains leaving Snow Hill were packed solid, with as little as 10 minutes between each departure, such was the huge demand.

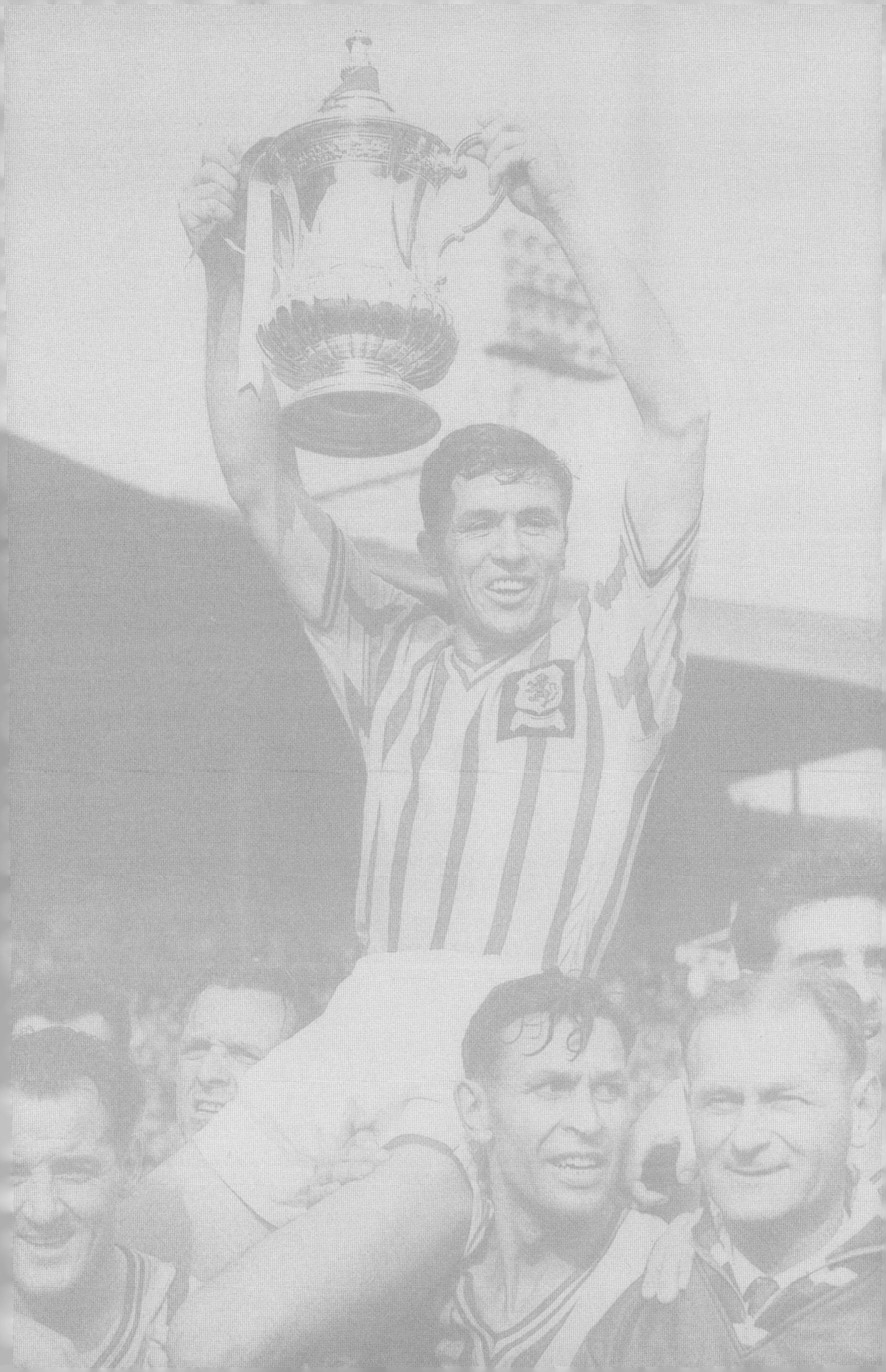

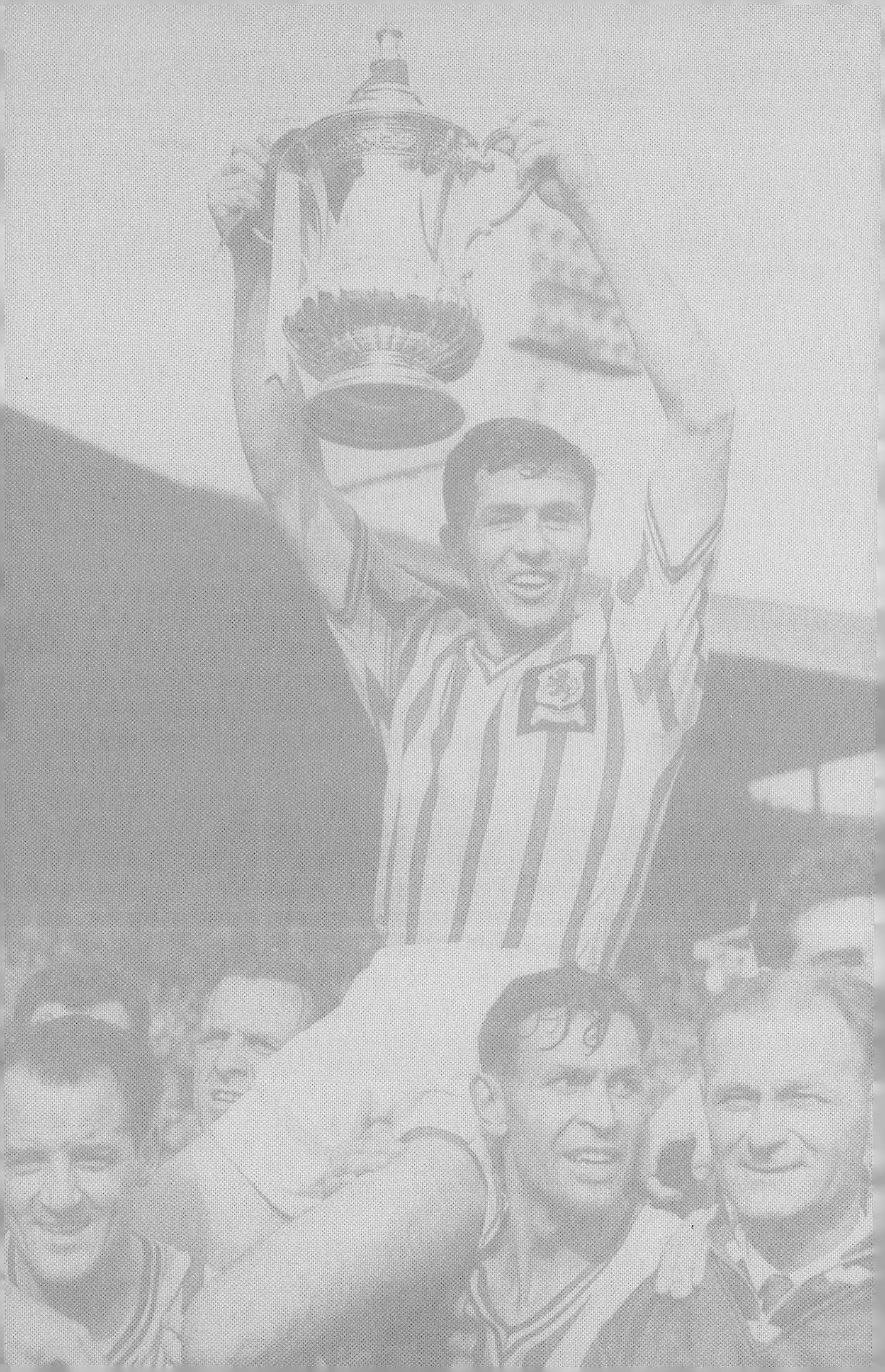

The bells are ringing for claret and blue

4th May 1957, Cup Final Day

"The fans stuck with us through thick and thin and to finally give them something to shout about was a terrific feeling."

Johnny Dixon

In the first editions of the Birmingham papers there was a Lord Mayor's message to Villa. "I know that the whole of the city will be with you today," he wrote. "I trust it will be a good game and that we shall have the pleasure of receiving you back home with the Cup on Sunday." The paper also carried the times and arrangements for the club's return to Snow Hill station on Sunday, their appearance at Victoria Square, Council House and then the route Villa will take to Villa Park.

Ticket touts were out and about from 7.00am, loitering around the Wembley approaches and offering 15/- (75p) tickets for £10 and 3/6d (17.5p) tickets for £5. Ordinary fans weren't helped by the amount of firms joining the mad scramble for tickets, because money was no object to the corporate organisations. And what better way to woo overseas customers who were visiting Birmingham for the British Industries Fair, than by giving them complimentary tickets for the FA Cup final? No wonder 50/- (£2.50) tickets were being snapped up at £80 pair.

After waking and leisurely breakfasting together, the Villa team were driven the short distance from their Brent Bridge Hotel base to Wembley Stadium. Nigel Sims vividly remembers the electric atmosphere that morning. "Villa fans were everywhere, a sea of claret and blue. When they recognised us, word spread and everyone ran towards the coach they were smiling and waving, giving the thumbs up, singing and applauding, it was marvellous. They all looked so pleased and happy. I was desperate to win the Cup for them as much as for myself. When we arrived at Wembley, Manchester United were already there, but we didn't bother about them, and made our way to the North dressing room."

Stan Crowther sat quietly in the Wembley bound coach thinking back to when he was a youngster listening to the post-war Final's on his brothers radio, "I'll play in the FA Cup Final when I'm older," he had told his mother. Now that dream was about to come true.

As the team got changed, the players said very little. They were all reflecting on what lay ahead. As they changed into their kit and went through their own individual routines, manager Houghton told them "Go out and enjoy it boys."

Billy Moore approached Sims and put his arm round Nigel's huge shoulder. "Nige, I want you and Stan to stay close to Johnny after we collect the Cup, I want you two big lads to carry him on your shoulders," he said. The fact that it was 'when' and not 'if' we collect the cup typifies the strength of feeling in the Villa camp.

An ex-player and now proud manager of Villa, Eric Houghton led his men out of the tunnel into a cauldron of noise. The Wembley pitch looked magnificent. Eric told his players "Win this boys and I'll give you the town hall!'

The crowd were in good voice for the community singing, though there were visible demonstrations and jeering when Birmingham City's adopted tune from last season, 'Keep right on to the end of the road' was sung as Villa's theme tune!

As the teams emerged it was Villa who looked the more relaxed outfit. They were smiling and looking around, taking it all in; United, on the other hand looked rather nervy, their players either looking down at their feet or straight ahead looking at the back of Matt Busby, their manager. The teams lined up either side of the half-way line as the Duke of Edinburgh made his way over to meet them – with Villa first to be introduced. A proud but clearly nervous Johnny Dixon introduced his team-mates as the Duke walked the line shaking hands with them "This is Pat Saward, left-half, Peter Aldis our right-back, Stan Lynn right-back," he began, to which the Duke responded, "You seem to have a lot of right-backs in your team!"

With kick-off looming and Johnny aware that he would be talking to Royalty, the enormity of the day had got to him and reduced the normally ice-cool Villa captain to a bag of nerves. After the formalities were over the Villans waved to their family and friends in the stand; Houghton's boys certainly seemed relaxed.

The teams for the 1957 FA Cup Final:

Aston Villa	**Manchester United**
1 Sims	1 Wood
2 Lynn	2 Foulkes
3 Aldis	3 Byrne
4 Crowther	4 Colman
5 Dugdale	5 Blanchflower
6 Saward	6 Edwards
7 Smith	7 Berry
8 Sewell	8 Whelan
9 Myerscough	9 Taylor
10 Dixon	10 Charlton
11 McParland	11 Pegg

The Villa captain won the toss and elected to play from left to right as you look down from the Royal Box, taking advantage of what little breeze there was as they faced the youngest team to appear in an FA Cup Final.

Immediately from the kick-off Villa seized the initiative but Blanchflower was on hand put the ball into touch. Taylor combined with Charlton but Smith was able to break the United raid and delivered a clever ball to Myerscough. United regained possession and clever play by Pegg teed up Charlton to have the first chance but Sims easily held his lob. As expected there was the customary probing on both sides. In another foray forward, United winger Johnny Berry cut inside and passed to Taylor, who hesitated, allowing Sims to dive at his feet.

McParland took a long throw but it was punched clear by Wood. Charlton collected it and ran into the Villa half but was tackled by Crowther.

Villa's midfielders were holding the ball well in the middle of the park, composed and uncomplicated. When United took possession they also looked impressive, short passing very quick and precise with six players involved in one move which broke down when Myerscough intercepted and from the half-way line booted the ball back to the safety of Sims.

With six minutes played Villa staged one of their hallmark counter-attacks directly into the United danger zone. Jackie Sewell sent a crossfield pass over to Peter McParland, who had made a run into the area. Mac headed the ball accurately but Ray Wood in the United goal caught it with ease. McParland's momentum pushed him on and turning slightly as Wood came forward off his line, the Irish centre-forward followed through with a legitimate shoulder charge.

Both players went down and Wood appeared to be in a bad way. Referee Coultas signalled for the trainers and for over two minutes anxious officials attended to the still form of Ray Wood. An unimpressed Duncan Edwards hovered over the Villa's prone centre-forward, appearing to berate him. Eventually, the ambulance men were able to stretcher the United custodian off the pitch.

Even though Peter McParland had suffered a nasty blow to the head himself, he was fully aware of the menacing Edwards, "He did have a go at me afterwards, he was having a right go and all that but I never took much notice to what he was saying - I didn't take any notice to anyone when they spoke, but he did have a go and I said to the ref to watch the No 6 and that was it. I never bothered after that; I just tried to get on with it. They would all try things on with you. It was hard tackling - we took it all then, we didn't bother about what's what, we got on with it and gave it back if you we got the chance."

Jackie Blanchflower put on Wood's goalkeeper jersey and a borrowed photographer's cap, and took up a position between the posts - he was going in goal, the game restarting with a free-kick to United.

The Manchester side had to reshuffle. Duncan Edwards dropped deeper to the centre-half position, leaving United's midfield significantly weaker. Every time McParland touched the ball the jeers and booing echoed around the ground. Villa tried to capitalise now their opponents were down to 10 men and dominated for long periods, with Sewell, having more time and space, looking particularly threatening in the middle of the park.

Billy Moore was on the pitch only five minutes after the Wood delay, Peter McParland needing treatment after coming off second best in a collision with Bill Foulkes elbow. The Manchester fans cheered – almost as if their side had scored - at Packy's misfortune.

Stan Crowther, having the game of his life strode past a young Bobby Charlton and skipped past makeshift centre-half Edwards but his shot lacked conviction and was safely gathered by Blanchflower. Jimmy Dugdale, meanwhile, was doing a sterling job, effectively keeping England centre-forward Tommy Taylor in check. When United's forward line threatened the Villa penalty area Sims would, in a single movement, seize the ball and release it immediately to set in motion another Villa counter-attack. Smith forced a corner, but big Pat Saward, moving upfield to try a drive, put his effort well over the bar. Villa showed delightful ball control in a move that had Roger Byrne and Edwards running around in circles.

Colman sent Berry away, but after beating two Villa men he was abruptly stopped by the Villa left-back Aldis. Another flowing claret and blue counter attack ended with McParland firing into the side netting from 10 yards after the winger was played through by his skipper. United, despite their handicap, were still playing with composure and to their credit insisted on playing cultured football rather than just hoofing the ball forward.

A terrific roar went up from the United contingent in the 33rd minute when Ray Wood made his way to the side of the pitch. At the referee's signal for him to come on the noise grew even louder. The 'keeper, after a few words with Coultas, made his way to the outside-right position. Wood, who appeared little worse for his knock, soon challenged McParland for the ball, to the delight of the Reds' fans.

Blanchflower, meanwhile, looked every inch a goalkeeper, time and again thwarting the Villa attack. On one occasion he came out smartly to hold a Sewell cross despite the close attentions of Myerscough and Dixon. It was almost as if he were born to the position.

The diminutive ex-Birmingham winger Roger Berry, now playing outside-left, won a free-kick when impeded by Stan Lynn, but the full-back atoned by heading away to safety. United were a rejuvenated side since the return of Wood and now displayed some of the touches their supporters had become used to seeing throughout the title campaign. At half-time the game remained goalless but it wasn't a pleasant stroll back to the dressing room for Villa's players, who were booed by sections of United supporters as they filed into the tunnel

Even in the sanctuary of the Villa dressing room, one player was visibly shaken, and it fell to tough taskmaster Billy Moore to tackle the problem of getting Peter McParland in the right frame of mind to carry on.

"I had to do something with the lad and do it quickly" said Moore. "I drummed it into him that the collision was a pure accident. As for the booing, I told him if he didn't like it I'd stuff his ears with cotton wool! That crack brought out the Irish sense of humour in Peter." Eric Houghton told his lads to go out and do much the same as they had in the first half and that the rewards would follow. With Mac's head sorted out the team made their way back to the pitch.

The Villa backroom staff came out for the second half in line, shoulder to shoulder with their heads bowed. The fans wondered what an earth they were doing. Billy Moore had lost his false teeth between the bench and the dressing room and if they weren't found – and quick, there would be hell to pay.

The crowd were surprised that Ray Wood hadn't come back out for the start of the second half, so Blanchflower carried on in goal. The sun was getting stronger now, with the whole arena bathed in sunlight. In Villa's first attack, McParland cut inside and connected with a probing delivery from the right. His effort struck the woodwork before United's stand-in keeper safely collected the rebound.

Villa's defenders were operating well as a unit. When United were awarded a free-kick following a foul by Peter Aldis, Berry floated the ball in but Dugdale headed it sideways and Saward cleared the danger. Nineteen-year-old Charlton, a late inclusion in the United line-up for the luckless Dennis Viollet, looked dangerous as he burst past Lynn and his pass fell straight to the feet of Taylor. But Sims, ever aware in the Villa goal, showed remarkable agility for such a large keeper, diving smartly down to collect off the centre-forward's toe. Villa had dominated for long spells in the first-half but now they were being penned in their own half, and were very much on the back foot.

After nine minutes of the second period Ray Wood emerged from the tunnel again. Referee Frank Coultas waved him on and the 'keeper returned in an unorthodox right-wing position. Now with an equal number of men on the field, United pressed more urgently Luckily, Nigel Sims and his trusted defenders also raised their game and were equal to all Busby's men could throw at them.

The best chance so far fell to centre-forward Billy Myerscough when McParland picked him out with an inch-perfect pass; but Villa's hopes of a breakthrough evaporated when the striker scuffed his shot and it went wide. Myerscough, clearly disgusted at his miss, threw up his arms in frustration.

But the pendulum was starting to swing in Villa's favour and they should have taken the lead in the 58th minute. Les Smith started the move, pushing an intelligent ball out wide to Sewell, who lobbed in a delightful ball to the far post, where the climbing McParland thundered a header against the post. Packy reacted and got his toe to the ball, but Blanchflower was able stick out his leg to kick it off the line. So close!

The booing started again – it didn't relent all afternoon for McParland – and it was about to go to a whole new level. Villa skipper Dixon took a short pass from the industrious Smith on the right before making a perfect centre. McParland honed in on it like an exocet missile to propel his header beyond Blanchflower and into net. It was 1-0 to Villa, and the claret and blue half of Wembley erupted.

When 'Mac' bagged Villa's first goal he thought back to the conversation he had with Billy Moore in the dressing room, "The crowd were booing it was always on the cards. Billy said, 'They are getting on at you, just play your game and stick one in the back of the net that'll shut them up,' that was his encouragement at half-time. He came over well, Bill, - he was a good man and a terrific trainer, he knew a lot of things and that was his advice to me." "They're getting on to you – sort it - simple as that."

"Billy was one of the main men for us in the Cup, he wouldn't stand any non-sense but you could argue the toss with him and he would say, 'right, that's it cleared up - get on with it."

There was cheering and rattle-waving, clapping and singing; this was a moment to savour. So much for United winning 6-0. It was totally hypothetical, but would Ray Wood have fared better against McParland's header? Not according to the Villa players after the game.

United were shaken. The champions looked rattled and a million miles from the composed football they were capable of. Five minutes later Smith and Saward combined to put their captain through, Johnny Dixon hit a terrific shot that smacked against the bar and came zipping back out. McParland lurking menacingly, reacting with lightning reflexes, getting his foot to the ball just as Billy Myerscough was also about to swing his leg at it. Hit with the usual 'Mac' venom, the ball blasted under the bar and smacked into the net.

Villa's fans were near hysteria. It was almost unthinkable – their team had a two-goal cushion and there were only 18 minutes left to run down. Could the claret & blues hang on? Surely they couldn't let this slip? They were built from the back on solid defensive foundations, and Crowther had played out of his skin all afternoon in what was undoubtedly his best game to date. Lynn, Aldis, Dugdale and Saward had also played massive parts and you couldn't single anyone of them out. They played as a team, defended as one and fought as a unit. Maybe, just maybe Villa could pull it off. Perhaps the men from Manchester weren't invincible after all.

Another sickening collision followed, this time between Blanchflower and Smith, the Villa man requiring the treatment.

With only seven minutes remaining, United knew they had no choice but to press and press. Then Tommy Taylor had a goalbound header pushed over by Sims – corner to United. The ball was floated in and again it was put out for another corner-kick. Duncan Edwards hurried over to take it and the ball came over from the left. Taylor got up highest and connected, the ball heading for the top corner. Sims had it covered as he backtracked but Stan Lynn, trying to head it off the line, inadvertently prevented the 'keeper from getting back far enough to claw the ball from danger. United had pulled one back, could they pull it out of the bag?

With the deficit halved, United sent Woods back between the posts, while Edwards moved further forward as did the rest of the United attack. Villa gained possession they wanted to run the clock down. Into the final minutes and Johnny Dixon, who had started the day nervously, before his ice-cool demeanour returned, was now taken over by a feeling of imminent joy, wondering if his team could hold out.

The Midlanders held firm, not allowing United to get the ball. Short passes went back and forth but it didn't matter. Then Coultas blew the final whistle – Villa had done it – they had won the F.A. Cup for the seventh time, a feat no other club had ever achieved. They had also denied Manchester United the double. The United fans were in shock they couldn't believe what they had witnessed. United only had to turn up on the day, they had thought; how had could a side of Villa's pedigree defeat the champions of English football?

One hundred miles north, in the tower of the Parish Church of St Peter & St Paul (Aston), the church bells tolled – ringing out for the first time since the war. The Bishop of Birmingham had said if Aston Villa win the Cup – the bells will toll! It was the first time the bells had tolled since the war. Not quite the same version as Johnny Dixon's, but the above was the story that Peter McParland has remembered all these years. Regardless- the bells did ring for the claret and blue.

Nigel Sims ran out of his goal and picked up Jimmy Dugdale. The Villa mascot, Andrew Pugh ran on the pitch and celebrated with his grown-up friends.

Johnny Dixon, a quiet, unassuming man and as proud a Villa captain as ever lived, led his battle weary team-mates up the 39 steps towards the Royal Box and to glory. A young Queen Elizabeth had witnessed history re-written. Johnny Dixon lifted the Cup – what a moment!

Aston Villa, a name famous in past glory days known throughout the civilised world, would now surely be muttered all over again to a new generation of football lovers. Sewell, Smith and Saward, Lynn, Aldis, and centre-half Dugdale all went up for their winner's medals; then Myerscough, McParland, with his big Irish smile, Sims, and lastly, the youngster of the team, Stan Crowther. Sir Stanley Rous described Stan as the best man on the field but sentiment clouded the judgement for the man-of-the-match award; it went to Jackie Blanchflower.

In planning Villa's game for the Final, manager Houghton had considered the United players individually. "We knew that Wood was an edgy type and we told the lads to harass him, particularly on the crosses, and not to let him have a free kick at the ball when clearing if they could help it. We thought we might keep him edgy in such a game and that he might make a mistake as a result." Eric Houghton had certainly done his homework.

The players were still sweating from their exertions when the national press started the wheels in motion. The disparaging stories penned during the match would be in circulation before the teams left the stadium – stories of how Villa had cheated their Manchester counterparts out of the double by intentionally maiming their goal-keeper. Not much was written about the legitimacy of shoulder charging. Unfortunately the national press in those days were not much different from today. Had Villa been based in the North West or London, nothing or certainly very little, would have been raised.

Johnny Dixon recalls the closing stages of the game, "The ball went out of play for a throw-in, while it was being recovered, I looked up towards the Royal Box. It struck me that we only had to hang on for a few more minutes and I would be up there, receiving the Cup. I nearly cried at the thought it was going to be ours. Then at last, there was the sheer delight of knowing Villa had won. It was fantastic when I went up to collect the Cup. Going up those steps was a wonderful feeling. Then the Queen handed me the Cup and I turned away from her to hold it up. The noise was unbelievable. To do something like that just once in a lifetime is tremendous and I will always be grateful for that."

Billy Moore who was responsible for getting into Peter McParland's head at half-time: "Peter was thoroughly sick at heart during the break, he was doubly fed up. The unfortunate collision with Ray Wood was bad enough, but to have to stand for booing in front of Royalty was even worse. So he went out there and snatched that vital first goal the way he had planned it. Had Wood been in the United goal I don't think he would have saved either of Peter's great efforts. But I felt sorry for them in losing a goalkeeper so early in the game."

McParland replied, "What a trainer Bill is, what a man to have behind you when things are going wrong! I never felt so down in the mouth as I did at half-time. The clash of heads with Ray Wood and myself was one of those things that can happen in the heat of the moment. After I had taken that header at goal – and I should have scored – sheer momentum carried me on. With Wood in possession and on his feet, I reckoned I was entitled to shoulder-charge him. I challenged quite fairly and was surprised when the referee gave a free-kick against me.

"All the upset of the booing was forgotten when I got that first goal. I could scarcely realise it at first. When it did strike home – what a moment it was! What a thrill. I shall treasure that moment as long as I live. And I would like to thank that great sportsman, Duncan Edwards, for the way he came over to congratulate me as we left the field. There were no hard feelings as far as he was concerned, at any rate!"

Peter McParland wasn't treated so kindly by Edwards team-mates though, being roughed up by some of the United players after the collision. "I was made the target for a personal attack that was obvious retaliation by players who considered I had purposely hit the goalkeeper," he said. "It was the worst handling I have ever experienced in football and it was a shocking thing to think it happened in a Cup Final at Wembley. I was struck on the jaw as I went for a ball in the air. On another occasion, when I leapt to head a ball an elbow was rammed in my back. Later I was hit in the back of the neck as I fell in a tackle with a United player sprawling across me."

After the first incident Mac aired his concerns to the ref, but Coultas insisted it was nothing out of the ordinary. When it happened repeatedly the Villa forward decided to get into the penalty area as often as possible, if they resorted to those tactics he may well get a penalty out of it. He had to restrain himself from striking back, which wouldn't have helped him or the team.

A beaming Eric Houghton commented, "I have impressed on you all along what a wonderful team spirit I have in my boys. Never in all my years at Villa Park have I known anything like it."

Chris Buckley, the Villa chairman, "We won worthily. I've been associated with Villa for 51 years, but never have I felt so proud of them."

Bill Smith the former Villa secretary, "It all takes me back to the day our coach Jimmy Eason and I first spotted McParland in a junior game. It was in 1952. I've got the ticket to that match in my pocket right now. I brought it to Wembley as a lucky mascot. It worked."

Derek Pace who had been dropped for the Final couldn't help grinning, "I'll let you into a secret. The club are applying to the FA for an extra winner's medal – for me. That will be ample compensation for missing such a match and spending those agonising last minutes helpless on the line."

The FA later refused Villa's request to have a special medal struck for the man known as Doc, even though the club pointed out that Pace had appeared in every round up to the semi-final, making six appearances in the competition.

The official reply read, "Sorry, but permission to strike a medal is given only in the case of injury." When the story broke in the press, one Birmingham paper recounted the following story of an Aston Villa player who didn't play in a Cup Final but received a Cup winner's medal, 'In Villa's first Cup winning season of 1886/87, George Frederick Price played in all matches, including the Cup-ties, except the Final. Just before the Final George had the bad luck to be injured. But a winner's gold medal was struck specially for him.'

Nigel Sims recalled what his manager had said, "Eric Houghton, barely two hours earlier, had promised us the Town Hall, if we lifted the Cup. We didn't get that, but we did get £50 each!"

Jimmy Dugdale revealed he was sick 30 minutes before kick-off, through nervousness. He hid the fact from his team-mates in case it had the same effect on them, though he believed that they all felt the same; even though everyone said how calm and sure Villa looked as they took the field.

"It all worked out well," said Dugdale. "There is such a wonderful team-spirit among us that we wanted nothing to hinder our chances. The biggest feeling of satisfaction I had in those few minutes before we were presented with our medals by the Queen was the thought of just reward for my team-mates – winner's medals for which they had worked so hard. I have never known such a team like Villa. They never know when they are beaten. If team-spirit, sportsmanship and club loyalty mean anything – and I think it means a lot – then Villa deserved to win the Cup Final before it was played." "The whole point is we deserved to beat United on merit. It is hard on any team to lose a player injured at any time. In a Cup Final it must be sheer misery and we are sorry that they lost Wood for such a long time. We would rather have beaten 11 fit United men. I mean that, sincerely. But although I may be accused of being wise after the event, I say that a fit Wood would not have made any difference. We would still have carried off the Cup. The great misfortune is that Wood's injury has taken so much praise from the people who deserve it – my team–mates."

Villa's official party made their way from the stadium across London for their celebratory dinner to be held at the Grosvenor Hotel.

A major coup for local Birmingham paper the Sports Argus, which was later publicised to the hilt, was the great lengths and trouble they had taken to ensure they got their special Cup Final edition from Birmingham to London for the Aston Villa supporters down in the capital. A photographer was on hand outside the Grosvenor Hotel in Park Lane to capture the moment club captain Johnny Dixon came outside to personally collect his copy of the paper from Mr Reg Roberts – the gentleman responsible for the 'Argus invasion.' At their Birmingham print works, the Argus Deputy circulation manager Fred Morris had started the ball rolling, handing the 'hot off the press' copies to a motorcycle despatch rider aboard a powerful 650cc BSA Thunderbolt, who was instructed to get down as fast as he could.

Club President Sir Patrick Hannon, a big racing man mentioned in his after dinner speech that winning the Cup had finally realised a 30-year ambition of his, unfortunately he knew little of football and mistakenly referred to the trophy as the Gold Cup (of Cheltenham fame) not the FA Cup. Chairman of the Football Association, the Lord Mayor of Birmingham and Villa Director, Norman Smith, all spoke at the function. Villa manager Eric Houghton – didn't, he wasn't asked or invited to.

"It was quite a party, once all the speeches were out of the way and we had pushed off to a nightclub in the West End, it lasted well into the small hours," was all a smiling Nigel Sims would say on the victory evening.

Villa fanatic Harry Moore remembers his friend's father telling him a story many years ago when Harry was still a child. His mate's dad was called Bob Sproson - Bob travelled back from the Wembley match by train on the Saturday night. Sharing the same compartment as him were Jimmy Dugdale's parents returning to Liverpool via Birmingham, the Villa defender's father could frequently be heard repeating, "To think our lad had the England centre-forward (Taylor) in his pocket, who'd of believed it!"

Entry for 4th May, Eric Houghton's personal diary; WON FA CUP WEMBLEY, 2-1 BEAT MANCHESTER UNITED – CELEBRATION DINNER, GROSVENOR HOUSE. Written in the hand of Eric Houghton in his own personal diary; the entry for 4th May 1957, was short precise and very much to the point.

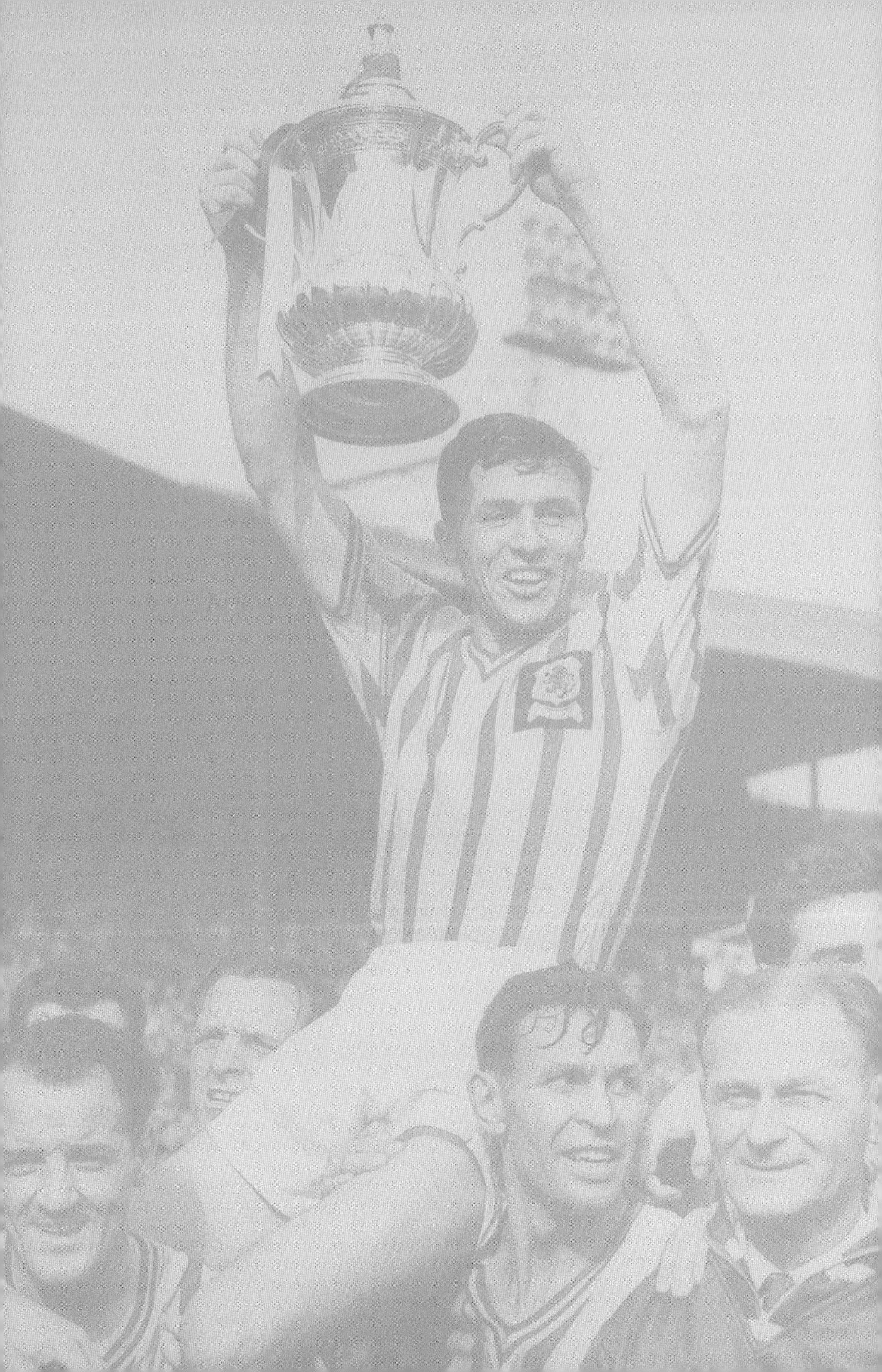

Seventh Heaven
The days ahead

The Villa team encountered scores of well-wishers at Paddington as they returned to Birmingham by rail the following afternoon. At Banbury and Leamington where the train made scheduled stops huge crowds greeted them gathering round the players compartment - all hoping for a glimpse of the famous 'pot.' Police were on hand to keep the supporters back as the team and Cup emerged from Birmingham's Snow Hill stations Great Charles Street entrance. The players climbed through the open roof of the coach as it relayed the team through the heavy thong with the assistance of a seven strong Police motorcycle escort to Birmingham's Council House where a very proud city laid on a Civic Reception. As the players alighted their bus the crowds broke through the temporary barriers and cut off the directors and officials travelling in the other two coaches.

The Lord Mayor, Alderman Ernest Apps was there to welcome the victorious side. Tremendous cheering and applause greeted the Villa captain as he emerged on the balcony to introduce his players one by one. The Lord Mayor's speech had been written in vain, each time he attempted to speak, he was drowned out by the roars and cheers. In the end he smiled and gave up. He shook the players hands and shouted, "It's a great day for Villa and a great day for Birmingham!"

Villa made the slow journey from the city centre back to their famous old ground that sat in the shadows of Thomas Holte's Aston Hall. They were greeted every step of the way by thousands of their loyal fans who lined the streets leading to Aston. The procession took in Corporation Street and Birmingham Central Fire Station, which had opened its doors and lined the station fire engines in a row. As the team passed by, the firemen saluted their Cup achievement by ringing their appliance bells.

Entry for 5th May, Eric Houghton's personal diary; Returned by train to Birmingham. Celebrations, Town Hall, Birmingham and Villa Park.

"That was one of the most memorable days I ever had," said Nigel Sims. "Coming into Birmingham along the road in that coach, there must have been millions - there were 250,000 people in the square (in front of Birmingham Council House). Unbelievable isn't it? I was a nobody, but not now! I had won the cup."

Villa Park was opened for the masses. To huge cheering, captain Johnny Dixon and Les Smith walked round the pitch as a show of appreciation to the Villa supporters. The players were spied in the directors' box by some observant fans, which led to the supporters spilling from the terracing and charging across the pitch. Up in the stand, high above the legions of claret and blue followers, the manager, players, trainer and then the chairman all took turns at holding Villa's latest trophy up, to show the adoring fans. The crowd then called for Derek Pace. They loved Doc and he had missed the Final, unable to guarantee manager Eric Houghton that he would last the full 90 minutes. His appearance raised the loudest cheer of the afternoon.

Of the Wembley trail Johnny said, "Even now (mid-1980's) I remember the run to the Final clearly. We started off in the mud at Luton, got a 2-2 draw and beat them in the replay at Villa Park. Then an away win at Middlesbrough and a home win, not without difficulty against Bristol City. In the sixth round we drew at Burnley and beat them in the replay 2-0 to play West Bromwich in the semi-finals. We drew 1-1 at Molineux and to be honest, we didn't have the run of the ball. But things went our way in the replay at St Andrew's, we won 1-0 and then beat United in the Final."

"It was a wonderful moment for everyone involved. We hadn't set the League on fire that season but after Christmas everything seemed to click. We were very fit, trainer Bill Moore made sure of that and once the heavy grounds came we were able to run the legs off other teams."

The main weapon in the Villa's arsenal for their Final victory at Wembley against Busby's Manchester United – confidence - "It was the magic ingredient, and this came through in our Cup matches" said Johnny. "When you've got confidence everyone wants the ball, and when you're lucky it does what you want it to. All the neutrals who went to Wembley that day were on our side. But we had a fine team which played controlled, direct football and were grossly under-rated. Eric Houghton and Bill Moore were a good combination, total opposites who complemented each other."

Regarding the controversy he said, "I don't think Ray Wood saw Peter McParland move in. Certainly Wood didn't move and Peter was very quick. McParland wouldn't hurt a fly, but he wouldn't duck a challenge either and Wood standing there holding the ball, that's just what is was – a challenge to be challenged. Peter took him up on it. What a pity that one moment overshadowed what for me was a tremendous Villa performance. United undoubtedly a great team had a habit of playing across the field. We were more direct and we forced them to play square balls as often as possible whilst cutting them to pieces with our accuracy. We never got the credit we deserved, at least in the newspapers or from the Wembley crowd, who turned from being on our side to following United after Ray Wood had been stretchered off. It's a game I will never forget of course. The faces on the fans gave it away when they left the ground after the win and when the fans are happy they get behind you – though Villa fans were always good to me, come rain or shine."

A leading national newspaper, the Daily Express ran the headline 'Manchester United Wuz Robbed' on the Monday morning, one of their leading reporters backed only by very poor quality grainy images from a black and white TV, implied the ball had crossed the goal line before being centred for one of Peter McParland's goals and should not have been allowed to stand. 'It was a goalkick, Villa had not won the cup at all,' exclaimed another heading. The Express had taken the liberty to send a reporter along to Villa Park on the same morning, naively expecting to find a very embarrassed manager admit that his side hadn't actually won the Cup, but had taken it by default. Eric Houghton was a gentleman, he had his own ways of dealing with controversies without lowering himself. The reporter was given a courteous welcome and was then invited upstairs to Eric's office, where he expected he'd sit down and conduct a serious interview with the Villa manager. Instead he found himself standing in front of a glass trophy cabinet holding a gleaming FA Cup. "There it is. We won it on Saturday and it's not going back." Eric Houghton had said all he was going to on the matter.

The following week another banquet, this time hosted by The Birmingham Post and Gazette in association with Birmingham's newspapers, was held at the city's Grand Hotel. The FA Cup trophy decorated in claret and blue ribbons took pride of place in front of the main table. Local journalist Alan Smith of the Birmingham Mail sang the praises of his bosses saying it was a far better bash than the one he had attended at the Grosvenor, where the fare had been basically chicken, peas and new potatoes. It seemed no expense had been spared for the 3000 or so guests who attended Birmingham's gala night. Here they dined on Pate Maison, Scampi's Mornay, Noix De Veau Poelee Nicoise, Pomme Rissolee and Petits Pois Au Beurre and finished in style with Ananas Au Kirsch, Dombe Pralinee, Friandises and Café. In the plush London Johnny Dixon spoke to the guests, hesitantly and quietly and very close to tears He proudly told the listeners what exactly this Cup win had meant for Aston Villa Football Club, the players and the supporters. "How lucky we are to have such loyal supporters; they were perhaps more confident than us that we would bring this Cup back!" he said.

Dixon also touched on the team spirit and the mutual respect that ran through the side. Among the guests were famous names from Villa's glorious past – Sam Hardy, Joe Bache, Harry Hampton, Frank Barson, Charlie Wallace, Tommy Smart, Billy Kirton and Dickie York. The legendary Aston Villa half-back line from the early 1930's of Gibson, Talbot and Tate stood side by side – very likely for the last time. Last but certainly not least, there was Albert Evans, the sole surviving team member of the glorious 1897 Aston Villa double-winning side.

It's common knowledge Aston Villa lost the famous old trophy back in 1895 after it was taken from William Shillock's shop window. If the Sunday People newspaper was to be believed a week and a day after the Final victory, lightning had indeed struck twice. A famous columnist of the paper wrote that after the club's Cup winning banquet at the Grosvenor House hotel, a party of players and officials had carried on the celebrations at Winstons nightclub in the West End. That was where the truth stopped. He then went on to say that they had taken the Cup with them, dumped it in the cloakroom and had left without it in the wee small hours. He further claimed there was widespread panic in the Villa hotel the next morning because no-one could remember where they had left the Cup. That part was also total fabrication. As the fleet of taxis left the Grosevnor bound for Winstons, the Villa secretary Fred Archer was seen happily entering the lift heading for his room, Cup clutched firmly in his hand. Very much a case of - Once bitten…

Mr J Broughton proposed the following minute –
"Our very grateful thanks should be extended to the Chairman for the excellent arrangements made for the FA Cup Final and for his splendid work during the past season."
Mr F.B Normansell seconded and stated the success started when the Chairman secured the three players last season.
Mr W.E Lovesey supported & endorsed the remarks of his colleagues.
Mr C.S Buckley returned thanks saying the secret of the success was due to the wholehearted co-operation of every member of the Board and the team spirit of the Club throughout
Aston Villa Football Club Boardroom minutes, Thursday 9th May 1957.

Tributes followed thick and fast. Among them, the Birmingham store John Lewis presented the players with fine engraved pewter tankards and the Aston Villa Shareholders Association presented the team members with special commemorative watches. The A.V.S.A also hosted a celebration banquet at the Birmingham Botanical Gardens, Edgbaston in October.

Luton away

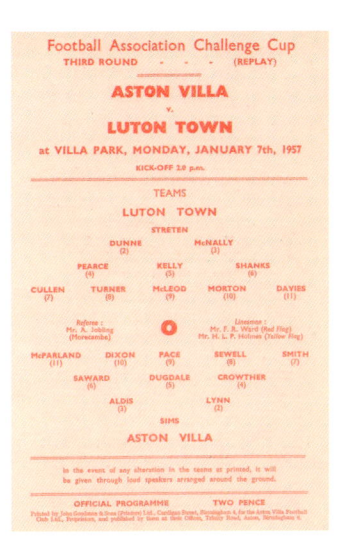

Luton home

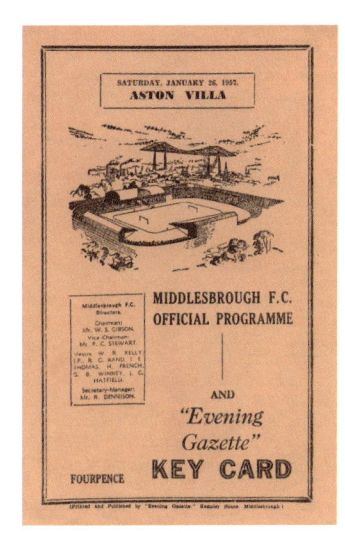

Boro away

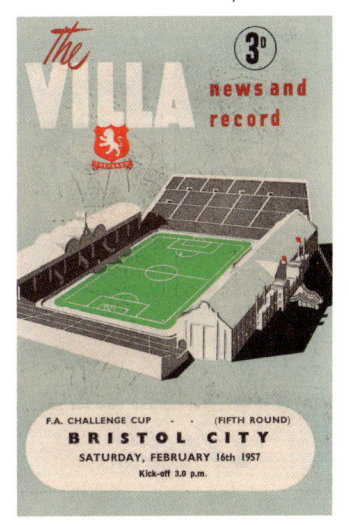

Bristol City home

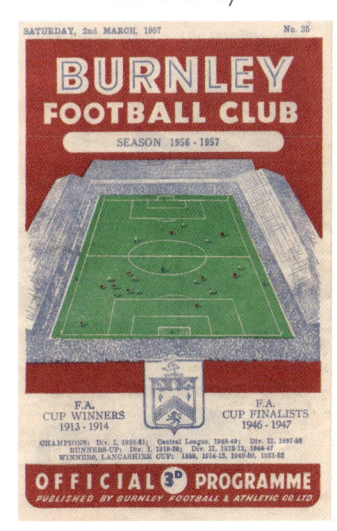

Burnley away

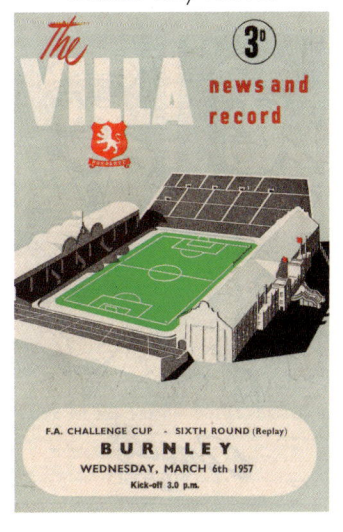

Burnley home

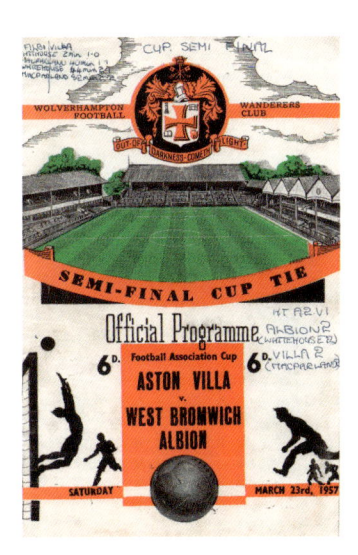

Albion semi-final at Molineux

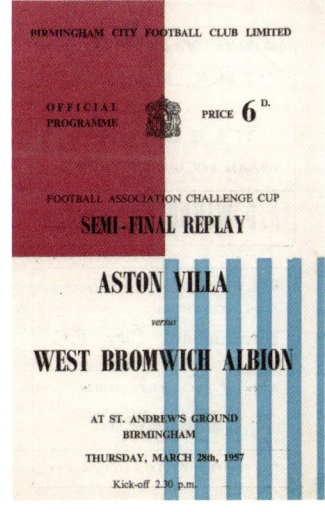

Semi-final replay at St Andrews

F.A. CUP SEMI-FINAL

SAT. MARCH 23

ASTON VILLA
versus
W. B. ALBION

at
MOLINEUX GROUND, WOLVERHAMPTON

ASTON VILLA

BACK ROW (l. to r.) D. Pace (inset); P. Aldis; S. Lynn; N. Sims; T. Birch; P. McParland; S. Crowther (inset).
FRONT ROW (l. to r.) L. Smith; J. Sewell; J. Dixon; P. Saward; W. Myerscough; J. Dugdale.

WEST BROMWICH ALBION

BACK ROW (l. to r.) D. Kevan; F. Horne; F. Griffin; J. Kennedy; G. Lee; B. Whitehouse; R. Bradley.
CENTRE ROW (l. to r.) W. G. Richardson; J. Dudley; W. Brookes; R. Barlow; F. Brown; G. Barnsley; J. Saunders; S. Williams; G. Williams; T. Watson; V. Buckingham (Manager).
FRONT ROW (l. to r.) J. Nicholls; K. Hadley; D. Howe; R. Allen; G. Summers; R. Horobin; M. Setters; L. Millard; W. Carter.

WOLVERHAMPTON WANDERERS FOOTBALL CLUB (1923) LTD.
Cup—Semi-Final
VILLA
WICH ALBION
WOLVERHAMPTON
ch 23rd, 1957
3 p.m.
BANK 2/6 (including tax)

TION CHALLENGE CUP COMPETITION No. 3331
REPLAYED TIE
NDREW'S GROUND, BIRMINGHAM
URSDAY, 28th MARCH, 1957
A v. WEST BROMWICH ALBION
KICK-OFF 2-30 P.M.
ADMIT TO GROUND
J TILTON ROAD
You are advised to take up your position NOT LATER than 2 o'clock

---

FOOTBALL ASSOCIATION CHALLENGE CUP COMPETITION

WEST BROMWICH ALBION
v
ASTON VILLA

SEMI-FINAL REPLAY
SEASON 1956-1957

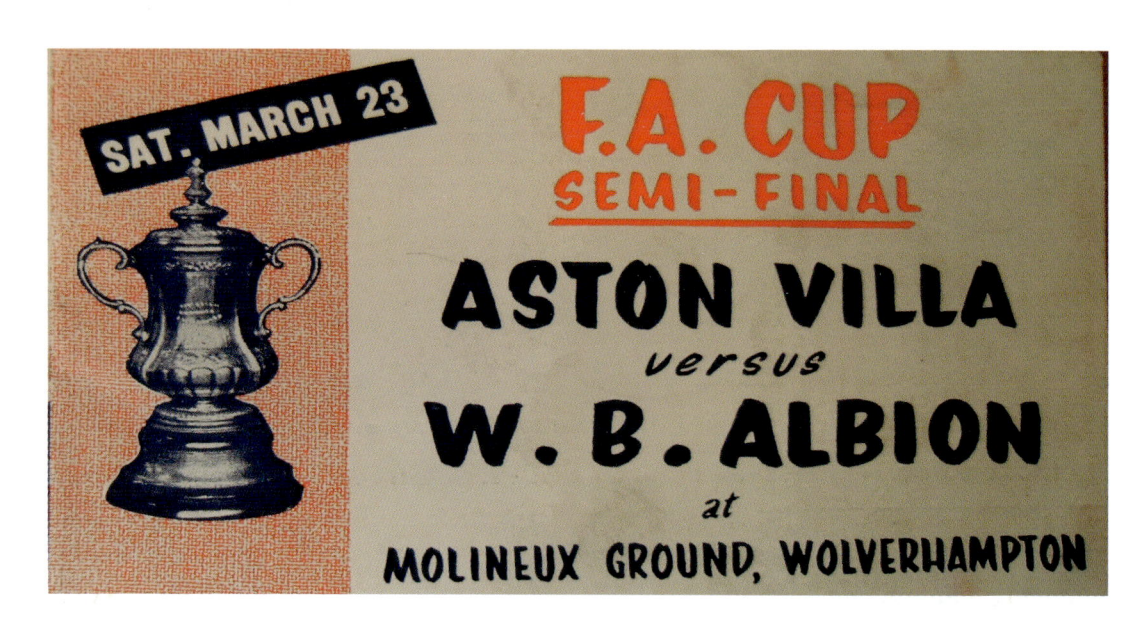

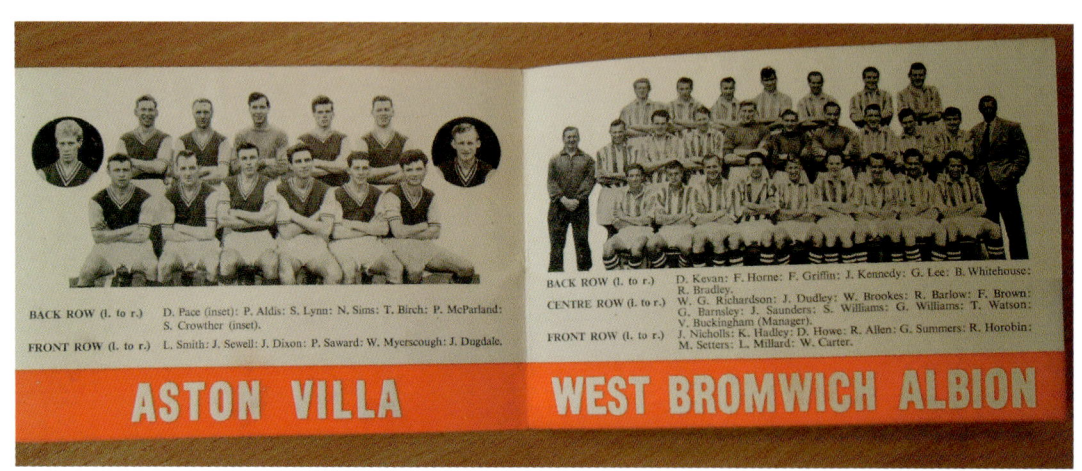

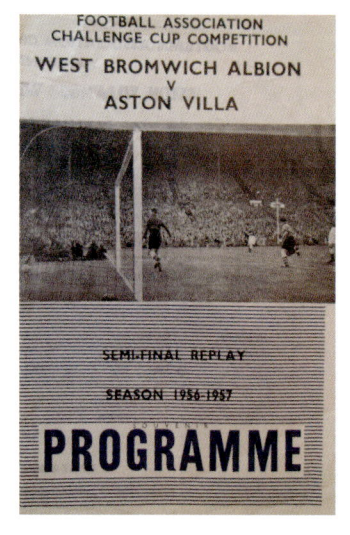

PROGRAMME

Souvenirs of '57

Albion semi-final at Molineux

Burnley home

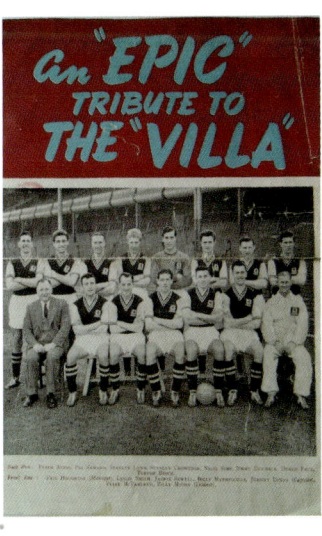

Albion semi-final at Molineux

Semi-final replay at St Andrews

Wembley Bound: Roy Fifield at New Street with his brother Edmond (right) and their friend Dave

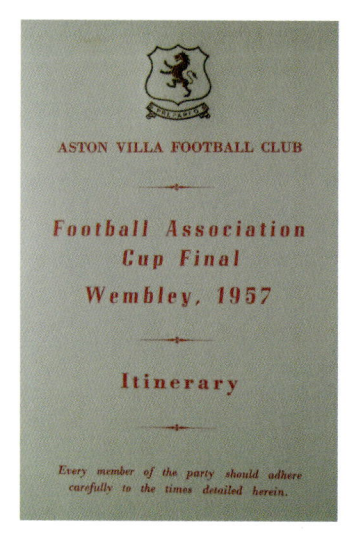

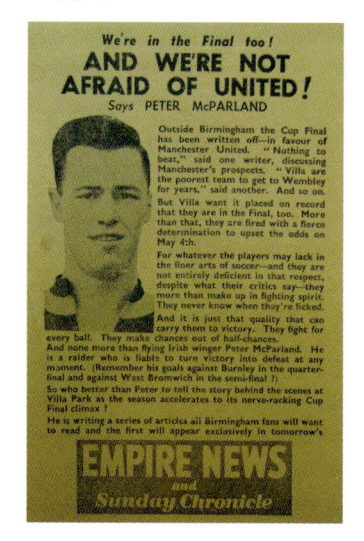

FOOTBALL ASSOCIATION — CUP FINAL
AT WEMBLEY STADIUM
ASTON VILLA
versus
MANCHESTER UNITED
PROGRAMME OF
SPECIAL TRIPS
TO
LONDON
AND
WEMBLEY
ON
SATURDAY, 4th MAY, 1957

BRITISH RAILWAYS

ASTON VILLA FOOTBALL CLUB

Football Association
Cup Final
Wembley, 1957

Itinerary

Every member of the party should adhere carefully to the times detailed herein.

We're in the Final too!
AND WE'RE NOT AFRAID OF UNITED!
Says PETER McPARLAND

Outside Birmingham the Cup Final has been written off—in favour of Manchester United. "Nothing to beat," said one writer, discussing Manchester's prospects. "Villa are the poorest team to get to Wembley for years," said another. And so on.

But Villa want it placed on record that they are in the Final, too. More than that, they are fired with a fierce determination to upset the odds on May 4th.

For whatever the players may lack in the finer arts of soccer—and they are not entirely deficient in that respect, despite what their critics say—they more than make up in fighting spirit. They never know when they're licked.

And it is just that quality that can carry them to victory. They fight for every ball. They make chances out of half-chances. And none more than flying Irish winger Peter McParland. He is a raider who is liable to turn victory into defeat at any moment. (Remember his goals against Burnley in the quarter-final and against West Bromwich in the semi-final?)

So who better than Peter to tell the story behind the scenes at Villa Park as the season accelerates to its nerve-racking Cup Final climax?

He is writing a series of articles all Birmingham fans will want to read and the first will appear exclusively in tomorrow's

EMPIRE NEWS
and
Sunday Chronicle

Wembley '57

FINAL TIE
ASTON VILLA v MANCHESTER UNITED
SATURDAY, MAY 4th, 1957 KICK-OFF 3 pm

EMPIRE STADIUM
WEMBLEY

NORTH TERRACE SEAT (Uncovered)
ENTER AT TURNSTILES (See plan & conditions on back)
ENTRANCE D4 (LEFT)
Row 19 Seat 296

EMPIRE STADIUM, WEMBLEY
The Football Association Cup Competition
FINAL TIE
SATURDAY, MAY 4th, 1957
KICK-OFF 3 p.m.
Price 10/6 (Including Tax)

THIS PORTION TO BE RETAINED
This Ticket is issued on the condition that it is not re-sold for more than its face value

---

FOOTBALL ASSOCIATION CUP FINAL

EMPIRE STADIUM WEMBLEY

ASTON VILLA v MANCHESTER UNITED

SATURDAY MAY 4 1957

DAILY EXPRESS COMMUNITY SINGING

Gladys Price with her husband Ivor

Villa '57 Cup team captured by renowned cartoonist Norman Hood

Aston villa archivist Laura Brett with Jimmy Dugdale's Final shirt

Stan Crowther with the Class of '57

Peter McParland with Irish Lion Billy Dumbrell

Governor of The Bank of England Mervyn King with Peter McParland, Jackie Sewell and Nigel Sims

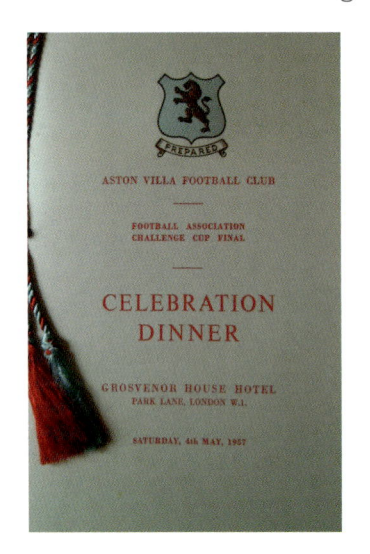

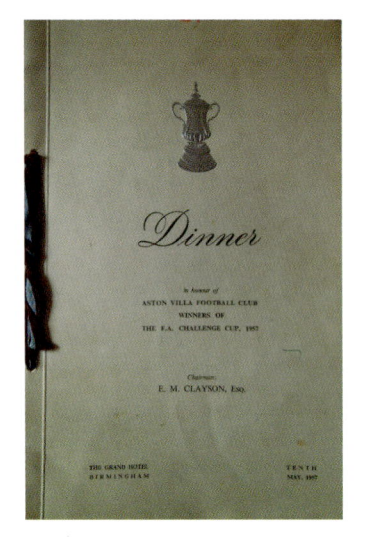

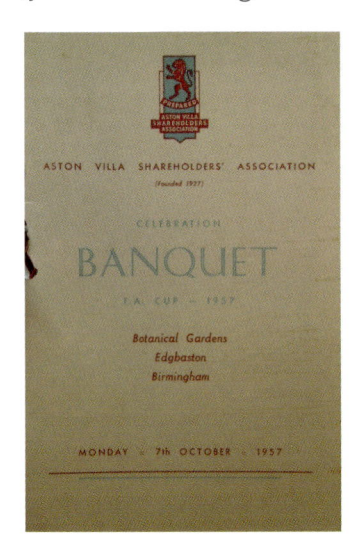

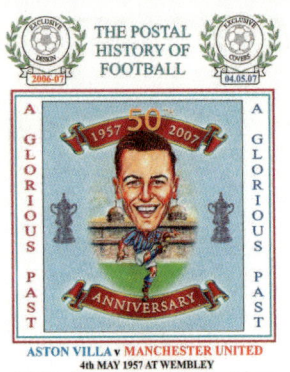

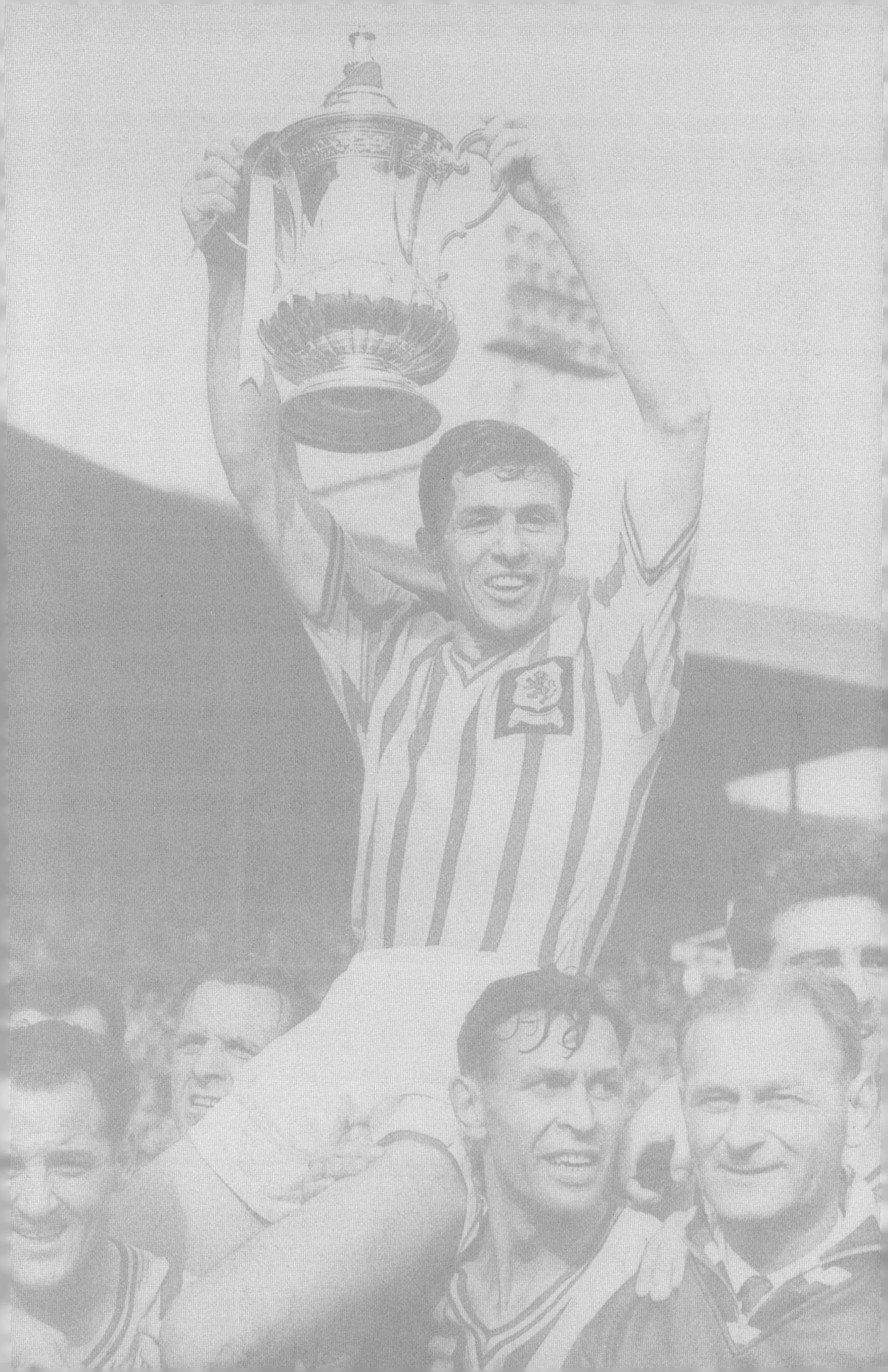

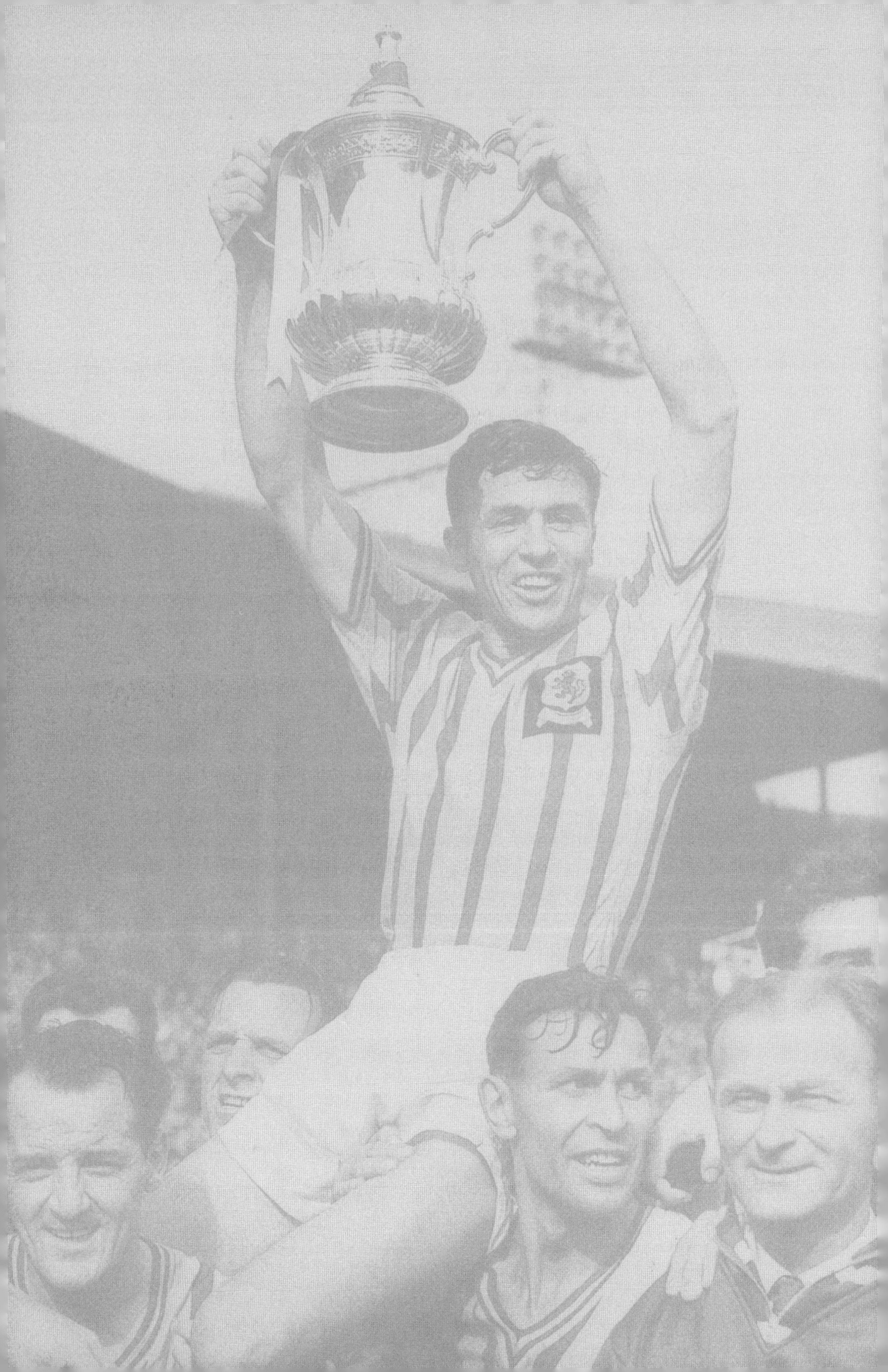

The men responsible for Villa's finest hour

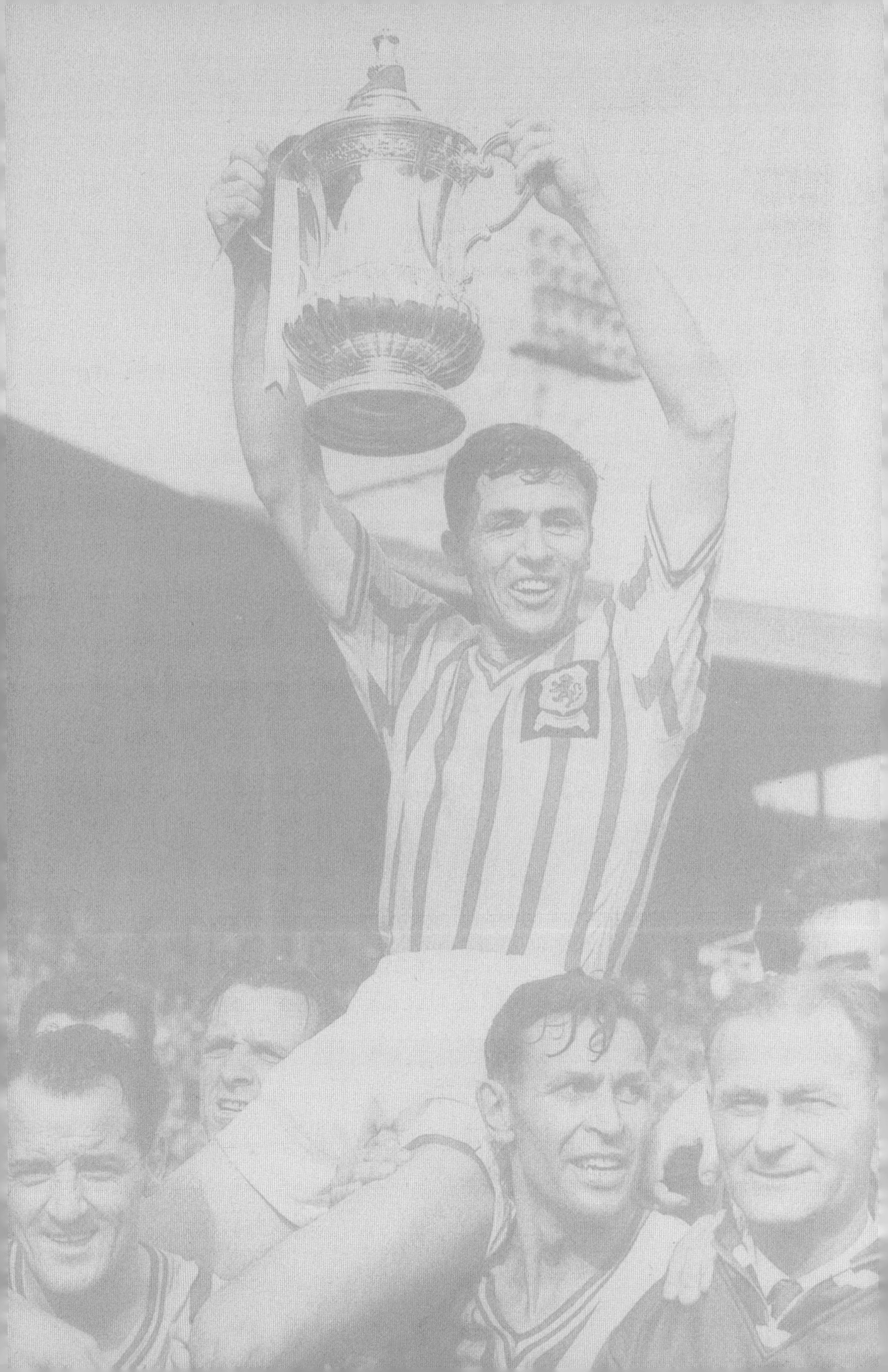

Manager
Eric Houghton

Eric Houghton was a prolific scorer during his teenage centre-forward years, both for his school team on a Saturday morning and then for the local village side on the same afternoon.

He started turning heads in non-League circles while playing for Boston Town before being recommended to Aston Villa by his uncle Cecil Harris, a capable two footed full-back who had himself appeared for the Midlands side. Harris, though, was restricted to only 26 appearances, playing in the era of Villa's distinguished back pair of Tommy Smart and Tommy Mort, and only getting a game when Smart was injured.

Houghton signed professional forms for Aston Villa on 24th August 1927 as a 17-year-old. With Villa having the revered Tom 'Pongo' Waring in the middle, the club converted Eric to play on the left flank, although he had to wait until January 1930 before pulling on the famous claret and blue jersey of the Villa first team.

The opponents that day were Leeds United. Although Leeds won 4-3 they were far more fortunate than they could have realised at the time as Eric Houghton failed to convert a penalty. He wouldn't miss many more and would go on to make a name for himself in the game, particularly as a dead ball specialist. He once scored from 40 yards from a dead-ball effort against Derby County in 1931.

Free-kicks and penalties were his forte. Between 1930 and 1947 Eric successfully converted 72 of the 79 penalties he was entrusted with, a strike rate of 91 per cent. He netted close to 80 penalties at all levels during his career. He also gained seven England caps and scored five international goals for his country.

Eric didn't let that debut miss affect his game. He went on to make 23 league and cup appearances for the first team in his first season, finding the net on 14 occasions, all those goals coming from open play.

In Eric's second season Villa finished runners-up to Herbert Chapman's Arsenal. Villa out-score the Gunners, banging 128 League goals – a top flight record which may never be broken. Eric weighed in with 30 of them, including nine penalties, but was still a country mile behind 'Pongo' Waring who smashed home 49 League goals, plus one if the FA Cup.

Houghton regularly reached double figures in the scoring charts for his beloved Villa during the subsequent 17 years. His official first team total of 170 goals (including 37 penalties) in 392 appearances would have been far more impressive had the Second World War not interrupted top class football. Eric hit 94 goals during the hostilities, including 21 penalties, but his 202 appearances were in regionalised unofficial matches Even though Houghton had represented his country seven times it wasn't beneath him to drop into the Villa's 'A' or third team at Jimmy Hogan's request to try to rediscover his shooting boots. In the 1936-37 season it seemed Eric's form had abandoned him. In a home game against Nottingham Forest, he contrived to miss the target from a yard out. The following week Villa won at Burnley, but Eric hit a penalty wide at Turf Moor. And as if that were not bad enough, he failed from the spot a week later at home to Bradford Park Avenue, although the goalkeeper saved that one.

A spell in the reserves to regain confidence didn't alter the situation and it was only during a match alongside Hogan's youngsters that things started to happen again. A revitalised Houghton came back into the first team fold and in his second match back hit a hat-trick, following up in the next match with a brace!

He signed off his claret and blue playing career by scoring from the penalty spot with the last kick of the game in a Central League match against Huddersfield Town on Boxing Day 1946. Notts County manager Arthur Stollery stepped in and signed Eric immediately after the game for the Division Three (South) club. He was at Meadow Lane until 1949, linking up well as an outside-right alongside England legend Tommy Lawton and a certain Jackie Sewell who would shortly be on his way to Sheffield Wednesday for a record transfer fee of £34,500.

Everyone was shocked that Lawton, the best centre-forward in the country, would even consider playing in the Third Division. But Tommy was a man of his word and when Arthur Stollery was sacked from Chelsea, he had asked Tommy if he would come and sign for him if he were able to acquire a managerial post. Stollery was appointed boss at Meadow Lane, County were somehow able to pay the required fee Chelsea were asking for Lawton and the rest is history.

Would Houghton have signed for the 'Magpies' had Lawton not been there? Between the three of them – Lawton, Houghton and Sewell - they accounted for nine of the 11 goals the Magpies scored in a club record 11-1 win over Newport County in January 1949.

Houghton's playing career ended the same year and he was installed as the new manager on 1st April 1949 in place of Stollery, who had departed in the February. Neil Houghton, Eric's son, said of his dad's time as manager at Notts, "The last thing he ever did as he was locking up was to go and check the dressing room. Tommy would often still be there concussed; he would come off the pitch in those days with the Tomlinson ball with the lace ups and his head would be all bumps, his forehead raw."

In Eric's first campaign at the helm, he led Notts County to the Third Division (South) title and held the position of manager at Meadow Lane for a further three seasons before signing back in at Villa Park in September 1953 to take over the manager's post which had become vacant after the sacking of George Martin the previous month. Having become one of a select group to have both played for and managed Villa, he quietly set about the task of reviving the sleeping giants of football, bringing in new young blood. One of his earliest signings was a young Belfast lad called Peter McParland and Villa finished Eric's first season in charge in 13th place.

The following season Villa would suffer the setback of losing many influential players. Danny Blanchflower and Tommy Thompson both requested and were granted transfers - an unheard-of phenomenon because players didn't usually want to leave Villa. Harry Parkes, Dave Walsh and Frank Moss jnr also played their last games in claret and blue. Yet against all odds Villa finished a very creditable six.

The following season 1955-56 was one of rebuilding. Notable signings included Jackie Sewell, Jimmy Dugdale, Les Smith, Nigel Sims and Pat Saward; less notable was the signing of Dave Hickson as a replacement for Walsh. Villa parted with £17,500 for Hickson and two months later he was gone, with a solitary goal under his belt. Villa were a team in transition and maintained top flight status only by goal average.

Early in the 1956-57 campaign, Houghton brought Stan Crowther into the first team in place of the injured Bill Baxter, who retired before the end of the season. Villa had the good fortune to remain mostly injury-free and were able to field a settled side throughout the majority of the campaign.

Houghton created a team that played as a unit, a team of well conditioned 90-minute men who would go on to take Villa to an FA Cup Final for the first time in 33 years. Eric said of his side, "We were more than a football team, we were a family." Houghton's second spell with the Villa came to an end on 19th November, the same evening that Villa were playing Heart of Midlothian in what was billed in the match programme as 'our second special floodlit game.' The main objective of the match was that Villa were interested in one of the Hearts players.

Nigel Sims recalls the event, "Eric came into the dressing room immediately after the match had finished. The scoreline of 3-3 was totally irrelevant; we could see he had tears in his eyes and looked greatly distressed. He then told us he had resigned. We were speechless, honestly, Eric loved this club, he wouldn't walk away, not Eric. Rumours had been gathering pace since August and we knew he had been very, very close to going when Billy Moore was forced out by the Board, but Eric didn't walk then - he rode it out."

In a hastily-released club statement, Villa informed the football world that their manager had left by mutual consent, which was perceived by many at the time as 'jump or be pushed.'

Eric never came to terms with the Board's decision. "I couldn't understand it," he said. "I had sold Danny Blanchflower and Tommy Thompson because they just wouldn't stay and with some of the money those deals brought in picked up Nigel Sims from Wolves, Jimmy Dugdale (Albion) and Jackie Sewell (Wednesday) and built a team who played for each other and were supremely fit. To get to Wembley we only used 12 men."

Another incident that Houghton struggled to come to terms with was the agreement he had with former Villa chairman Fred Normansell. In those days a handshake - between gentlemen - was as good as a written contract, one that both men would honour. Eric explained, "When I took over I was promised a £2,000 bonus for getting Villa to Wembley, but there was nothing in writing. I also wanted £500 for Bill but I ended up with £650 for myself and Bill got only £100, less tax. He went in and collected his cheque then walked out of the club."

Normansell a caring, popular and highly respected gentleman died before Villa's triumphant day at Wembley and ex-Villa centre-half Chris Buckley, who succeeded him as chairman in July 1955, refused to honour the agreement.

After leaving Villa only 18 months after their Wembley triumph, Eric was taken on as chief scout by his ex-Villa team-mate Billy Walker, who was now manager of Nottingham Forest. He then had a short spell as manager of non-league Rugby Town before becoming a director at Walsall. In a third spell at Villa Park Eric took a seat on the Board, he sat for seven years before becoming Senior Vice-President in 1983.

Eric Houghton always had time for the supporters young and old; he would chat for as long as anyone cared to listen, sometimes about a few of the greats of Villa – the likes of Billy Walker, Pongo Waring, Frankie Broome and George Cummings, all former team-mates of Eric's.

He spoke of their achievements, never his own. Eric was a modest man. He refused to take the acclaim for Villa's finest post-war achievement – the 1957 Cup win – generously crediting the victory to his fitness-fanatic Geordie trainer Billy Moore. Even when the new executive suite in Aston Villa's North Stand was named The Houghton Suite in recognition of his service to the club, he replied, "It is very nice to be honoured in this way, but I can think of a lot of players who are more worthy of it – my old friend

Billy Walker for instance. So although the suite is named after me, I feel as if I am accepting the recognition on behlf of all the great players I have played with for Aston Villa."

Eric was a Villa man to the core, a true gentleman who was extremely loyal to those around him. He rated Nigel Sims and Jimmy Dugdale as "the best signings I made in my life." Only when pushed would Eric reveal his finest ever claret and blue side, more likely than not because it would mean omitting and possibly upsetting former team-mates or lads he signed. He did state that he could name two or three other sides of equal strength.

Houghton's sporting prowess wasn't limited to football. He had also turned out for Lincolnshire Cricket Club in the Minor Counties Championship. After the war he captained the Warwickshire second XI and during the 1946/47 season he made seven appearances for the Warwickshire first XI making his debut against India.

He was also a successful businessman co-owning the Houghton & Parkes sports shop situated in Six Ways, Erdington along with fellow Villa player Harry Parkes. On Eric's move to Notts County the partnership ended but on returning to the West Midlands he later started a similar venture - opening another sports shop, Houghton & Bradford in Sutton Coldfield with ex-Birmingham centre-forward Joe Bradford. Neil Houghton fondly remembers working in his father's latter shop during the school holidays. In March 1992, he was presented with a plaque, an acknowledgment from the Football Association to commemorate over 50 years service to football.

Eric Houghton died in Birmingham on May 1st 1996, but remains to this day one of an elite group of only 11 men who have scored 100 or more goals for Villa. His 170 total puts him in third position behind Billy Walker and Harry Hampton.

Gordon Lee a player under Houghton having signed professional terms for Villa in October 1955 had this to say, "A man like Eric Houghton leaves a mark on you. He was a first class man, sane, sincere, dedicated and loyal. I owe much to him and without doubt his influence has helped my career in management. You must remember that in my time at Villa Park youngsters like me had to battle all the while against household names for a place in the team, so I know how it feels to be in that situation. Eric was helped of course, by having Bill Moore as his trainer. They were totally contrasting as men, but complemented each other. Bill was like a bottle of pop, fizzing all the while with his passion for the game bubbling out."

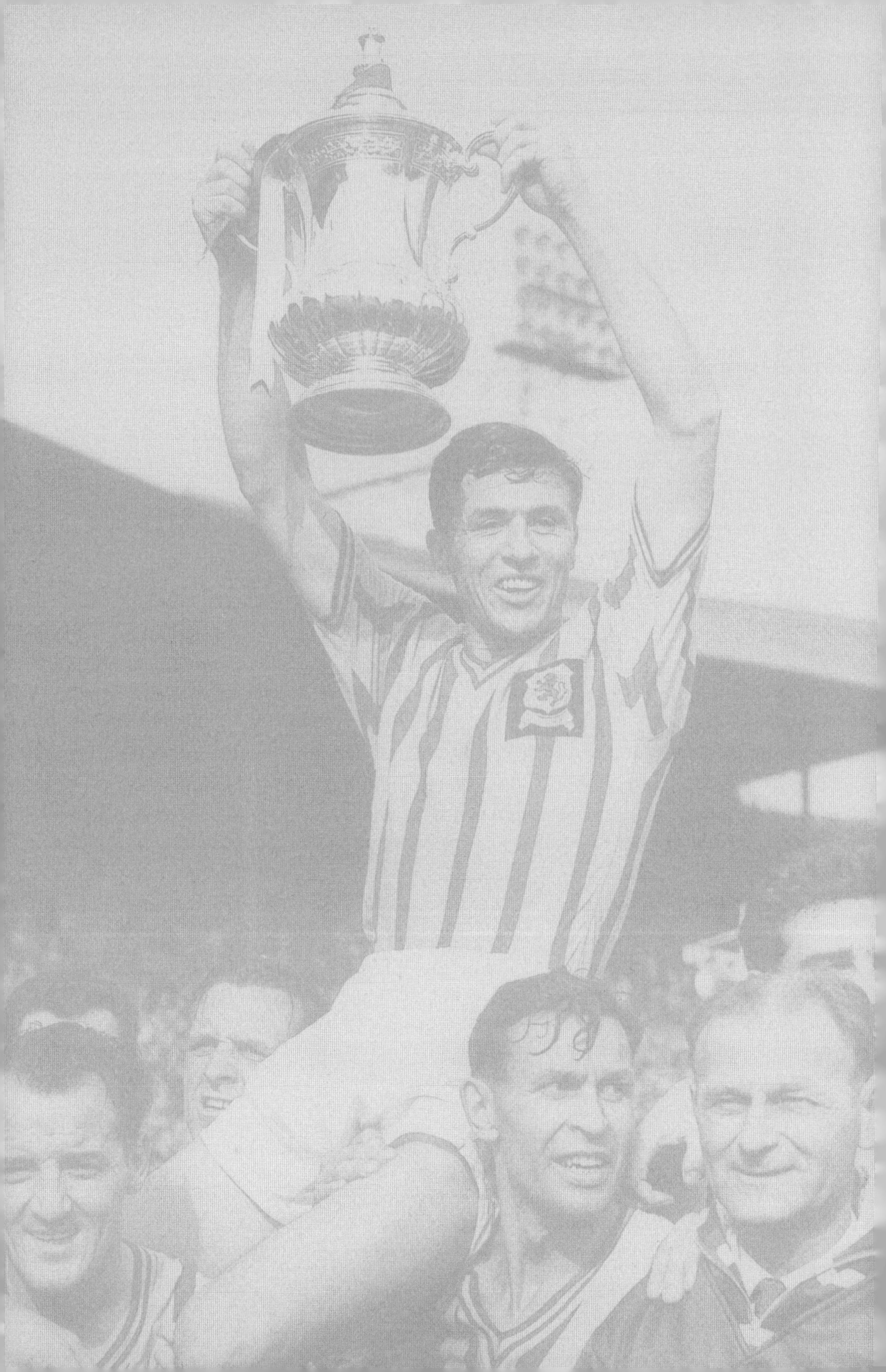

No 1 goalkeeper
Nigel 'Nigger' Sims

David Nigel Sims came into the world on August 9th 1931 in Coton in the Elms, a little village near Burton, Staffordshire. He was the third son of proud parents Jack and Edith. From a very young age he knew he wanted to be a professional footballer, his older brother Jack was a promising player who turned Birmingham City down. Before long, mother Edith decided to drop the name David, and called the youngster Nigel; she realised as he got older he would be called Dave by his mates and she didn't like the thought of that. She would have liked the name 'Nigger' even less.

Nigel was a big lad for his age and excelled in most sports; he was a more than useful centre-forward for both the school and the Coton Village Junior team. When Nigel was 12 his brother Jack, who was centre-half for the village senior team, made him go in goal as they were a man down. He excelled that day – against adults too. And the first save he made is still remembered by Nigel as his best ever!

He soon outgrew the village side and went to play for Stapenhill when he was 16. During his time playing for the Swans he caught the eye of a Wolverhampton Wanderers scout. After a few trials he convinced the club that he was worth a risk and signed on at Molineux as a member of the ground-staff for £4 per week. He became good friends with England captain Billy Wright who always had time for the new intake of youngsters at the club. After six or seven months, Nigel's ability and appetite for the game earned him a professional contract. As a 17-year-old he made the agonising decision to undergo surgery on his feet and that decision ultimately paid rich dividends, even though spent the next eight years at Molineux and appeared less than 40 times for the 'Old Gold.' There was no way he would dispossess Bert Williams, the regular Wolves goalkeeper, other than when Williams was injured.

But Eric Houghton threw a lifeline to Sims – who grabbed the chance with both hands. He moved across the West Midlands in March 1956, when Villa were a team in transition, and close to going down. Sims went straight into the side, replacing Welsh stopper Keith Jones and playing the last nine matches, of which Villa were able to win five and retain their top flight status.

The following season Nigel made the No 1 jersey his own. He was now the number one choice between the posts; it had taken a long time but he had finally achieved it. He went on to play his part in Villa's FA Cup triumph and was also in the victorious side that gained promotion from the second flight at the first attempt in the 1959-60 season. The winner's tankard Nigel received after Villa lifted the inaugural League Cup of 1961 rounded off his honours attained while at Villa Park.

He was expected to make the full England team but with the international selection committee having board members from both Wolves and Birmingham sitting on it, the call never came. It was a huge surprise to left-back Peter Aldis that his goalkeeping team-mate, never 'got the nod,' "For two years Nigel played out of this world," said Aldis. "There was no-one – and I stress no-one - equal to his ability during this purple spell. He was always a good player, but in this particular period he was exceptional and should have played for England. His anticipation was outstanding, and for a man of his size his mobility was extraordinary. It was a privilege to play in front of him." Nigel had to make do with representing Young England in the traditional eve of Cup Final fixture and playing for the Football League.

On his release from Villa in 1964, Nigel played the summer months in Canada, for Toronto City under Malcolm Allison. After a brief spell at Peterborough, Nigel emigrated to Canada and turned out for a two other Toronto-based sides - Falcons and Italia. While at Italia, Nigel Sims picked up the last honour he would achieve in the game of professional football, helping his team to the title of the Eastern Canada Professional Soccer League. He also sustained the injury that would be responsible for bringing his career to an end - a career that ran for nearly three decades!

Larry Canning said of Nigel Sims, "I would regard Sims as the best goalkeeper at Villa Park throughout the post-war period of 40 years or more. He had virtually everything a player could want for that particular job. Big, strong, agile he went for everything in his area and usually got it. Nigel was exceptionally powerful in coming off his line to go for balls, either in the air or on the ground. I never played against him, but I would suppose that he presented a very formidable obstruction to opponents going for goal because of his sheer physical dimensions. One of his greatest strengths was that unusual combination of size and agility. He was particularly good at using adept footwork to get the ball or take up good positions. To put it briefly – he was very quick for a big man!"

Nigel lives with his wife Marjorie, near the Gower peninsular. Nigel's book titled 'In Safe Hands' was published in 2012, the proceeds of the book going to help with surgery costs for injuries sustained in his outstanding career between the sticks. Was he England's finest uncapped goalkeeper - or the footballer with the film star looks?

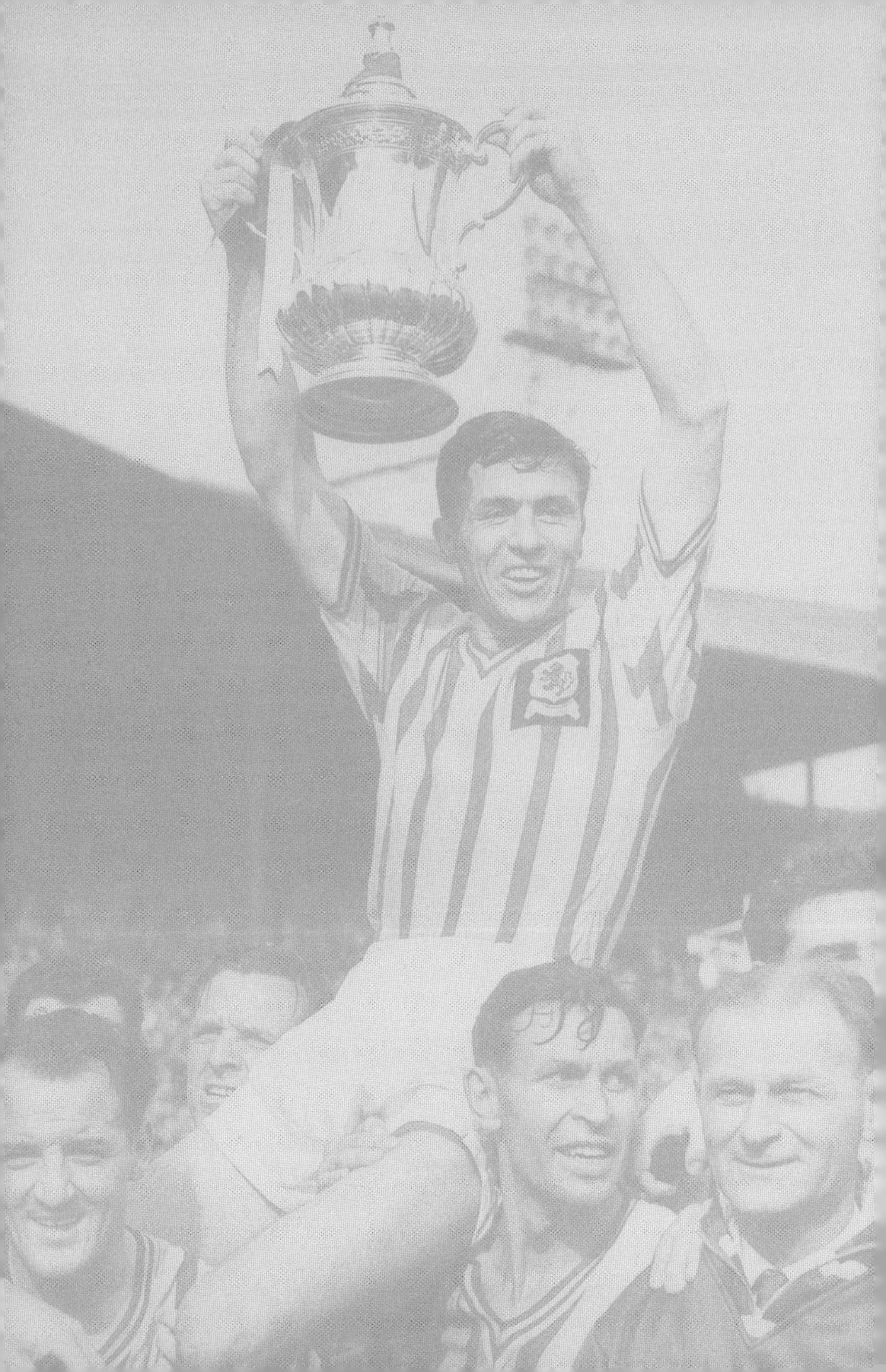

No 2 right-back
Stan 'The wham' Lynn

Remembered affectionately by the fans as Stan the Wham because of his powerful dead ball shooting power, Stan was known by Villa's players by the not-so-flattering name of Vera. Needless to say, Stan preferred the fans' moniker!

Lynn is part of Villa folklore. A right-back, he was revered by the Villa supporters for his full-blooded tackling as much as his striking ability; he made in excess of 320 appearances in the claret and blue jersey, scored 38 goals for the club of which 19 were penalties; he bagged a hat-trick in a game against Sunderland to become the first full-back to achieve the feat in the top flight.

And in a match against Cardiff City, the Bluebirds' custodian Graham Verncombe, bravely (or stupidly) saved one of Lynn's special free-kicks with his chest. The keeper prevented a goal, though he knew very little of it until quite a while afterwards – he had been knocked unconscious.

Stan originated from Bolton, having been born in the Lancashire town on 18th June 1928. His football career kicked off shortly after the Second World War with Accrington Stanley of Division Three (North). He signed for them in 1947, and chalked up 35 appearances for the Owd Reds in three seasons at Peel Park. At the same time Stan worked as a grinder in a local mill.

Both Derby County and Newcastle United took a keen interest in the young defender but his mill role meant he was unable to sign for either club due to a Control of Engagement order. Initiated by the government, it was enforced to prevent workers in key industries from leaving to go to what was deemed as unproductive labour and it remained in place until March 1950.

That same month manager-less Villa reacted immediately and went calling with a £10,000 transfer fee – a figure Lynn always claimed he wasn't worthy of. Stan was seen as the ideal replacement for the ageing Harry Parkes, another player with a kick like Muffin the mule, and made his debut for the Villa in October 1950, playing 10 matches that season. The following campaign Stan was out of contention until November, coming into the side away at Fulham, where he scored one of the goals in a 2-2 draw.

He was drafted into the team in the absence of Peter Aldis, though Stan wore the No 2 shirt and Harry Parkes moved to left-back. The 1954-55 campaign saw Stan make the right-back position his own and he played more games that season than anyone else, chalking up 46 League and cup appearances and weighing in with seven goals. Only Johnny Dixon and Tommy Thompson scored more!

Lynn served admirably in Villa's defensive line for over a decade, picking up a Second Division champions medal in 1959-60 and a 1961 League Cup winners tankard to accompany his 1957 FA Cup winner's medal. Harry Moore, a Villa fan of over 60 years, recalls the time he spoke to Stan – as a starry eyed 15 year old - at an organised meet-and-greet a week or so before the Wembley showdown. Harry asked, "How will you play knowing that the Queen will be there?" Stan replied in a matter-of-fact manner, "I won't even know she's there; I'll play my own game."

In October 1961 Lynn's career took a downward spiral when he left Villa and joined perennial strugglers Birmingham City, a side who had escaped relegation by just two points in each of the previous two seasons.

In Lynn's first season with Blues, they exceeded all expectations and finished six points above the trap door. In Stan's second season at St Andrew's, they finished yet again two points, but only one place, above the relegation zone. In the campaign of 1963-64, the margin was even closer, down to a solitary point, before Birmingham finally achieved what they had seemed to strive for – relegation. After being so close for six seasons, they had finally managed it. And full-back Stan Lynn was the club's joint-highest scorer!

Stan remains one of the highest scoring full-backs in the history of the game. He quit League football in 1966 and died in Birmingham in 2002, aged 73.

No 3 left-back
Peter 'Elvis' Aldis

Peter Aldis was a defensive lynch pin for Villa. He made close to 300 appearances for the claret & blue, the majority of them alongside fellow full-back Stan Lynn – a partnership which first saw light of day in Peter's debut against Arsenal in March 1951. How many supporters present at the game would have been aware of the significance of the day? They were witnessing another fantastic full-back pairing; history was in the making that afternoon.

The partnership comfortably stood the test of time and remained until that fateful day in May 1959 when Aldis made his last appearance in the Villa jersey, the infamous 1-1 draw against West Bromwich Albion which condemned us to relegation. Quite simply, Lynn and Aldis should have been afforded a similar title to Villa's great pair of full-backs from the 1920s and 1930's – Mort and Smart – otherwise known as 'Death & Glory.'

By comparison with his partner, Peter's scoring feat could not have been more modest – a solitary goal in 295 matches. But what a goal! Even though he wasn't a great scorer, the saying – 'a scorer of great goals' could have been written especially for him. His sole effort was a 35-yard header against Sunderland in a 3-0 win at Villa Park, September 1952, and it held the English League record for being the longest headed goal.

Born in Kings Heath, Birmingham in April 1927, Peter played for his local side Hay Green while working at the Cadbury's chocolate factory. He was spotted turning out as the team's centre-half and Villa came in for him in November 1948, signing him on as an amateur under the leadership of ex-Scottish International Alex Massie, their former wing-half. Peter signed professional forms in January 1949, and it was during George Martin's reign as manager that he was handed his debut.

Among Peter's attributes were his exceptional ball distribution, his fitness and his tackling ability. Under the guidance of the coaching staff, these were honed to perfection as he turned out for Villa's second string in the Central League.

Peter's finest moment in a Villa jersey was the Wembley Cup win of 1957, just a week before he turned 30. It was the only honour he won during his time at Villa Park but it was something to cherish.

Joining Hinckley in 1960 and staying there four years, he became one of only two players ever to appear in 13 different rounds of the FA Cup. He then moved to Australia where he took up the post of player-coach of Slavia, during which time he was voted Australian Player of the Year. After one season he coached Wilhelmina and then joined Melbourne Lions in the same capacity.

After returning to England he spent the 1969-70 season at Alvechurch as player/manager, once again getting the chance to pull his boots on.

He always talked fondly of his Villa career. "How can you quibble at being paid for doing something you would do for nothing?" he asked "Like most things in life we did what we wanted to do and got satisfaction of doing a good day's work for reasonable pay. At one time I worked in Cadbury's – chocolate block 6; playing football was a very reasonable alternative to that. And when I started we used to train at the HP Sauce ground. George Cummings was one of the coaches, he used to spend hours banging balls up for me to head. It's a wonder he didn't kill me – even if it did give me a flat head." Of the Cup side of 1957 he said, "We weren't classy but we enjoyed each other's company; there were no little cliques within the club and we worked for each other. That's what got us to the Final and that's what won us the Cup."

In August 1986 he made a compassionate plea to Villa fans through the Villa News & Record. Peter and his wife Grace took the decision to sell his prized Wembley shirt to raise funds for a charity after losing their only son, Gary, who died after a two-year spell in St Bartholomew's hospital battling leukaemia.

Peter also wore his 'second' 1957 shirt when he competed in the 1989 London marathon. He thought it was a good idea at the time but later regretted it. Lightweight, super absorbent material wasn't around in the 1950s. "I was not only on my knees when I finished the marathon," he said, "the old jersey stretched to the point where it was covering them!"

In his programme notes, ex-Villa wing-half Larry Canning who had regularly played in the defence alongside Aldis, wrote, "Aldis was a tall, very elegant player who sensibly concentrated on what he was best at, namely clearing his lines very quickly with good long passes, probably to Peter McParland. He was never encouraged to do more than that and one of his strengths was that he was seldom caught in possession. Ball playing was not his style and as a result one seldom saw him dribble his way into trouble. Peter always gave a good, solid performance. If I were asked to use one word to sum him up, it would be – elegant!"

Peter died in November 2008, which was a cruel year for the '57 side. Jimmy Dugdale and Les Smith had passed away in March, their deaths separated by only a week.

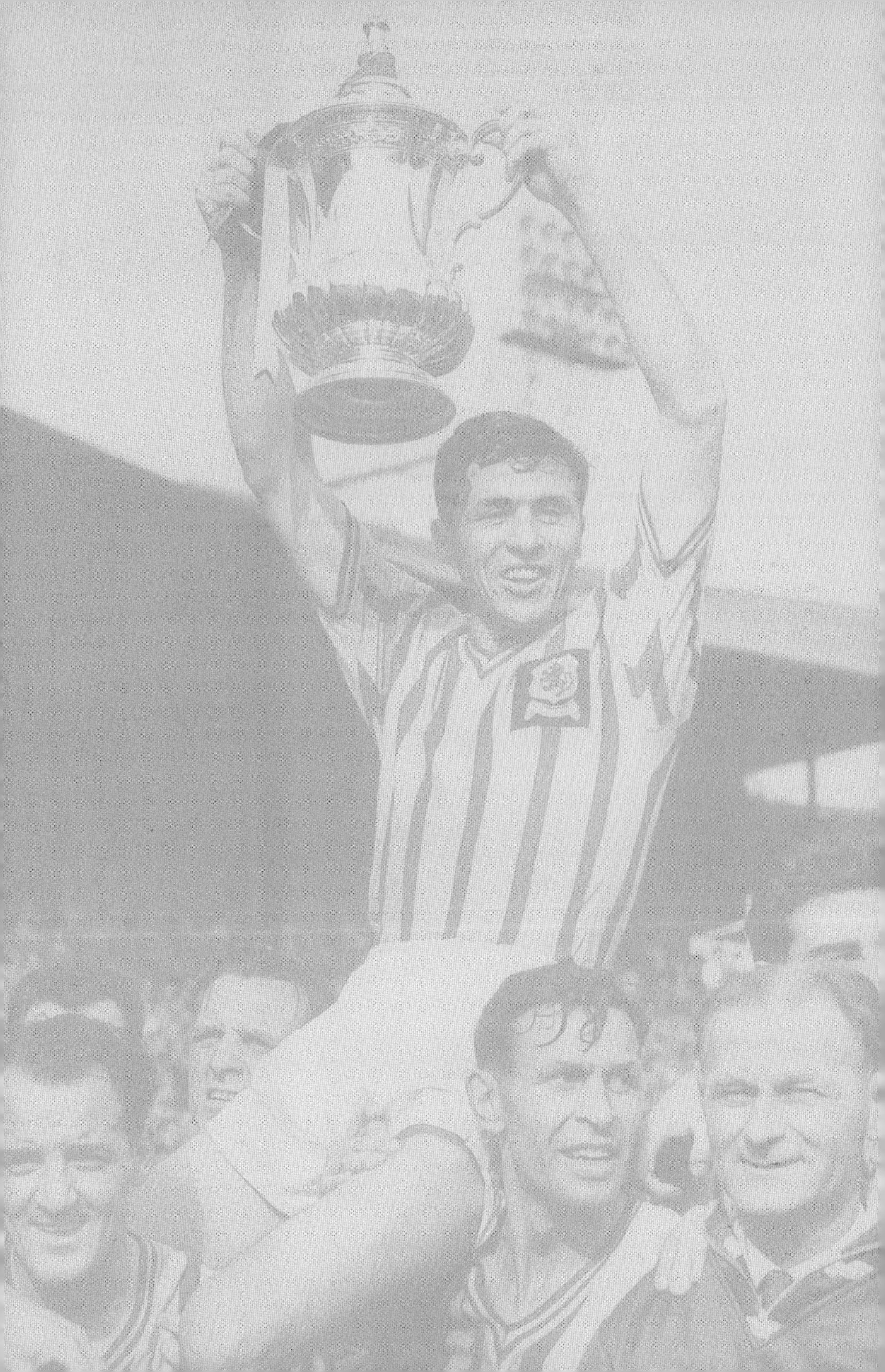

No 4 right-half
Stan 'Teezy Weezy' Crowther

Signed by the astute Eric Houghton for the princely sum of £750, Stan left non-league Bilston behind in August 1955. Less than two years later Crowther appeared in the first of two successive FA Cup Finals. The second one, in 1958, created football history – because it was the first time a player had legitimately turned out for two different teams in the same season's FA Cup competition.

Having played in Villa's third-round tie away to Stoke City and the second replay, Stan was Cup-tied. But United, having lost eight players in the Munich air disaster in February, were given special dispensation to sign Stan and field him in the same competition (see Stan Crowther's foreword). Yes, Ernie Taylor did go to Manchester United under the same dark circumstances as Stan, but Taylor wasn't Cup-tied, having not featured in Blackpool's third round tie away at West Ham.

Crowther was the baby of the 1957 Cup side, having been born in Bilston, Staffordshire, in September 1935. After starting his footballing career with his school team - Stonefield Secondary Modern – as a full-back, he was snapped up on amateur terms by West Bromwich Albion in May 1950. He had been told as a youth he could have his pick of 12 League clubs and for two years he played in the Baggies' nursery side, Erdington Albion. But Stan wasn't offered the chance to sign on for another two years with them.

"I knew it hadn't gone well, playing full-back didn't help," he said. "It wasn't my position so I left; there was no hard feelings." Stan ended up playing back at Stonefield for a year, and the centre-half role was ideal for his game. This led to him joining his local side Bilston. The 'Steelmen' had a few big name players in their side, lads who had appeared for the Wolves and Albion prior to the Second World War, and they played their football in the Birmingham Combination. He remained there, turning in good performances – initially for the reserves at centre and wing-half - for three seasons. But he was well aware that he was attracting the attention of some big League clubs – because his boss used to tell him.

He played in Villa's second and third teams during his first season with the club and it was only when Bill Baxter damaged his cartilage, nine games into the 1956-57 season that Crowther was finally given his chance. He took it with both hands. Although not entirely confident about his own ability, he was tall and strong – and talented. From making his claret and blue debut in a 0-0 draw at home to Bolton Wanderers in late September 1956, he went on to feature in 24 League games and every round of the 1957 Cup run. His best performance for Villa - by a mile - was reserved for an audience with the Queen, in the Wembley showdown against Busby's Babes. Due to circumstances beyond his control, unfortunately, Stan never received the 'Man of the Match' award he so richly deserved; that went to United stand-in keeper Jackie Blanchflower. In his second season Stan had to relinquish his beloved No 4 shirt on a few occasions to Vic Crowe, who was coming back from injury. In those games Stan slotted effortlessly into Jackie Sewell's berth at inside-right. He made 62 appearances for Villa, scoring four goals in a five-match spell, before departing against his will to Old Trafford. His time in Manchester didn't work out as he had hoped and 10 months – and 20 games - later he moved on to Chelsea.

His spell at Villa Park holds his fondest memories, a fact which is reflected by his achievements while with the club – a Football League Representative match and three appearances for England U-23s, plus an FA Cup winner's medal against the club that ultimately took him away from his beloved Villa.

In his time at the Villa, Stan was known affectionately by his team-mates as Teezy Weezy – he was very proud of his blond locks. Peter McParland remembers this well, "The one day we were training up at the HP Sauce factory and it was blowing a gale. We were playing a little practice match at the time and the ball was going all over the place. Eric Houghton stopped the game and called us into the centre circle; he started giving us a rollicking for what was going on. Stan was stood beside me, and the next thing he's down on the deck with his head between his hands, and I said "what the hell are you doing." Stan replied, "That bloody winds blowing my hair up." "Stan was always brushing his hair forward; he thought that if he didn't, he would lose it!"

On another occasion Stan was walking along a corridor in Villa Park when he passed Eric Houghton going the other way. Eric said, "Stan, the chairman says you have to get your hair cut. Without pausing Crowther replied, "Tell the chairman to get his own f***ing hair cut!" Peter remembers, "Old Eric was stunned when he told the story back to us."

Larry Canning said of Stan Crowther in his programme notes for the Villa News & Record of the 1980s, "He (Stan) seemed to arrive from nowhere and blossomed very quickly to be an important part of that team that won the Cup. He proved himself to be a very good, stylish player who was simply an excellent, natural passer of the ball. In retrospect one can say that it was a sad thing that he did not have the career his ability warranted."

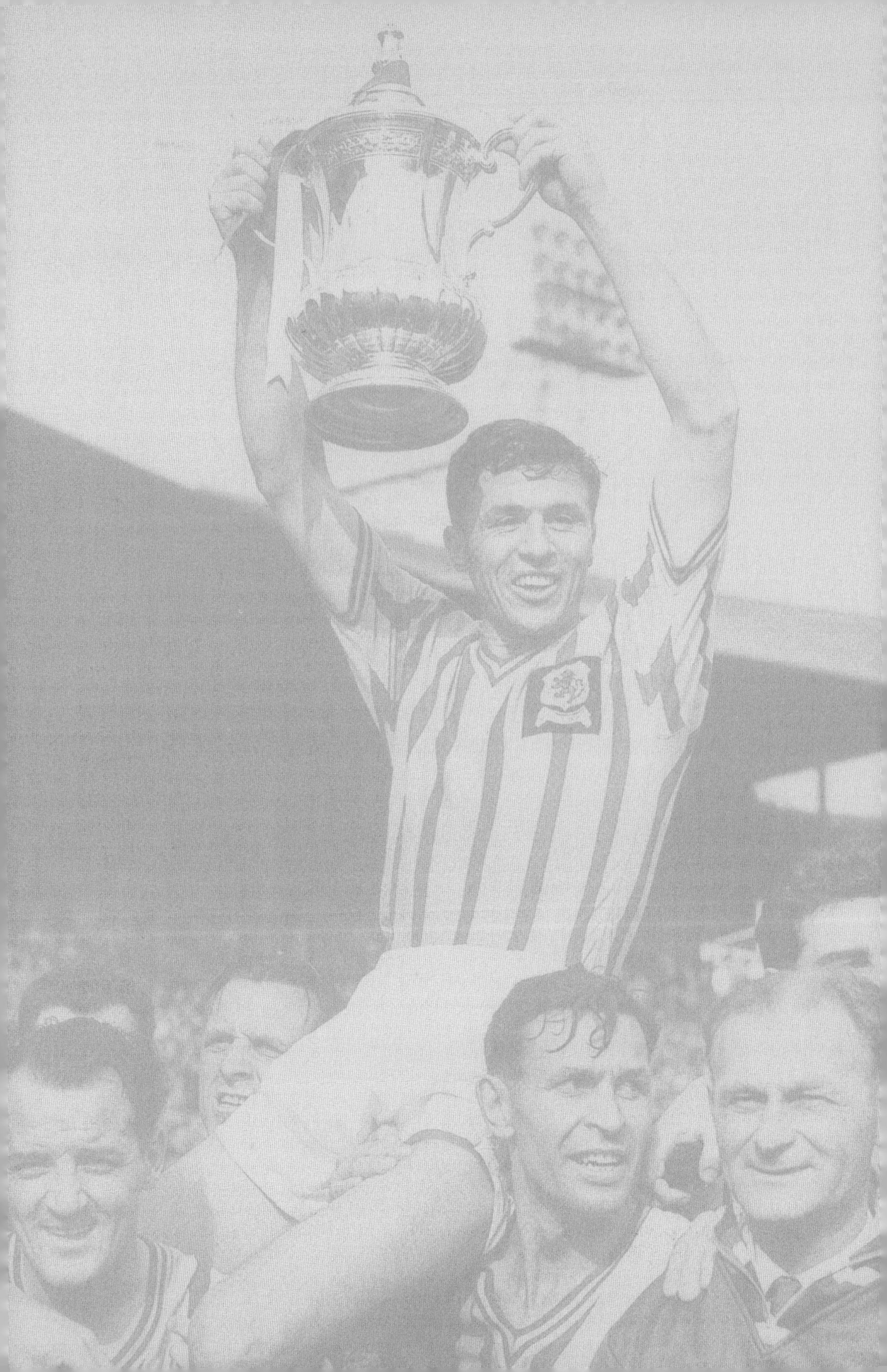

No 5 centre-half
Jimmy 'Laughing Cavalier' Dugdale

Along with Nigel Sims, manager Eric Houghton cited Jimmy as being his best signing during his managerial career. It has been documented that those two acquisitions were arguably the best bits of transfer business Villa had conducted since the war, and yet strangely enough neither went on to gain full international recognition. "I came close once," Jimmy recalled, "I played for England B in Yugoslavia and after the match was told that I was almost certain to be selected for the senior side in a game against Hungary, but it never happened. For that matter, why wasn't Johnny Dixon ever given a chance by England? As a person, player and captain Johnny was the best bloke I ever came across in the game, and that's saying a lot."

Dugdale was a dependable and solid centre-half who was snapped up from West Bromwich Albion for £25,00 in February 1956. He began his career at The Hawthorns, where he signed amateur forms in 1950. A year later he was rewarded with a professional contract from the Baggies, his excellent form continued and this led to his three caps at England 'B' level and also representing the Football League and the Football Association. Jimmy's finest moment up to that time was his appearance at Wembley in the 1954 FA Cup Final, where he played a huge part in Albion's 3-2 win against the much fancied Preston North End, the Baggies defence ensuring that the great Tom Finney had an indifferent match.

Born in Liverpool in January 1932, Jimmy started playing football at seven or eight years of age; he played full-back for Croxdale Rovers Youth Club as he reached his teens and progressed to adult football from the age of 15 – starring for Harrowby in the West Cheshire League, where he turned out in both wing-half and centre-half positions. It was in this league he came up against former Villa legend Tom 'Pongo' Waring, whose career had all-but ended. Harrowby's boss Jack Doyle was so impressed with the 'mature above his years' Dugdale, he wrote and recommended him to West Bromwich Albion. "I know he wrote to Albion about me, and got them interested, but to this day I've no idea why he chose the Albion. He never spoke about them or followed them. Funny thing, that."

With Joe Kennedy's emergence at The Hawthorns, Albion didn't stand in Jimmy's way and sanctioned his move 'down the road'. Many clubs had tracked Jimmy's availability but it was Villa who won his signature. "I remember the day I signed quite vividly, the then chairman, Mr Chris Buckley, invited me into the old boardroom, offered me a large scotch and told me very clearly that he has spent a fortune to get me. I think the figure was £20,000"

Dugdale was signed by the claret & blue in July 1956 as a replacement for the near departing Con Martin who, after eight years and 213 appearances, was calling it a day and returning to his native Ireland.

Villa were struggling at the time of Jimmy's signing. They had lost comprehensively 4-1 at home to Chelsea in the previous game – and occupied a relegation position – before he made his debut three weeks later in a 1-1 draw at home to Arsenal. Dugdale's signing added a much-needed, steely determination, strength and stability to the Villa defence, his performances were instrumental in Villa retaining their top flight status. Of the Villa's remaining 14 fixtures in the 1955-56 campaign - Dugdale featured in them all - Villa lost only four. Prior to his arrival Villa had lost 14 of their 28 League matches.

In the build up to the 1957 Final he was described in the press as 'the finest buy Villa have made since the war'. That season he won his second FA Cup winner's medal, completely marking Tommy Taylor out of the Final, and helped put his former side out at the semi-final stage, causing controversy in the process. His clash of heads with good friend Ronnie Allen led to the Albion forward having to go off.

Jimmy, known by his Villa team-mates as the Laughing Cavalier, played his last game in the claret and blue jersey in March 1962. He notched up an impressive 255 appearances, he played his part in Villa regaining their top-flight status and then featured in the club's winning of the League Cup in its inaugural season. Jimmy remembered the League Cup success over two legs against Rotherham, "We were trailing 2-0 after the first leg in Rotherham, but we pulled back to win the second match 3-0 at Villa Park in the last few minutes of extra-time. It was quite a game!" He also recalled fondly, two other games he was involved in, both at Villa Park, "One was against Charlton Athletic when we won but finished up winning 11-1, although to be fair to Charlton, they used three players in goal during because of injuries. Then there was a game with Liverpool when I think we were losing 4-1 when I had to go off injured. Those were the days before substitutes but I wasn't missed too much because after I went off, we pulled back three goals to draw 4-4.

Jimmy was a hard man but also a caring one. Gordon Lee, who played alongside him in defence - albeit very briefly - said of him, "Jimmy had a heart as big as a gas holder and competed for everything. He was The Rock of Gibralter."

In October of the same year Jimmy moved down two divisions to play with Queens Park Rangers though he was forced to retire the following May after two unsuccessful cartilage operations. On hanging up his boots, Jimmy became a publican before taking up a steward's position with Villa's Lions club; he also served as a steward for six years at Moseley Rugby club and in a similar capacity at the Conservative Club at Halesowen. He later had to have both amputated and passed away in February 2008. Of his Villa career, former 'Villan' Larry Canning said, "Whenever I watched Dugdale playing for Albion before he moved to Villa, I used to imagine he based his game on ex-WBA centre-half Jack Vernon. Dugdale would do exactly the same; he rarely booted the ball a long way, he used his brains by pushing passes to his wing-halves or inside-forwards who could use it constructively. He was always in there where it hurts, in the wars with cut eyes and other injuries because he was so brave and honest a player. Yet although he was always regarded as tough, he was never dirty. He never went in to kick people but he got kicked often enough himself."

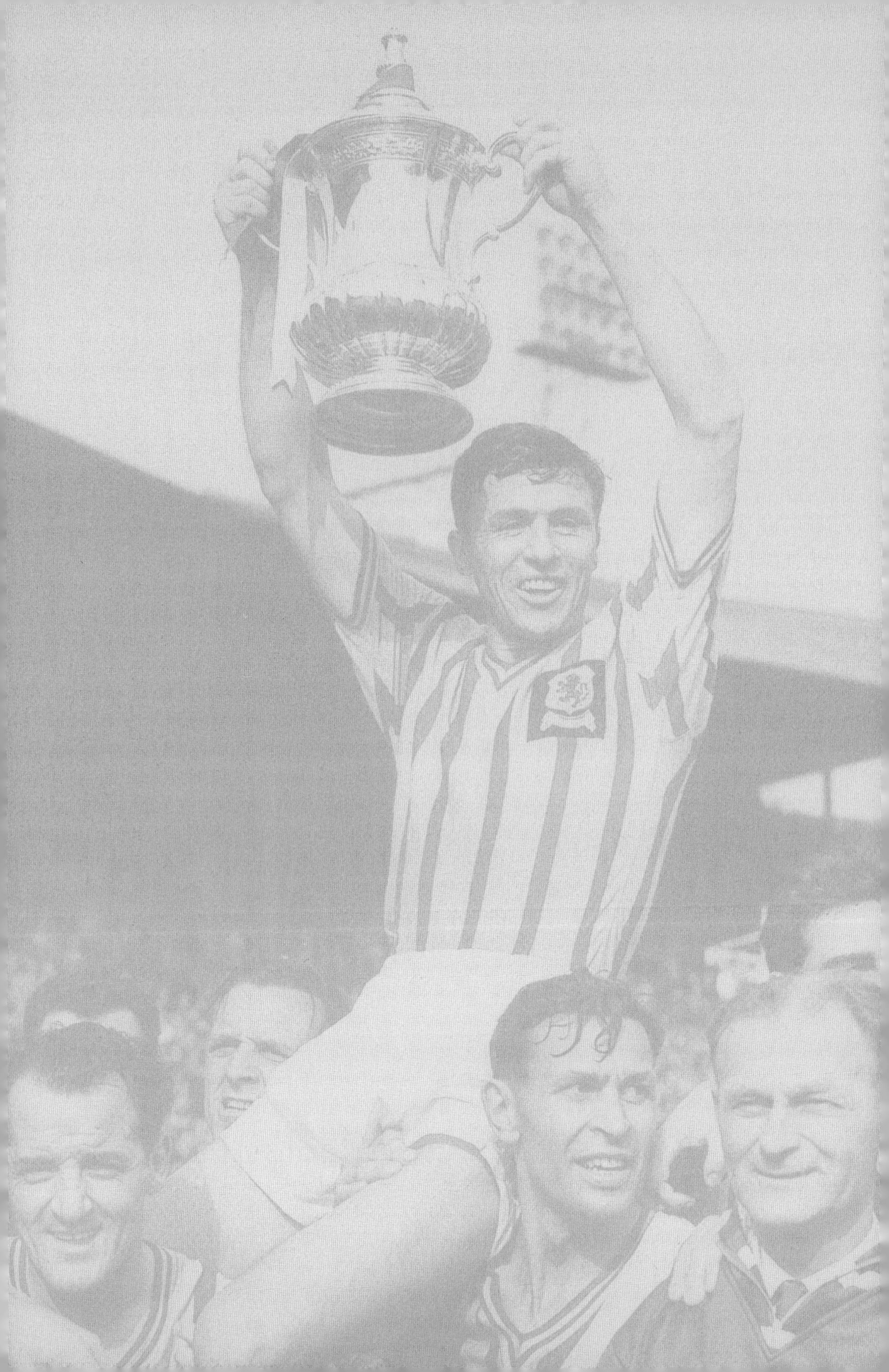

No 6 left-half
Pat 'Seaweed' Saward

Born in Cobh, County Cork, Ireland in August 1928, Pat's football career started late and he was well into his teens when he played for Cobh County Schools. He showed little interest in the game because he thought he was no good at it, but Croydon Sea Cadets managed to get him to play intermittently as an inside-forward. "I'm not good enough," he told them finally, along with all the other Croydon-based sides who were chasing him.

Eventually Pat joined the Navy and football was shelved totally. When home on leave, he would go along to Selhurst Park to watch his older brother Len play for Crystal Palace. Together they would have a kick about and it was during one of these occasions that Len was able to convince his younger sibling that he could make the grade as a professional, resulting in Pat signing on with Beckenham, the Crystal Palace nursery club. It was there, with help from manager 'Dusty' Miller, that Saward finally realised his worth on the field.

From being an amateur/trialist at Palace, Pat signed professional forms for Millwall in July 1951, staying at The Den for four seasons in which he notched up 118 appearances and scored 14 goals. While at The Den, Pat Saward earned the first of his Republic of Ireland caps.

Villa signed Saward in August 1955. The Midlanders had finished their 1954-55 campaign in sixth place, level on points with Manchester United and only a point adrift of runners-up Wolverhampton Wanderers. Pat had been used to mixing it in Division Three (South) with players of far lesser calibre. Doubts started to surface once again but Pat waited patiently. He made his debut as an inside-forward in mid-October in an enthralling 4-4 draw at Villa Park against United. Villa had gone 2-0 up, mid-way through the first half only for United to lead 3-2 at the interval. With Manchester leading 4-3 late into the match Pat Saward marked his debut with the equaliser. He would bizarrely score his second and only other goal in what would amount to 170 appearances for the Claret & Blue in the following season's corresponding fixture.

Saward remained in the side for five games – Villa won two and lost two - and then was left out of the team until returning for the odd game in April 1956. The Villa's campaign had been a disaster and the club stayed up by virtue of goal average alone – and Saward somehow blamed himself for the dip in the club's fortunes. Transfer-listed, he very nearly went to back down to Division Three level with Norwich City, but Villa gave him another chance – this time at wing-half. It proved to be an astute switch as Sward helped Villa win the FA Cup for a record seventh time. Norwich, meanwhile, finished the 1956-57 season bottom of the pile in Division Three (South). Even during his six years at the Villa, he would maintain that brother Len who played for Palace, Newport and Cambridge, was a far better player than him.

As well as a total lack of confidence in his ability, Pat would also get very nervous. In order to switch off from football after training he enrolled in a psychology course, "I started it as something to fill in the evenings," he said. "But I got so interested that I went three nights a week. Then when the Cup run came along I had to ease up."

Before the Final there were fears that Pat might be nervous at Wembley, but not only was he one of the calmest players on the field, he was also described as being the most improved wing-half in the country! Pat went on to accumulate an FA Cup winner's medal, Second Division Champions medal and 18 Eire caps. In his time as assistant manager at Coventry City, Saward is credited with unearthing future Villa European captain Dennis Mortimer. He also had spells with Brighton and Al Nasr of Dubai as manager.

Pat died in September 2002 in a Bottisham nursing home on the outskirts of Newmarket.

No 7 outside-right
Les 'The Smudge' Smith

Outside-right Smith, was signed by the Villa at the same time Jimmy Dugdale arrived from The Hawthorns (February 1956), they both made their debuts in the game against Arsenal at Villa Park. Les also featured in all of the claret and blues' remaining fixtures of the 1955-56 season and became an instant hero to the Villa fans by scoring a brace in the last game of the season at home to West Brom. The 3-0 win, resulted in Villa maintaining their top-flight status as they avoided the relegation trap door only on goal average.

Les was born in Halesowen in December 1927. He signed on as an amateur for Wolverhampton Wanderers in June 1945, signing professional forms the following April. Smith remained at Molineux for more than a decade but due to the quality in depth at Molineux, competing against players of the calibre of Johnny Hancocks and Jimmy Mullen, he was severely restricted to first team appearances, making only 90.
His career mirrored that of Wolves reserve goalkeeper Nigel Sims; Smith finally jumped ship in February 1956 when Eric Houghton and a fee of £25,000 persuaded Smith and Wolves respectively that a transfer across the Midlands made good sense.
 In his first four games for Villa he played alongside inside-right Jackie Sewell, a very clever ball player recently acquired from Sheffield Wednesday, but before this partnership could blossom Sewell was injured and had to miss the last quarter of the season. Les then struck up a good understanding with Tommy Southren but this arrangement was only going to be a temporary fix. The following campaign, a revitalised Jackie Sewell and wide man Smith combined better than anticipated – they went together like bacon

and eggs!

Built on a defence of granite and now boasting a forward line as dangerous on the right, and hopefully as destructive as the left side of McParland and Dixon, Villa clearly meant business.

Smith weighed in with 13 League and cup goals in Villa's victorious Wembley campaign. His predecessors Southren, Ken Roberts and Colin Gibson had never been as prolific at finding the net.

Smith's only honour in his time at Villa Park was his 1957 Cup winner's medal, and he had to retire prematurely when he ruptured an Achilles tendon towards the end of Villa's instantly forgetful campaign of 1958-59, the curtain falling on his claret and blue career in a League match at Nottingham Forest in April 1959. In a fraction over three years Les had made 130 appearances and notched 25 goals. He played half as many games again in Villa's colours as he had for Wolves – and it took him a third of the time to reach them. Les died in March 2008.

No 8 inside-right
Jackie 'The Little General' Sewell

Born as John Sewell January 1927 in the village of Kells, Whitehaven, Jackie came from a large family of football stock. He played alongside six of his uncles when he was only 16 years of age, turning out for Kells Centre, a miners' welfare team in Cumbria. Turned down early in his career by Barnsley boss Angus Seed, who thought the young Sewell was too light, he made an impact on the game like very few before him. He took his disappointment well and within the month he was playing for Kells against Workington (Jackie also guested for Workington and Carlisle during the Second World War).

Notts County had sent scouts up to run the rule over a certain Workington player but two players ended up going to Meadow Lane for trials. In his trial game, Sewell did his chances no harm by bagging a hat-trick and in October 1944 he was duly signed on as an amateur. Within 10 months he was signed as a full-time professional. In his six year spell in Nottingham, he helped them to promotion from Division Three (South), although he received very little recognition. Tommy Lawton, it seemed, was solely responsible for a period in County's history known as the 'Lawton era.'

In March 1951 Jackie left Eric Houghton's Notts County for Sheffield Wednesday for what was a British record transfer fee of £34,500. Jackie told me, "I had no idea I'd been sold, the first I heard was from the lady who ran the digs I was staying in. She kept saying "congratulations" and then asking "is it true?" At the time I thought it was a ludicrous amount to pay for a footballer. But I never thought I'd see the day when players changed clubs for a million pounds. Like the game itself, times have changed."

Jackie's first season at Hillsborough saw the Owls go down, though he hung around and was instrumental in them coming straight back up as champions.

Sewell scored three times in six appearances for England, and he played against the legendary Ferenc Puskas in the infamous 6-3 defeat by Hungary at Wembley, although his international career was over – far too abruptly – before he signed for Villa.

Sewell was signed by Eric Houghton - the same Houghton who had sold him to Wednesday from Notts County – in December 1955, and went straight into a relegation-haunted Villa side. Like the other new signings, he played his part in keeping the club up.

He was described as having almost a telepathic understanding with his right-wing partner Les Smith, and their partnership proved very successful. It was surely as instrumental as the McParland-Dixon left-sided attack. That duo hit a combined 30 League and Cup goals; Sewell and Smith contributed 31.

The highlight of Jackie's Villa career? "Villa's Wembley triumph of 1957 – that must count as the high-spot of my time at Villa. There was a marvellous spirit in the side and we were tremendously fit, a fact that I think took us to Wembley. Apart from the Final – and although we were the underdogs against Manchester United, we all felt we could win – the match that sticks out was in the sixth round against Burnley. We drew up at Turf Moor and then beat them 2-0 on a quagmire of a pitch at Villa Park. It was a marvellous performance by us considering the conditions and even now I can remember one of their full-backs, Doug Winton, who later came to Villa, saying to me during the match that he couldn't wait for the final whistle because of the conditions. Yet we could have played on all day."

After falling out with Joe Mercer, Jackie went up to Humberside to sign and play for Hull City, though he and his wife were extremely grateful for the way they were treated by Villa during that time as their infant son Paul was seriously ill. "My son was born in Birmingham and I'll never forget the help we got from everyone, and at the Dudley Road Hospital when there were problems in the early weeks," he said.

With his playing career coming to an end, he had accumulated many honours – a Division Three South champions medal, a Division Two champions medal, an FA Cup winner's medal and six England caps, as well as Football Association caps for tours of Canada and Australia.

Jackie later moved into management with Lusaka of Zambia, "I spent 13 happy years in Africa, based around Lusaka, where I helped establish a multi-national side. I came back to England with hopes of going into management but that never worked so I settled in Nottingham with Bristol Street Motors." He still resides in Nottingham and lives close to his son Paul.

During our book launch of In Safe Hands - Nigel Sims' Football Memories, Jackie Sewell came along to Villa Park where he left a large crowd spellbound with his stories and memories. It was an absolute honour to have Jackie share our day. He is someone who is still held in high esteem. "The supporters were always good to me," he said. "They were a marvellous set of lads at Villa and I always enjoy the occasional visit I make back to Villa Park these days."

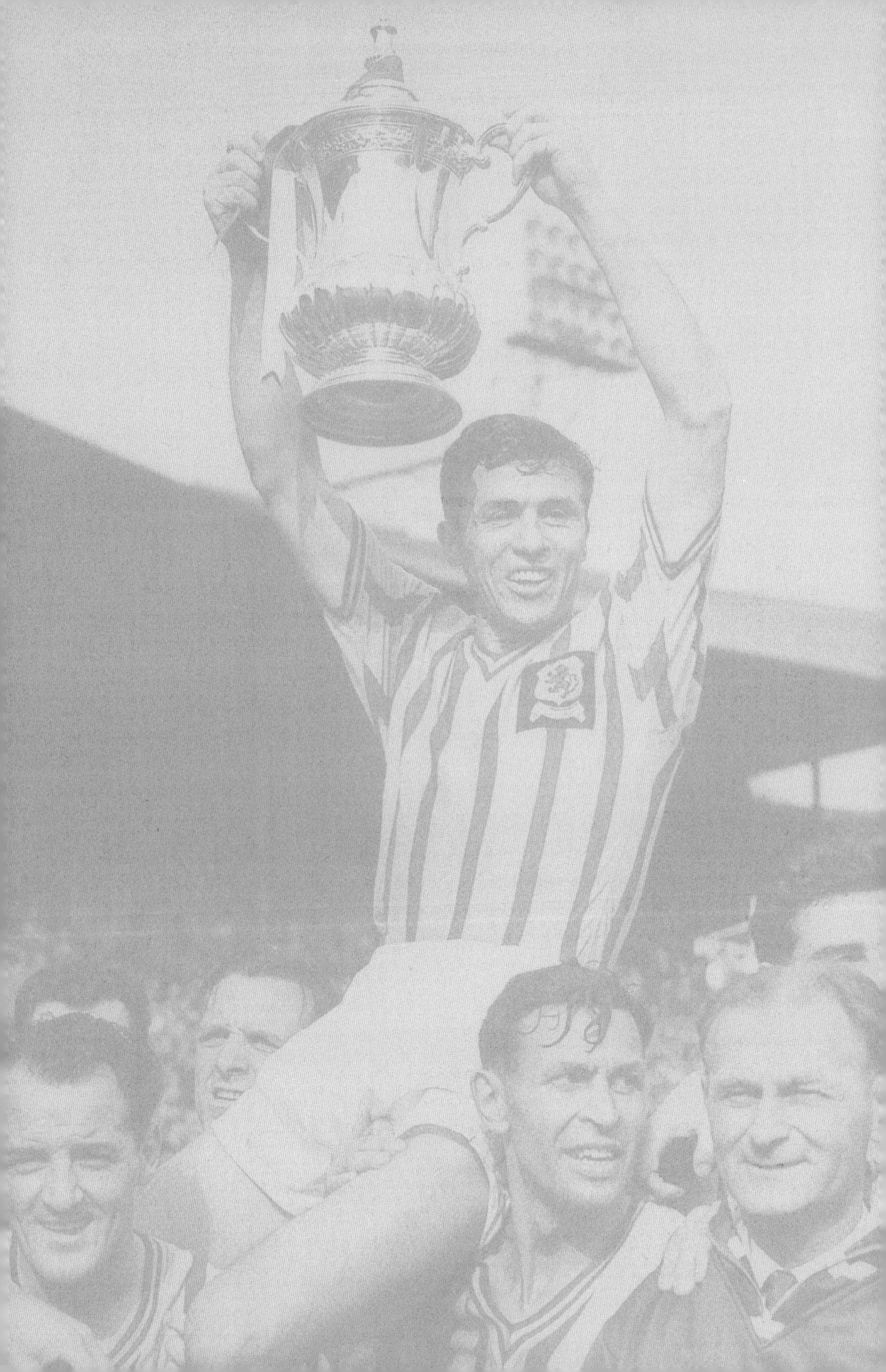

No 9 centre-forward
Billy 'Whooping Cough' Myerscough

Out of the entire Cup-winning side, the Wembley fairy tale must have appeared far greater for Billy Myerscough than for any other player involved. Bought in from Walsall in a part-exchange deal that took Villa forward Dave Walsh in the opposite direction in July 1955, Billy didn't feature in a single first team fixture for his new side for the entirety of the 1955-56 campaign. Yet 12 months later he was a Wembley hero.

William Myerscough was born in Farnsworth, Lancashire in June 1930. He played for Manchester County FA before signing amateur forms for Manchester City, although he was never offered a full–time professional contract and drifted north of the border to Ashfield FC, a club situated in Possilpark in Glasgow.

Walsall, who had finished the 1953-54 season bottom of the pile in Division Three (South) for the third year running and had luckily being re-elected on each occasion, were prepared to give the forward a chance and signed him on professionally in June 1954. Billy repaid them by scoring six goals in 26 appearances, prompting Eric Houghton to take him as part of the Walsh deal.

His debut in the claret and blue came in December 1956, when he deputised for the injured Jackie Sewell, but after two games Villa's regular inside-right was restored, and he was back plying his trade in the Central League for the reserves.

He was later recalled at the expense of the injured Derek Pace, playing in his preferred centre-forward role, in a morale-boosting 1-1 draw up at Old Trafford. When Villa played this match they knew if they could safely negotiate their semi-final with West Bromwich Albion, they would set up a Final showdown at Wembley with either Manchester United or Birmingham City, so the game assumed extra significance. After three consecutive League games, Billy was given the nod to play against the Baggies in the semi and came up with the winner in the replay at St Andrews. Two days after sending his side to Wembley, Myerscough scored his first League goal in a 2-0 victory over Preston.

With Derek Pace unable to guarantee lasting the full 90 minutes of the FA Cup Final, Houghton had little choice, in those days before substitutions, but to hand the coveted No 9 shirt to Myerscough.

Billy made 74 appearances in his five years at Villa Park, finding the net 17 times, and his semi-final header being was the most important of his career. His last match was in the 1958-59 season under new boss Joe Mercer, and he ultimately gave way to the fast-emerging Gerry Hitchens.

He became a bit of a journeyman in his later years, having spells at Rotherham, Coventry City, Chester, Wrexham, and Macclesfield. And Billy's passion for the game was, without question, re-ignited as an amateur in October 1967 he had a season at Manchester Meat Traders.

William Henry Myerscough was the first member of the team of 1957 to pass away. Billy died in Manchester in March 1977; he was just 46.

No 10 inside-left
Johnny 'The Blur' Dixon

Villa's Wembley '57 captain was born December 1923, in Hebburn, a small town situated on the south bank of the Tyne. Johnny started playing football while very young and turned out for a few local youth teams, notably Jarrow and Hebburn boys and Durham County Boys. In turning out for Jarrow at the tender age of 12 years old he was their youngest-ever player. After leaving school he went to Reyrolle Works and featured in their side. At the age of 17 Dixon had spells with non-league outfit Spennymoor United and then Newcastle United, where the Magpies took him on as an amateur trialist.

With the outbreak of the Second World War, and with League football put on hold, Johnny guested for various Northern teams - Hull City, and all three of the big North-East sides, Middlesbrough, Newcastle United and Sunderland. Initially he played regularly in the black and white of Newcastle, but gradually drifted out of the reckoning. With his career seemingly going nowhere, Johnny was persuaded by his brother Ernie, who had returned from the War, to submit a transfer request. Ernie who had once had high hopes of being a professional footballer, was determined that his brother would succeed where he had failed. On receiving Johnny's request for a transfer, the club - no doubt to save face - responded and gave him a 'free' confirming exactly what he had thought. He was surplus to requirements.

"I wrote to Villa asking for a trial," he said. "I had no connection or special interest in them. I wrote simply because they were a great name."

They gave him a game and brother Ernie proudly watched on as 'wor young un' signed amateur forms in August 1944. So keen was Dixon that he spent 18 months travelling back and forth from Tyneside to Birmingham to turn out for his new team. After he turned professional in January 1946, both Johnny and Ernie relocated to 'Brum.' Dixon made his debut for Villa in the last campaign of the war years, when they played in the Football League (South). He capped a fine debut at home to Derby County by getting the Villa's fourth goal in an emphatic 4-1 victory – only to knock himself unconscious in the process. He lined up up in the attack alongside such notable greats as Frank Broome, George Edwards, Ronnie Starling and Billy Goffin. Dixon played two remaining games that season with future manager Eric Houghton at outside-left. He had six games under his belt and had found the net three times.

In his next season 1946-47 normal service was resumed – the return of Division One football. Dixon featured in roughly half of the games that season but within three years he was a virtual ever-present and remained so until Villa's relegation in April 1959. By then, Johnny had captained Villa to an historic record breaking FA Cup win, and - sadly at the time of writing – he remains the last player to do so, following in the footsteps of Archie Hunter, John Devey, Howard Spencer, Joe Bache and Andy Ducat. It might not have happened, because Johnny was only made made captain of the side six or so matches before the Wembley showdown. "I was very fortunate," he said. "The club was decimated by injuries so there was no big deal about making me skipper. The truth was that there was hardly anybody left that they could ask, but I took it as a great honour and enjoyed the experience. I enjoyed playing football and thought everybody else did too. As long as I could run about, work hard and provide wholehearted endeavour, I assumed that my team-mates would do the same. It seemed to work."

"Although the League has always been the big test of a team's ability, it was the Cup games that got everyone talking. You'd be saying to rival players, 'I'll see you at Wembley.' From Christmas onwards it was the Cup that captured the imagination most of all. Wembley was a big part of that. I didn't get to go there as often as I would have liked, but it had something special about it, aside from the Cup itself. I suppose it was knowing that all those great players down the years had played there, both in the Cup and in internationals."

"I know a lot was said about the fact that Peter McParland charged their goalkeeper, but you could do that in those days. You could do it to any other outfield player, so why not the goalkeeper? It was very sad that Ray ended up with a broken jaw, but it was nothing intentional. The goalkeeper expected a challenge from one of the forwards. Usually it was the forwards who bounced off.

"I remember Eric saying to us before we went out, 'I've got to talk to you about something very important. Now who's going to carry Johnny around the pitch when we've won the Cup?'

"We were the underdogs, but we were confident. We had a supremely fit team,

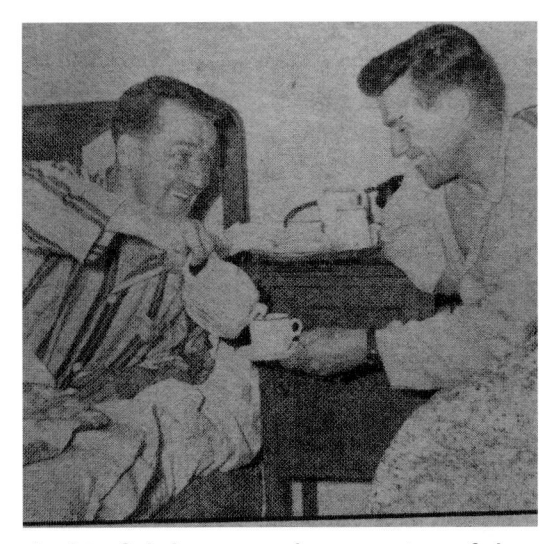

Jackie & Johnny on the morning of the big match.

Big decisions lie ahead for Referee Frank Coultas, £10 or a gold medal?

Cartoon.

Mascot Andrew Pugh's lap of honour.

Face of expectancy.

Eric Houghton leads his team into battle.

"Shake hands gentlemen, I want a good clean contest."

How many full-back's?

An airborne Peter Mac collides with Wood.

Ouch, I bet that hurt.

Villa's defence holds strong.

Blanchflower has no choice.

Blanchflower has no chance. 1-0 to the Villa.

McParland bangs in his second.

Myerscough, to you-to me.

Your ball Jim.

WEMBLEY 1957

Mind the step.

What a beauty!

One looks particularly pleased.

Say cheese - the World's media.

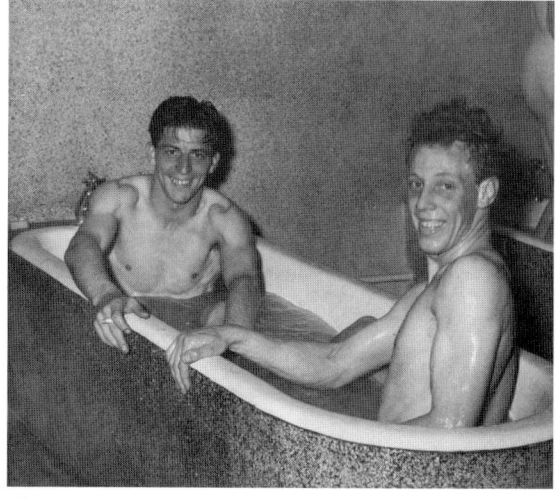

Save water, bathe with a friend. Billy and Stan.

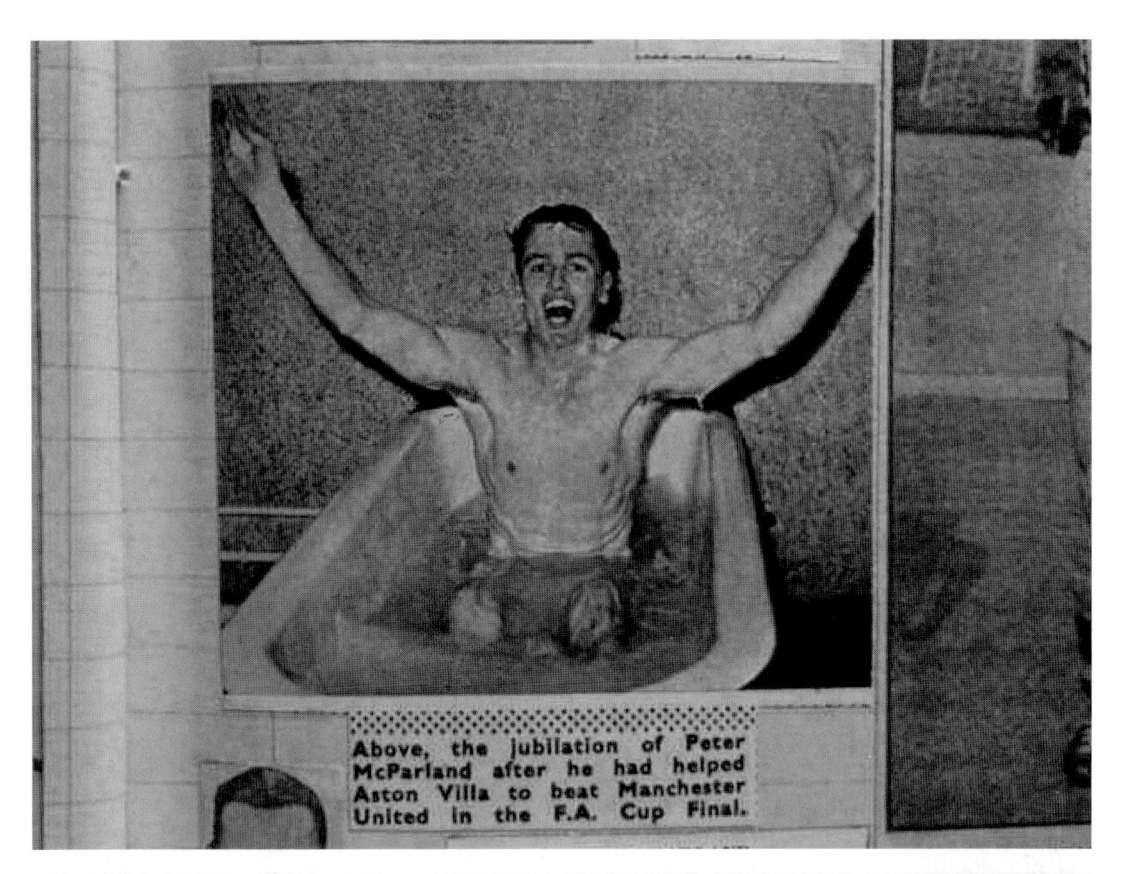

Above, the jubilation of Peter McParland after he had helped Aston Villa to beat Manchester United in the F.A. Cup Final.

Captain Marvel

Seventh Heaven

Lord Mayor's speech at Grosvenor banquet.

"It's ours, win your own.

Johnny receives his Argus.

Sports Argus leaves B'ham on a BSA.

Parading trophy to Trinity Road.

The 'Wham' and Elvis take the strain.

Another street scene.

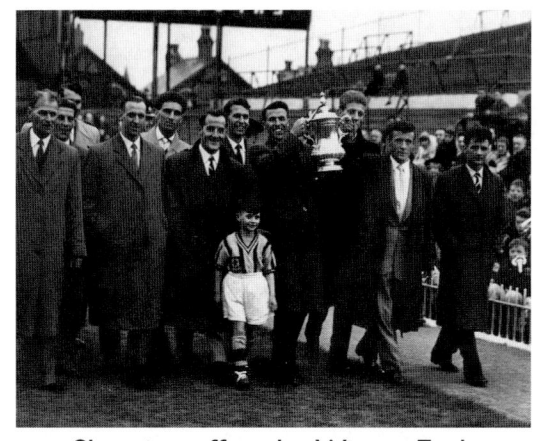

Showing off at the Witton End.

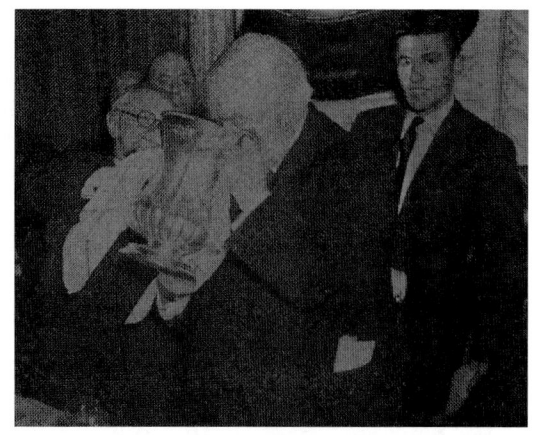

Aston Villa president at B'ham dinner 10th May.

Billy Moore and Eric Houghton.

Seated Joe Bache (centre) and Sam Hardy (right) meet Dixon, Dugdale, Saward and Lynn, dinner 10th May.

Villa face French Cup winners Toulouse.

Annual cricket match v Albion 1957.

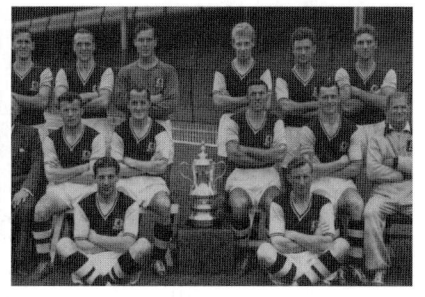

Back in more familiar kit.

Johnny meets his match - wife Brenda.

Banquet at Botanical Gardens, Edgbaston 7th October.

JOHNNY DIXON, ASTON VILLA CAPTAIN, BEING CHAIRED BY HIS TEAM IN THEIR BUKTA OUTFITS AFTER BEING PRESENTED WITH THE CUP BY H.M. THE QUEEN.

Like the winning teams

Bukta Outfits are *Consistently Good*

ASK YOUR LOCAL OUTFITTER FOR TEN COLOUR CATALOGUE OF "1001" COLOUR COMBINATIONS INC. CONTINENTAL STYLES. If any difficulty write to SOCCER, BUKTA HOUSE, STOCKPORT, CHESHIRE trained by Eric and Billy Moore, and the fact we were so fit helped us on the big Wembley pitch. We were noted as one of the fittest sides of the time and also had a team that gave everything and worked for one another. It was a great occasion and the reception we got from the crowd was fantastic. Apart from the Villa fans, I don't think anyone thought we would beat Manchester United. They had a great side.

"But we had greatly improved during the season and when you have got that team spirit going and you combine that with the level of fitness we had achieved, we knew we had every chance of pulling it off. When we arrived back in Birmingham, the reception we got was truly marvellous. The supporters had stuck with us through thick and thin and to finally give them something to shout about was a terrific feeling.

"A day like that is something you never expect to experience. I consider myself very fortunate to have been part of it all. It was a truly great occasion."

In a twist of fate Johnny Dixon's last game in the beloved claret and blue jersey was in the final fixture of the 1960-61 season. It was fitting that Villa had regained their rightful place back in the higher echelons of English football after a solitary season in the second flight. The game against Sheffield Wednesday, in which Johnny scored in a 4-1 win - and also broke his nose - was remembered also for a young Scottish full-back, Charlie Aitken, making his first team debut. Johnny's career of 430 appearances ended as Aitken's 660 appearances was beginning. Between them they provided three decades of unbroken service!

Johnny Dixon was described as natural and completely unspoilt by his sweetheart Brenda, whom he married at Aston Church in May 1961. Among the many guests were some of his team-mates including Stan Lynn, Vic Crowe and Ron Wylie. At the time of Wembley in 1957 Johnny had been one of the few bachelors in the team, when asked why, he said he was too busy playing football.

Johnny hadn't been ready to call time on his career; he thought he was good for a while longer, "I felt I could have played on, I thought I had two or three years more in me, but it was not to be. Joe Mercer thought I had come to the end, and I was put in charge of the third team. One day I went to a reserve match as a spectator and we were short of players so they asked me to step in. I scored three or four goals – I can't remember exactly, because it was such a long time ago – and as the first team was having a bad time Joe asked me how I felt about coming back. He played me in the reserves and said 'see how it goes' with a suggestion that I would be considered for the first team the following week. But the team won at Highbury that weekend and nothing was said after that. Then Joe was sacked, Dick Taylor took over, Bill Baxter moved up to first team coach and I took over the Central League side."

Dixon, like many before him as well as countless other talented Villa players since, was never rewarded with international recognition. On the subject his ex-Villa team-mate, full-back Harry Parkes had this to say, "England must have had a brilliant team for Johnny not to play." Eric Houghton less diplomatically replied, "Of course Johnny should have played for England; plenty of worse players did!"

When his professional and coaching career finished, Johnny opened up a hardware shop in Wylde Green, Sutton Coldfield.

Johnny Dixon's 144 goals for Villa earns his inclusion in a group of just 11 men who have scored 100 goals or more for the club; he scored on his debut and in his last game – with plenty in between.

Ex-Villa team-mate Larry Canning said of the '57 skipper, "There is no individual who played such a valuable part in keeping the club in Division One when times were bad, shown such an all-round collection of skills, and conducted himself for so many years with such character and dignity. Dixon had been a Powderhall sprinter, that's how quick he was. But what I liked about him most was the way he always did the simple things well. He was an absolute delight to play alongside because he was so honest and straightforward in all he did. Dixon was an extremely unselfish player who would only attempt to score if he was in the best position to do so. If a colleague was better placed he had the judgement to pass the ball. He was tall with square shoulders and a good physique and simply lived for the game. He had good close control and a very powerful shot."

Johnny Dixon kicked a ball around for 60-odd years, first for fun, then for a living and finally for charity when he appeared regularly for Aston Villa Old Stars. His name was first on the team sheet – not many men can claim to have bought a pair of football boots for personal use in their 70th year.

He lived for his football, once remarking that he disliked the sight of a substitute warming up on the touchline, "I go as far away from the bench as possible and turn my back, in case it's me they're trying to call off."

His love of football was plainly visible in a story recalled by his wife Brenda. She had told Johnny how she was feeling unwell one morning, "Johnny helped me into the cane rocking chair on the patio, saying the fresh air and sitting in the sun would make me soon feel better. He had to go out, he was playing for the Villa Old Stars in a charity match; well, two matches actually. I didn't feel better, in fact I was starting to feel worse, the hot sun was beating down on me and I was unable to get out of the rocking chair without assistance. I was stuck until Johnny returned. By the time he came home I was burnt to a crisp. And the stomach ache – that was appendicitis!

Johnny was still turning out for the former Villa players into his early 70s. Nobody could tell him he should be slowing down and taking things easy at his age. If he was substituted it didn't go down well with him. Johnny said, "If I don't get to play the entire game I might as well stop coming." This was the opportunity the team's management had been waiting for – letting him go gently, for his own good. They said they couldn't guarantee he would play the entire match and had him sitting on the bench. Johnny wasn't interested in being the sub and packed it in!

Shortly afterwards Johnny's memory started to deteriorate; he could no longer remember places he frequented. It was the onset of Alzheimer's.

Johnny, a devoted husband, loving father to Andrew and Helen, and also a grandfather died in January 2009. Vic Crowe, an ex-Villa team-mate, passed away the following day. They were both great claret and blue servants, and are deservedly revered as Villa legends.

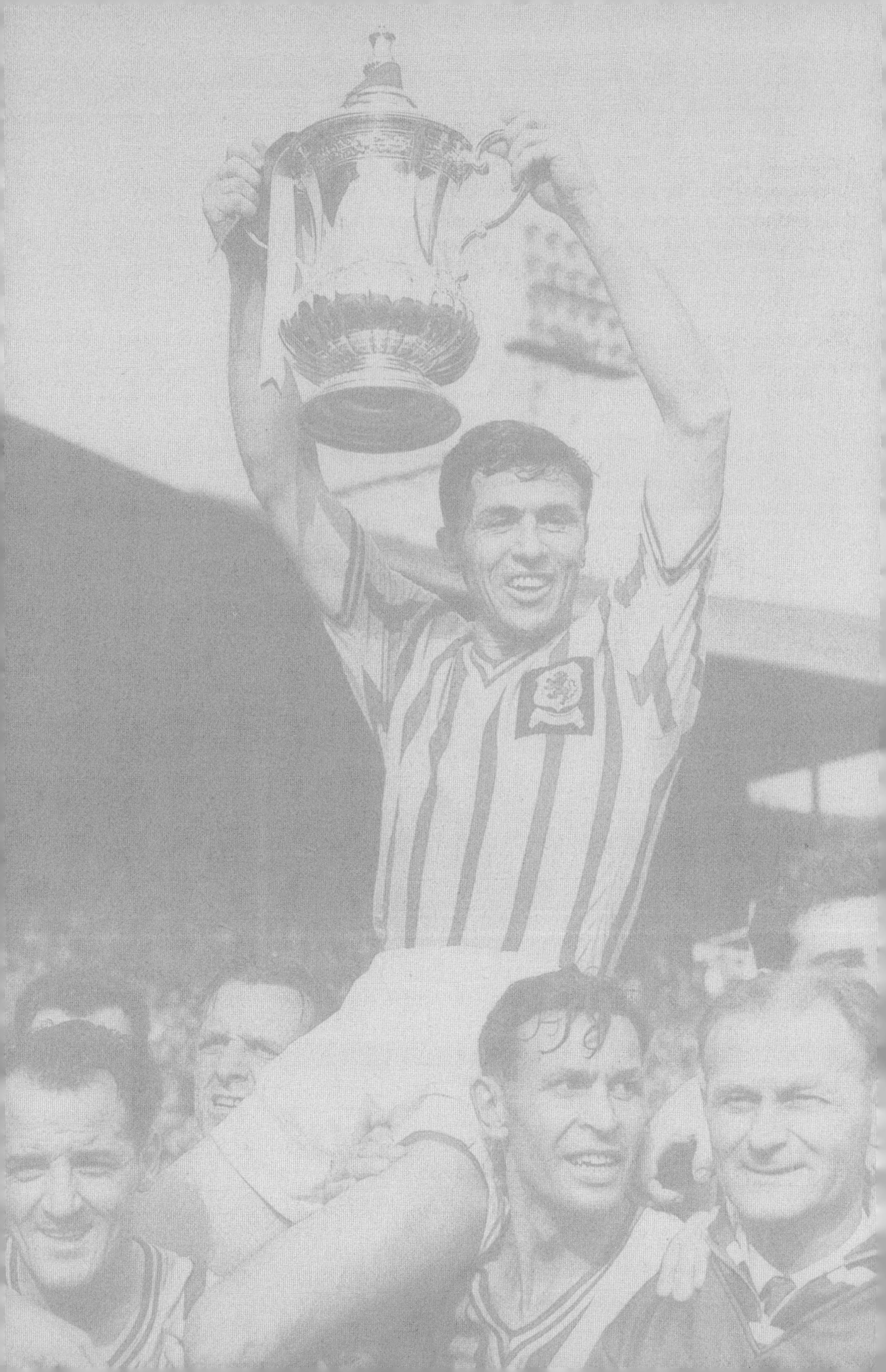

No 11 outside-left
Peter 'Packy' or 'Mac' McParland

Spotted and subsequently signed by Villa boss George Martin while playing in the League of Ireland for Dundalk, McParland was born in Newry, County Down in April 1934. He played Gaelic football at scholol and got his first taste of conventional football for Newry schoolboys; he then progressed to the Dundalk Junior side before making the transition to adult football when he signed for Dundalk United in the same month he turned 18. At the time he was serving his apprenticeship to be a coppersmith but then Villa came calling. They had watched him several times and knew he was worth a risk because he had all the attributes of greatness – he was fast, his play was direct and he packed a shot. Villa bought (or stole might be a better description) McParland for £3,880 in August 1952. It was a fee the Irishman repaid time and time again during his Villa career.

Peter made his debut the following month, at home to Wolverhampton Wanderers in a 1-0 defeat, although it was his only appearance that season. He had to wait 16 months for his next taste of first-team action, coming into the side on Christmas Eve in place of Norman Lockhart. George Martin had since left Villa Park to be replaced by Eric Houghton and Wolves were again the opponents, though this time at Molineux. Peter did his chances of cementing a place in the team no harm that day; he netted Villa's second in a 2-1 win, scoring past Nigel Sims, who making one of his rare appearances for the Molineux club.

McParland's name would become a regular feature on the team sheet from that point on, not only playing in all but one match until the end of the season and scoring five times in those 19 appearances, but for the next seven and a half seasons until to his transfer to Wolves! In that time he missed just a handful of games, only injury or call-up duty stopping him from turning out in the claret and blue.

Peter's goals early in his Villa career not only helped lessen the blow to his club of losing two potent strikers in Tommy Thompson and Dave Walsh but assured the Villa management that here was an ideal goal-scoring replacement. Peter McParland's star never shone as brightly as it did in Villa's record-breaking Cup campaign of 1956-57. He rewarded his managers faith in him by notching 12 League goals in 36 games - an impressive ratio for a winger – and even more remarkably scored seven (in nine games) of his team's 17 FA Cup goals, including his brace in the Final.

His 22 League goals in the Second Division campaign of 1959-60, alongside Hitchens' 23 and Thomson's 20, were instrumental in Villa returning as champions to their rightful place in the top flight, after a solitary sojourn in a wilderness that consisted of such outposts as Scunthorpe, Lincoln and Leyton Orient.

The following season Mac's goals helped bring more silverware to Villa Park. His first and Villa's third, deep into extra-time in the second-leg of the League Cup Final against Rotherham United, ensured a 3-2 on aggregate triumph as Villa became the first team to win the trophy. McParland wrote his own name in history – he the first man to score in both FA Cup and League Cup finals.

Even though Packy had played in an FA Cup Final and appeared in the 1958 World Cup Finals for Northern Ireland it wasn't beneath him to regularly turn out for the Villa's third string for midweek matches in the Birmingham League, "I turned out against teams such as Brierley Hill and Cradley Heath. The Villa and Albion both had sides in it where all old pros and other teams would give you a kicking. It was a tough old League – but it was fun. Don Howe stills talks about it and says it gave him a good grounding." Youngsters who would never aspire to professional status saw it as a trophy to take an ex-international such as McParland out of the game.

Peter still regularly attends Villa matches and recounts his career for the claret & blue with fondness, "I suppose the '57 Cup final was the highlight," he says. "It's every player's dream to play in a Wembley Final; scoring the goals that won the game was a bonus. But another match I remember was a League game against Manchester United, at the time the famous Busby Babes were just starting. It was a great game at Villa Park, ending in a 4-4 draw after we'd twice pulled back from two goals down. And we had a chance to win the match 5-4 in the last minute when Dave Hickson's shot was going in but Pat Saward ran in to make sure – and headed past the post!"

Peter left Villa Park in January 1962, making the short journey to Molineux, he stayed there for one season but managed to find the net on 10 occasions in 21 matches. Mac turned up at Home Park the following year and made 38 appearances for Plymouth Argyle, again scoring regularly as he hit the target 15 times. He later had two spells in the Southern League for Worcester City and sandwiched between these had a very brief time in Canada playing for Toronto Inter-Roma in the Eastern Canada Professional Soccer League and a short period with Peterborough United. McParland also appeared in the North American Soccer League, where he had two seasons alongside former Villans Vic Crowe and Phil Woosnam in the Atlanta Chiefs team. Glentoran, in his native Northern Ireland, was his last port of call; here the curtain would fall on Packy McParland's playing career in the combined role of player/manager between 1968 and 1971. After hanging up his boots Peter was in great demand, and his coaching skills took him to all corners of the globe – the United States, The Middle East, Cyprus, and Libya to mention a few. Of his coaching role in the Far East, friend and former team-mate Johnny Dixon said it was for Peter McParland to teach Irish to the Chinese!

Peter McParland's domestic club honours, along with his Football League XI representative medals and his 34 caps for Northern Ireland - including the 1958 World Cup Finals, add up to an impressive tally. Peter has a place alongside team-mate Johnny Dixon in an exclusive club of only 11 members – men who scored 100 or more for the claret and blue cause. He boasted 121 goals in 341 appearances – and this from a wide player. The young man from Newry did good!

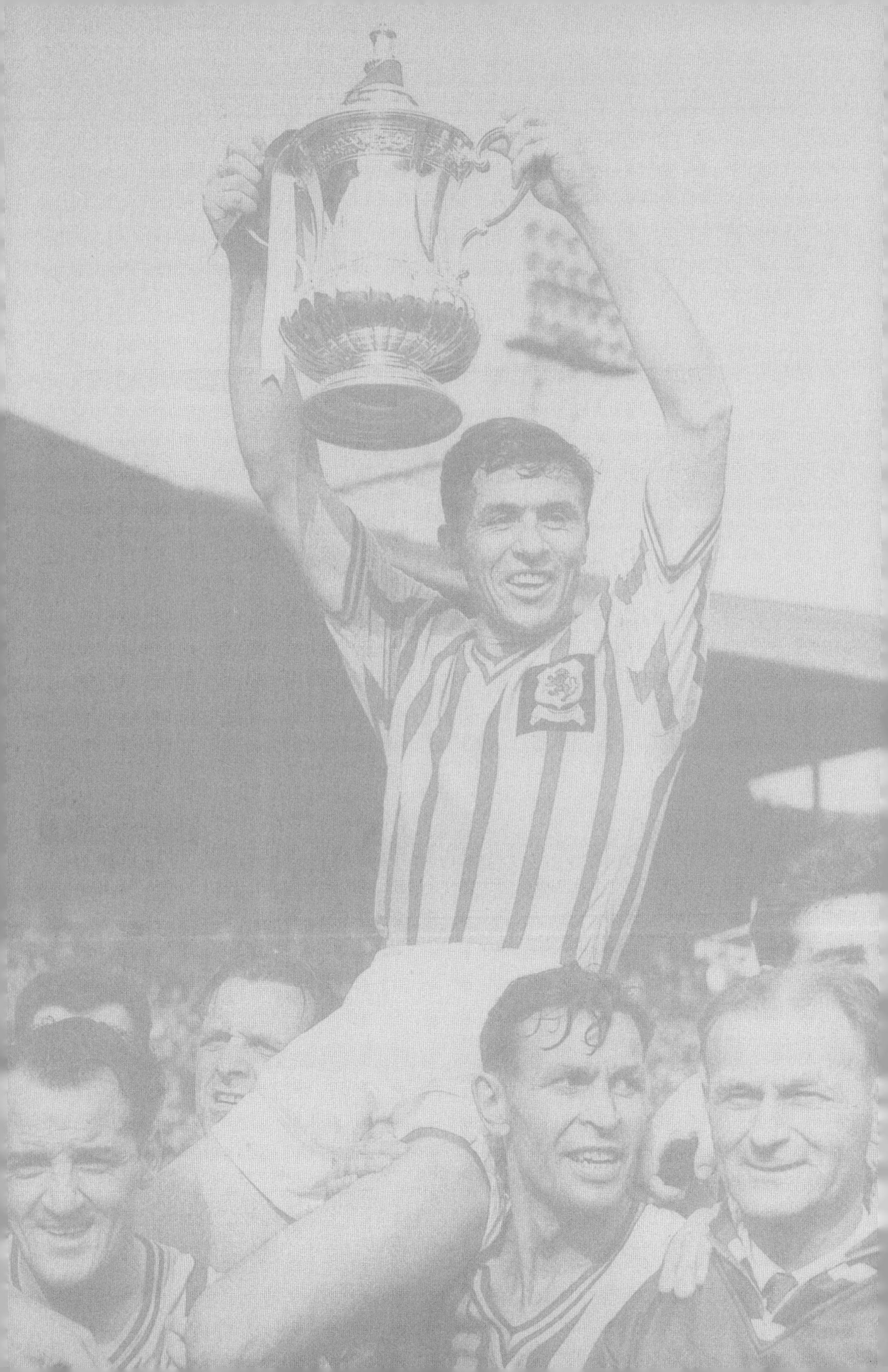

Special mention of
Derek 'Doc' Pace

Derek Pace didn't feature in the Wembley spectacle but to failure to mention his considerable contribution in these pages would have been nothing short of a travesty. Pace played in six of the Villa's nine FA Cup matches, finding the net in both fourth and fifth rounds.

Manager Eric Houghton had agonised long and hard whether to include Pace and had sought the advice from the specialist who had been treating his injury. But there was no guarantee that the player would be able to last the entire 90 minutes and it was in the back of Eric's mind that to stand up to the expected United onslaught, Villa would need 11 men – though he jokingly said that 12 would be better – on the pitch for the entire game. His worst fear was starting Pace only to see his striker go off after only 10 minutes. So Billy Myerscough got the nod.

Of the Wembley omission Pace responded, "Being left out never caused any resentment. Bill was my best friend, and we were all so elated at winning. In fact, I remember the FA Cup Final for something totally different – I lost Jackie Sewell's false teeth! Jackie had worn his magic molars for the presentation to the Duke of Edinburgh and then passed them on in a handkerchief to me for safe keeping. When our first goal went in, we all jumped up and by the time I'd come down to earth again, I couldn't find Jackie's false teeth. I thought he'd kill me. But in due course I found them again."

Derek John Pace was born March 1932 in Essington a few miles north-east of Wolverhampton. His first taste of football was playing for the National School team in Bloxwich, appearing as centre-half even though he was rather small. He tried to emulate his boyhood idol Stan Cullis, the Wolverhampton Wanderers centre-half, and excelled in the position to the point that he captained Walsall Schoolboys.

On leaving school his football continued, though he had moved into an attacking role, playing in the Bloxwich Combination League He turned out for Bloxwich Scouts and if they had no match Derek would appear for another local side, Walsall Wood. He scored over 40 goals in his time with Bloxwich.

Villa came in for the newly converted inside-forward in September 1949 after being discovered by former Villan George Cummings at a time the club were without a manager following Alex Massie's departure. "As a 17-year-old beginner I was over-awed by the great names still in existence at Villa Park in 1949," he said. "I took over from Trevor Ford – how about that for a start! Then there was Ivor Powell, Dickie Dorsett, Frank Moss, Les Smith (Sir Leslie), what a fantastic player – all skill and sunshine. In those days the old pros went out of their way to help the youngsters and I for one was very grateful."

Pace's signing for Villa coincided with his National Service call-up to the Royal Army Medical Corps, which led to his 'Doc' moniker. He represented the Army at this time against Ireland.

Derek stood 5' 7" and three-quarters and was very insistent on including the small addition, "Well, all my life I've always heard people talk about my lack of inches and for a forward that was bad news; Jimmy Greaves was hardly a giant, but certainly got among the goals." Due to his stature Doc was never going to be a Nat Lofthouse, but being extremely tough and tenacious, he proved to be a handful for opposing defenders. Trevor Ford was offloaded to Sunderland in October 1950 for a fee the Villa board just couldn't refuse - £30,000. Derek must have thought that this would open the door for him but the club went out and purchased another forward, Dave Walsh. Derek finally made his debut at home to Burnley in March 1951 and scored in a 3-2 win. Along with a multitude of forwards – Miller Craddock, George Edwards, Dave Walsh and Ron Jeffries – Doc was seeking to make the No 9 shirt his own. Even full-back Stan Lynn wore it that season.

The following campaign Pace was restricted to only seven first team outings, finding the net twice. Colin Gibson an outside-right who had signed for Villa two months before Derek, would also turn out in the role as central striker, 'Doc' certainly had his hands full!

In all Derek featured in eight campaigns for the claret & blue and could always be relied on to score. In a rather meagre total of 107 appearances he netted a very respectable 42 goals. He left on Boxing Day 1957, signed by future Villa boss Joe Mercer, who at the time was managing Sheffield United - for a fee of £12,000. Arguably Doc's best display at Villa Park was in February 1960 when Villa were sampling Second Division football. He bagged a hat-trick that afternoon but unfortunately he was playing for the opposition and single-handedly condemned Villa to their sole defeat on home soil that season. He spent roughly the same length of time at Bramall Lane as he did at Villa but was far more valuable to the Blades' cause, being United's leading scorer for six seasons. During his time in Sheffield he banged in 175 League and cup goals in 302 appearances. "I think United got the best of me," he said. "I don't know what it is, but I was always conscious of the fact that they had spent good money on me, and that they had confidence in what I could do. Mind you, the size factor was there too. In fact, on the day I signed I travelled to Sheffield by car. I had reached Chesterfield when I decided to stop for a cup of tea, and near the café was a newspaper placard announcing my impending arrival at Bramall Lane. I paused to read it, and a man came out of the shop, took one look at me, glanced at my picture in the paper, muttered 'Another little un' and cleared off!"

After brief spells at Notts County and Walsall he retired from the playing side in May 1967. His career total of 233 goals in 444 matches shows just how prolific, given the opportunity, Derek Pace could be. He went on to try his hand at management with non-league Walsall Wood but this lasted only two years.

Even at the height of his fame in professional football Derek Pace still served his first club, Bloxwich Scouts, as their President and coach. In later years Derek was a North Stand season-ticket holder at his beloved Aston Villa. He passed away in October 1989 at the age of 57.

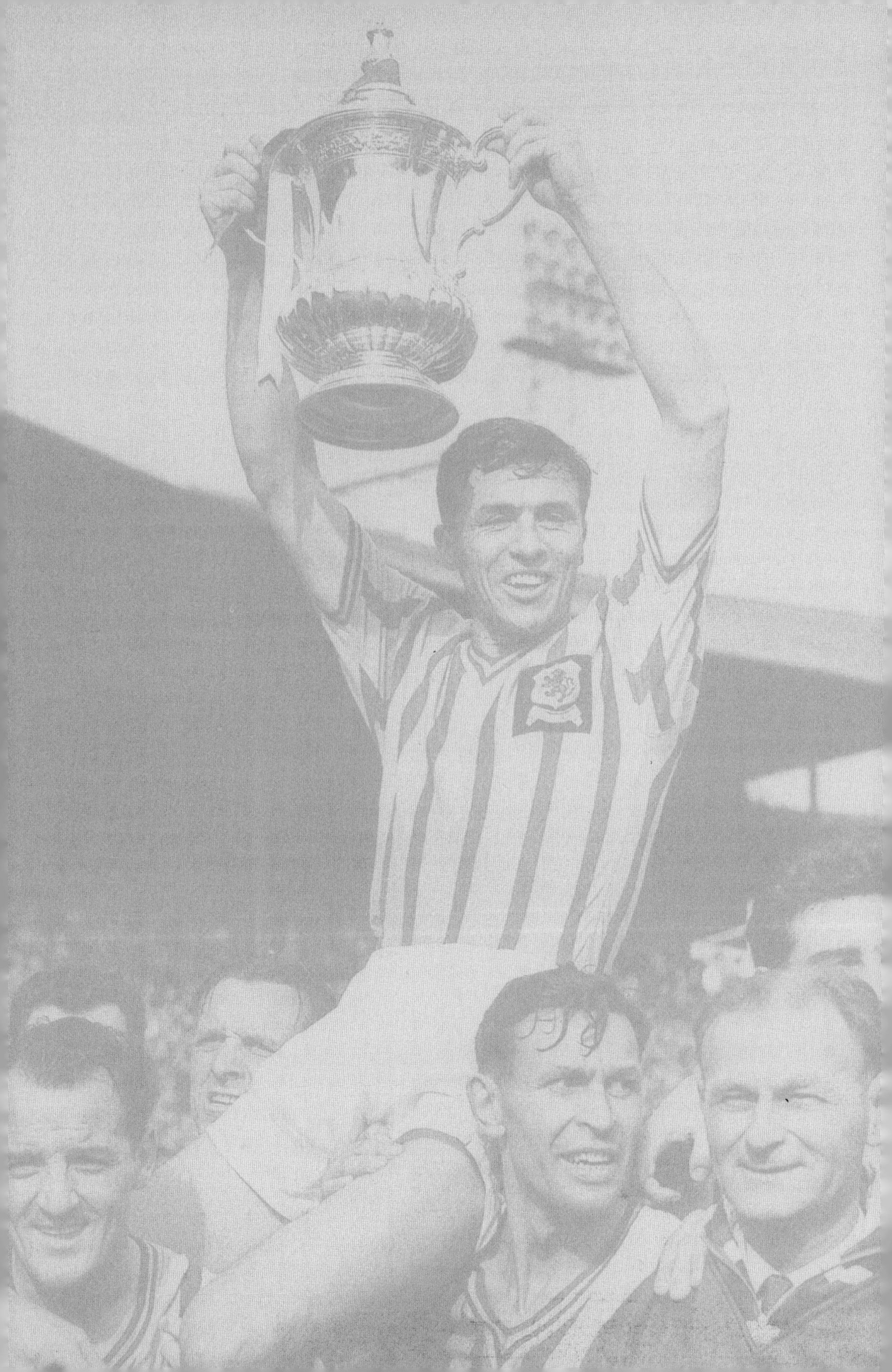

Trainer
Bill Moore

Billy is remembered by the surviving members of the class of '57 as being instrumental in their lifting the famous FA trophy. Manager Eric Houghton certainly put the cup success down to Moore, insisting "Bill was the best trainer in the country and made sure we were super fit." Moore's training techniques were not just hard; they were demanding. But they were ultimately responsible for making the players very possibly the fittest side in the entire Football League. When Villa had to plough their way through pitches that were more suited to growing vegetables – the third, fifth and sixth rounds all spring to mind – it was their conditioning that saw off the weaker opposition.

A Geordie by birth, hailing from Washington, Tyne & Wear, but a Midlander by adoption, Moore had what can best be described as an unspectacular playing career. He played for Lincoln City and had four outings for Stoke City before moving down a division with Mansfield Town.

After the war Moore made the transition from player to trainer, taking the journey from Field Mill to Merthyr Tydfil. After cutting his teeth in Wales, his next port of call was Meadow Lane where he was appointed trainer of Notts County.

Eric Houghton was manager of the Magpies at the time and recognised that Moore was more than capable of handling the game's bigger players of the day, people like Tommy Lawton and Jackie Sewell. When Houghton got his calling in 1953 to return to Villa Park, he didn't hesitate to take Billy with him as his right-hand man.

It was Billy Moore's view that every man who plays football for a living has a right to be in the best condition to give of his best. He never spared himself in his efforts to provide that fitness and expected players to show the same spirit.

In his time at Villa the players adored him and he had their total respect. Stan Crowther said, "We loved him. He could 'eff and blind' but he knew what he was doing, everything was for a reason." Villa 'keeper Nigel Sims added, "If Billy had told us to run through a brick wall, we would have. As a team we were very confident in each other's ability, and Billy's never-say-die attitude was instilled in the side. In the dressing room before the Cup Final, Billy came up to me and putting his arm round my shoulder he told me, 'Nigel, I want you and Stan to stick close to Johnny Dixon, so when we collect the Cup, the pair of you can carry him on your shoulders.' Not if – when!"

It wasn't just Moore's worth to Aston Villa that was recognised. In November 1956, he was selected as trainer to the England national team for their match against Wales at Wembley.

In the memorable 1956-57 season Moore was assisted by the second-team trainer Phil Hunt, chief scout and coach Jimmy Eason, ex-Villa manager Jimmy Hogan and third-team player-coach Dickie Dorsett.

Sadly it was Bill's last season. He had been promised a £500 bonus for his part in the club's Wembley appearance but the club reneged on the agreement and Bill received only a fraction of what he was entitled to - £100, less tax. It didn't sit easy with Bill and when he came out of the office with his cheque he was no longer on the payroll. Speculation was rife; did he walk or was he squeezed out?

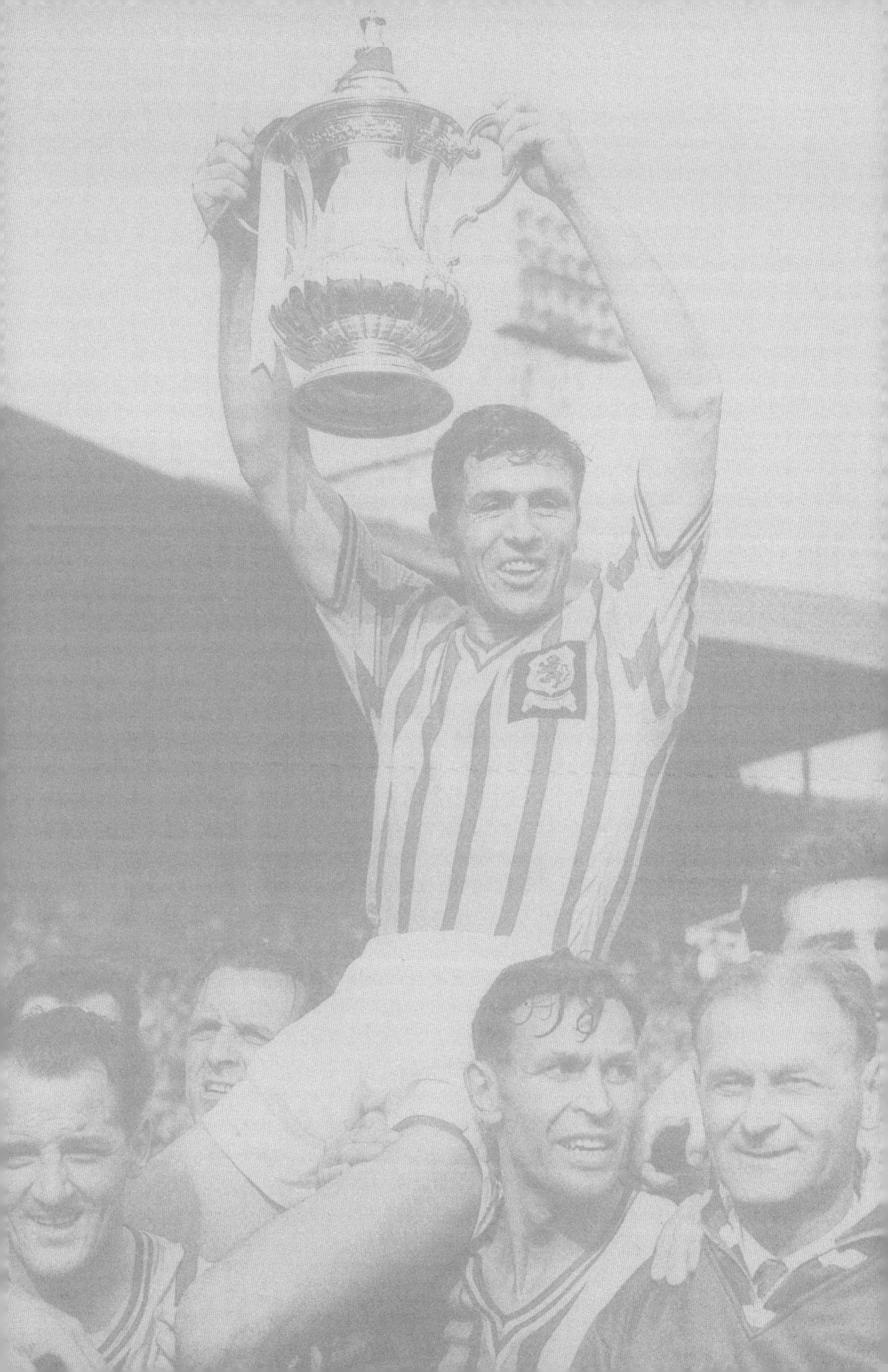

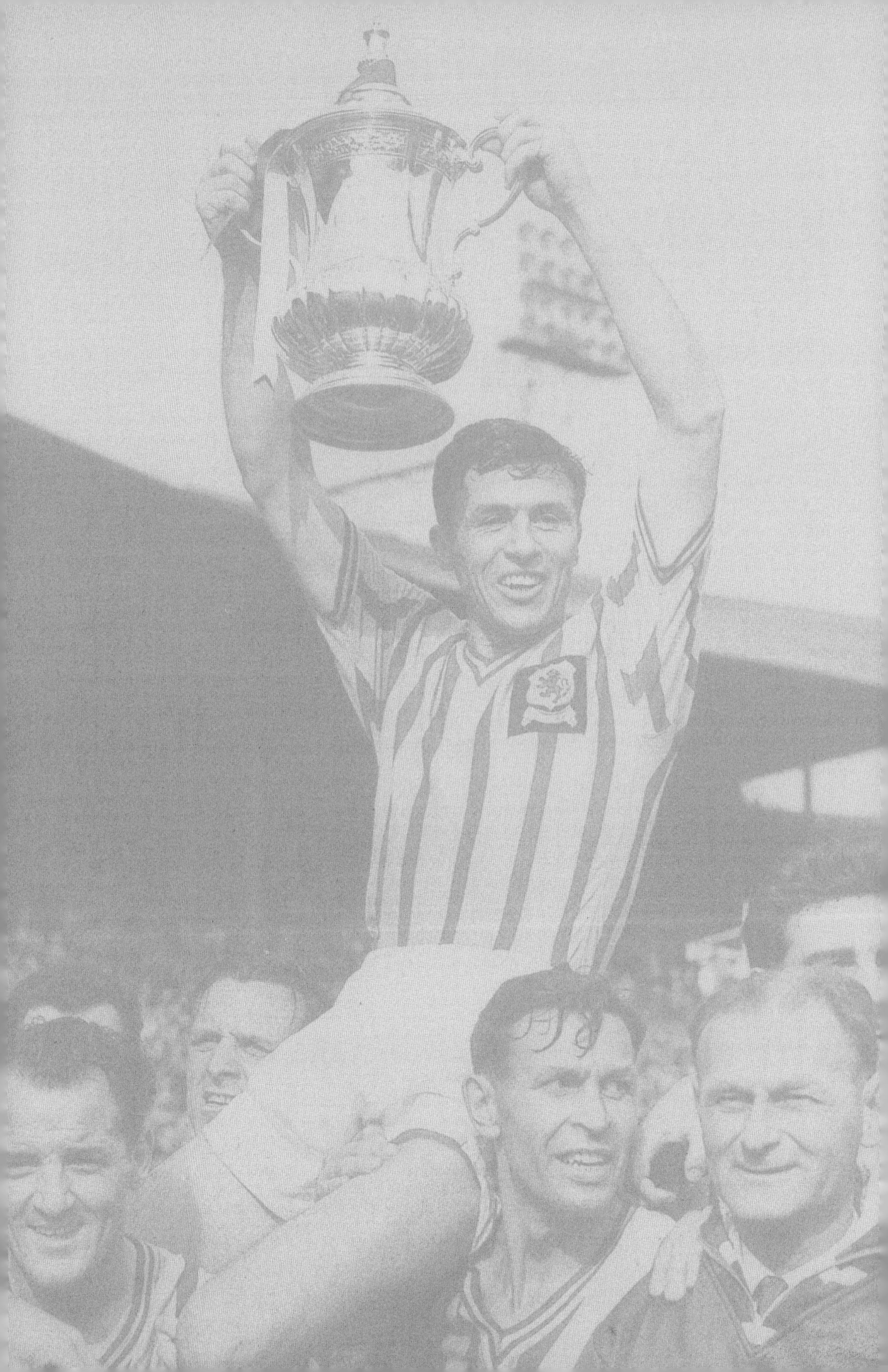

Recollections & Memories

I had a difficult decision to make for the Final – Pace, who had recovered from his groin injury, or Myerscough? After a specialist's report on Pace, and knowing the Wembley turf was heavy on legs and groins, I decided to play safe with Myerscough. Even so we used only 12 players from round three to the Final, including three replays. We applied for a medal for Pace, but were refused. All he received was the same as trainer Billy Moore and myself – a complimentary programme.

Although I was proud we won the Cup, it was not all sunshine and roses. A few days before the Final, I had orders from the chairman via secretary Fred Archer that no children were to be allowed in the official party. My wife and three children, together with Mrs Moore and family, had to travel by road with friends. Yet I was informed later that the first to board were two grandsons of directors. Why the team manager and trainer coach of a Cup Final team should be subject to such inconvenience on so important an occasion surprised me.

I shall always appreciate a good tip given me by my friend Arthur Turner, then manager of Blues. They had been beaten at Wembley the previous year and Arthur said, "For goodness sake don't stay near London early in the week, Saturday never seems to come." So we treated it as an ordinary League match. We trained at Villa Park on the Friday morning and left on the noon train, visiting Wembley Stadium in the afternoon and staying Friday night at the Brent Bridge Hotel, Hendon, about four miles away.

Although luck was with us that afternoon, our boys put on a much better performance than many thought possible. Thanks to Bill Moore we were certainly one of the fittest teams ever to step out on the Wembley turf. After our great victory – Villa's first FA Cup win since 1920 – what was to follow was very disappointing.

We had put Villa back on the map but they had been so long in the wilderness the directors did not seem to know what to do. Normally the celebrations of the winning finalists go on until the early hours but our banquet concluded by 10.45pm.

I was not allowed the privilege of sitting at the top table nor of making a speech to thank the trainer and the lads for a great victory. The banquet itself was a dull party – an opinion expressed to me by several experienced football personalities who were present. It was most embarrassing for me to take the players and wives out to nightclubs to seek our own celebrations. Two of the younger directors accompanied us.

However, we were given a great reception from the Birmingham sporting public on our return on the Sunday – scenes I shall never forget.

No Cup Final bonus had been given to myself or Bill Moore so just before we were due to report back for training in July I approached the chairman on the matter. When I was with Notts County I had a clause in my agreement, stating 'In the event of the club gaining promotion or reaching the FA Cup Final, the manager to be paid £1,000.' I had discussed this with Mr Fred Normansell on my appointment and he said, "You get us to Wembley my lad and you'll get double that."

Knowing his keen desire and ambition I believed him. When I approached the board on the matter it was a different story. I informed them of my conversations with the late chairman, but their attitude astounded me. They finally granted me a sum considerably less than half the amount promised in my first contract.

Some managers I know have received bigger bonuses for avoiding relegation. Failure paid more than success. Bill Moore was also 'awarded' a small bonus.

The following season we started off in moderate fashion. Our enthusiasm and team spirit had been shaken and Bill Moore departed. I had been trying to arrange a two-year contract for Bill which the directors had almost finalised. The appointment was fixed for 12.30, but they were late arriving and Bill left for his lunch, so it never came about. I have often wished I had gone with him but my attachment to the club was decisive. Messrs Normansell, Rinder, Devey and Co had always instilled into me that the club comes before any individual. After Bill Moore left I felt my right arm had been cut off. Football management is a two-man job. Less than 12 months later I was dismissed; the chairman invited me to resign, but I refused.

About that time we were installing the floodlights and were arranging an opening match. I had several good reports of a Hearts wing-half and had arranged the friendly with them so we could have a look at him. The player, the great Dave Mackay, should have joined Villa, but I was dismissed the same evening and he joined Spurs. I was negotiating for him at around £15,000.

Eric Houghton

Dad was upset I remember because there were no facilities for the family to travel officially. I was away at boarding school and was due back at school in Oakham, Rutland, on Thursday. The Cup Final was always played on the first Saturday in May, which was the start of the cricket season. I said, "What about the Final dad?" He replied, "Well you're captain of cricket, you have other responsibilities!" So, off I went back to school. It was a rugby-playing school, so the 'round' ball as they called it was not viewed with any great interest.

So I got back on the Friday and my housemaster called me in and said the headmaster wanted to see me down at school house, which was the other end of the town. I went down there and I can remember his words now, "I gather there's some round ball event taking place in London, I think you ought to go, as long as you are back here on Monday morning that's fine," and he gave me the train ticket. So off I went. I did as the head requested and returned back to school on the Sunday.

I let mother know. She said they were staying at the Grosvenor on Park Lane and to "get a taxi to bring you from the station." I'd never been to London by train on my own before. I took a taxi but the driver must have misunderstood me as he drove me straight up to the front doors of the Dorchester hotel, where there was a chap with a green bowler. I realised the mistake and as he opened the taxi door I jumped out and walked off down the street; this chap looked at me as if I was barmy because instead of going into the Dorchester I set off to the Grosvenor.

Dad asked someone to look after me while the banquet was going on – a good friend of his. There were a lot of people in the hotel waiting to see the players. Dad said, "Look after Neil, buy him a drink if he wants one and I'll settle up with you afterwards. I remember him saying to Bill Clements, the chap concerned, "What do I owe you for Neil's drinks?" Bill replied, "Well, he's had nine Double Diamonds!"

I remember the match pretty distinctly really, even though it was a long, long time ago. My sister and brother were there; they went down to the game with my mother. I remember her saying that she thought if she went out (away from her seat and down to the concourse) they'd score, and they did. I didn't see my dad before the match, the first time he saw me was briefly before the banquet, but he knew I was being allowed from the school to go down.

But it was interesting, the things you remember about the build up; dad deliberately took them down late, he didn't want them to go down too early. I recall him taking them to Cadbury's over at Bournville, he was trying to find a ground that replicated the turf at Wembley because they were concerned that the Wembley turf was stamina-sapping. He managed to persuade Cadbury's, who had probably the best pitch in the area for grass, to let Villa train over there.

Neil Houghton (son of Eric Houghton)

The story of how Aston Villa came to win the FA Cup in 1957 for a then record seventh time began not in the third round at Luton Town but just over 12 months earlier at the beginning of December 1955 when manager Eric Houghton nipped along to Sheffield Wednesday and persuaded them to part with Jackie Sewell

When he had been transferred from Notts County where he had been under the masterful tutorship of Eric, to Wednesday, Jack had earned the sobriquet of "Britain's costliest football". The fee was a mere £34,000.

Villa acquired him for just half that. It is fair to say that we did not see the best of Sewell, who was often maligned for his apparent lack of effort but he became every bit as influential for Villa as his contemporary, the revered Don Revie, who had a 'plan' named after him that really belonged to the Hungarians.

But Sewell could not revive Villa on his own. It was three significant signings in February 1956, Nigel Sims and Leslie Smith from Wolverhampton and Jimmy Dugdale from West Bromwich, who not only performed the miracle escape from relegation but who became the nucleus of the Cup-winning team.

When the third round draw was made on 10th December mid-table Villa had just been annihilated 3-1 at home by League leaders Manchester United. A trip to Luton, who were one place above us in the League was not greeted with enthusiasm. But the new pale blue shirts worn for the first time unannounced in a 2-0 success against Charlton at a near-deserted and derelict Valley raised the spirits. The last Christmas Day match ever away at Sunderland was depressing not just for the result, a 1-0 defeat, but because the weather had turned decidedly wintry and the Boxing Day return clash had to be cancelled. Villa ended 1956 on the slide. But so did Luton!

The snow had melted come third round day, the consequence was mud and lots of it. At ground level football pitches these days are not always as green and smooth as they appear to be but there are those of us old timers who miss the fact that each round of the Cup used generally to be played on a different type of surface.

LUTON TOWN v VILLA

The importance of the FA Cup can be gauged by the fact that Villa stayed overnight at a hotel in Bedford. I stayed overnight at home but awoke in great excitement because I was being allowed to travel with my father in the coach that the Barn Social Club had reserved on one of the two excursion trains. Birmingham to Luton by train is still not a straightforward journey. The train took us via Water Orton and Leicester and took exactly three hours to negotiate its way to Luton, arriving two hours in advance of the 2.15 kick off.

It was a dank, miserable day, a description which might just as easily apply to the match, and the return journey, although it was slightly quicker. I have no recollection as the whether any charabancs made the trip but if they did their journey time would have been no better. Few would have had the wherewithal to go by car.

VILLA v LUTON TOWN

Forty-eight hours later the two teams took the field at Villa Park. With insufficient time to prepare a proper Villa News we had to make do with a twopenny piece of card. It was extortion really, as the full programme only used to cost three pence – so not many bought it and it has become something of a rare item. The working supporter wanting to be there either had to have an accommodating boss or book leave in advance just in case. Little wonder that the crowd, 28,536, consisted of a large percentage of pensioners.

The draw for the fourth round had been made just before most spectators were setting off to the ground. The winners – and nobody expected it to be Luton – would be away to Second Division Middlesbrough.

After thrashing Everton 5-1 at Villa Park nobody who saw Villa's total capitulation at White Hart Lane the following week (losing 3-0) could have contemplated that this team was about to win the Cup! Except for one thing - with Sims injured against Everton we were obliged to bring in Keith Jones for what unsurprisingly turned out to be his last big game. Even though he did save a penalty – or rather, in sheer amazement, he turned to catch the ball as it rebounded off the post!

MIDDLESBROUGH v VILLA

I had to be up early ahead of the trip to Middlesbrough on Saturday 26th January. The train was scheduled to leave New Street at 7 am. I was not only traveling in the 'Barn coach' but we would be having lunch on the outward journey, plus dinner on the way back. To me, it was sheer luxury. I hasten to add though that it was a treat to myself. My father could not have afforded to pay for us both. Train fare was £1.25 and the meals £1 each.

The train reached Teesside three hours ahead of the 2.45pm kick off. Unlike all the other supporters there was no need for us to go in search of a meal.

A certain Brian Clough opened the scoring for Boro but over fifty years later at 3-2 it remains in the memory as one of Villa's greatest ever performances away from home, certainly in the FA Cup.

The fifth round draw gave us Bristol City at Villa Park. The momentum was growing to such an extent that somebody decided we needed a song. Blues had purloined the Harry Lauder epic, Keep right on to the end of the Road on their fruitless run the previous season. In truth singing was a bit beneath the dignity of the fans of 'the greatest football club in the world,' but Blues were still in the Cup and the Birmingham Mail saw the chance of drumming up a few more sales.

So again, somebody added football words to another First World War song, It's a long way to Tipperary - and the rest is history! It says something about the song as a Villa anthem that that is exactly what is has become – history. Blues have kept their dirge, West Ham theirs for nearly a century, Spurs and others too. You never hear 'Tipperary' but then the town is in the 'Republic' and we have cause to be sensitive about such things.

The immortal John Charles (at least as far as Leeds and the Welsh are concerned) made a rare appearance for Leeds at Villa Park at what was frequently being referred to as the Hall of Memory– so long was it since we had won anything. The 1-1 draw followed two days later by a 2-2 against Manchester City again at home saw an improvement in our league position.

VILLA v BRISTOL CITY

Goalless in the heavy going at Bolton was seen as adequate preparation for whatever the Bristolians had to offer. Except our one cause for concern was that unusually for a Second Division team they had the England centre-forward John Atyeo. When he scored the equaliser just after the interval hearts sank.

But Jackie Sewell was enjoying a purple patch and his diving header, which broke the tension, was a thing of beauty even though many thought he might conceivably have tapped it in. Contrary to the alternative words to our song, Bristol City had not been 'miles too slow'. Relief had greeted the final whistle.

Two days later at home to Portsmouth, Sewell scored what remains the most audacious goal ever scored at B6 and hardly anyone was there to see it. Fans were unwilling to risk taking the afternoon off work and besides; many were now saving up for the next round wherever that might be.

Unusually the sixth round draw was televised for the first time ever, not at lunchtime but just ahead of the early evening news. There was a tense delay while the last two balls were given an extra shake. But every Villa supporter watching knew the outcome in advance - Burnley away! The remainder of the draw saw Blues v Nottingham Forest, Albion v Arsenal and Bournemouth v Manchester United.

United won, obviously, but came mighty close to losing at Bournemouth. Albion controversially won their replay at Highbury when the referee allowed a goal with the linesman standing flag raised for offside. Blues, well they held to their part of the second city bargain to keep the Mail happy.

As luck would have it our League game at St. Andrews was postponed following a deluge. Villa Park was in such a poor state that a bit of rain was hardly likely to make things worse so instead lots more of us than usual got to see the reserves hammer Huddersfield Reserves 6-0.

BURNLEY v VILLA

Burnley always seemed like the back of beyond. It was four hours away by road and not much quicker by train. Especially a direct train that had to negotiate a way around Manchester that is difficult to this day. It would probably have been easier to change trains and stations in Manchester. Worse, there was no dining car.

But the Cup was the Cup and a fifth of the 50,000 crammed into a ground that did not hold anywhere near 50,000 were wearing claret and blue. Sorry, we were all wearing claret and blue but we knew who was who, even though those were still the days of intermingling.

The only reason the result is not considered better than Middlesbrough in the annals of Aston Villa is because we won at Middlesbrough and, truth to tell, we were a little disappointed to 'only' draw at Burnley.

The Cup draw contained so many ifs buts and maybes that all we knew ahead of the replay was that a second city Final was still on the cards – though outside the Birmingham Mail, Manchester United were deemed a certainty to get to Wembley.

VILLA v BURNLEY

Birmingham City – rivals – phooey. We borrowed their red change shirts for the replay. Burnley chose to play in all black, obliging the referee to remove his jacket for the second half. At 4.45pm on Wednesday 6th March 1957 joy was unalloyed in Aston.

An Arsenal v Burnley semi-final would have taken place at Villa Park but far more exciting, I was going to get to see Villa in the semi-final for the first time. Controversially the FA chose Molineux. Tickets would be at a premium but Wolves fans, recognising a 'killing' were only too willing to dispose of their one-third allocation.

After a 1-1 'success' in the league at Old Trafford the Manchester sports paper commented, 'that United would have to improve if the two sides were to meet at Wembley.' IF.

We won 4-1 at home to Cardiff for whom Gerald Archibald Hitchens scored the one then a 0-0 against Arsenal, which meant that barring a complete meltdown, relegation was no longer an issue.

ALBION v VILLA

It was every man for himself getting to Wolverhampton and even more so coming back! There were, of course, still two main lines between the two places. New Street to High Level and Snow Hill to Low Level. Most Villa supporters opted for New Street to avoid passing through West Bromwich on the Snow Hill route.

My place was standing at the South Bank end low down just to the right of the goal. Remarkably I had almost precisely the same view of three of the goals as appeared in the published photos.

It was generally considered that Villa had been lucky. It was also generally considered that we were lucky five days later when the whole thing was reprised at St. Andrews. In so far as we were lucky when a shot struck Stan Lynn on his heel when he was retreating 25 yards from goal and the ball curled wide of the far upright we were lucky. But an organised defence is important in football and we had an organised defence. Plus the moment of inspiration Albion lacked when Billy Myerscough quite literally used his head.

Odd thing about the Lynn back-heel is that I had a perfect view of that too which is perhaps why I wax lyrical about it. My original ticket had been a 2/6d one for the Spion Kop. But a Blues season ticket holder who had no interest in taking the afternoon off work for a skirmish that did not concern him let me have his 6/- ticket.

Traveling home on an Inner Circle No 8 knowing Villa were in the Cup Final was even more exciting than in the five years that same journey had been my escape route from the horrors of school. Five weeks and 11 games remained before Wembley. Highlights were 2-0 at home to Preston two days after our triumph. Preston had the great Tom Finney, alongside him ex-Villan Tommy Thompson – sorry Tommy but Sewell had more nous! Roy Chapman's brace at St. Andrews (2-1). Then when Jackie Sewell showed Sheffield Wednesday what they had given away (although they had won the Second Division without him!), a game in which sadly goalkeeper Arthur Sabin was to play his first of only two first team matches.

The fourth of the Monday afternoon league extravaganzas. A 2-2 draw against Sunderland seen by only 8,252. Attendance at all four games totalled only 42,605. Easter Saturday at Newcastle (2-1). Easter Monday 4-0 v Wolves to show who was boss then next day a 3-0 defeat at the Molineux.

Finally as tame a performance as can ever be excused, a 3-1 reversal at home to Luton, where the real adventure began. It's a long way to Tipperary

It is forty-three years since this First World War tune rang out around Wembley Stadium at an FA Cup Final. A song adopted by Villa supporters in mocking response to the Harry Lauder dirge Keep Right On to the End of the Road. This tune, of course, was so effective that it inspired Don Revie to his finest hour.

Unfortunately, nobody had told Arthur Caiger who for years tried vainly to lead the Wembley crowd in community singing. So we had One Song to the Tune of Another long before the panellists in I'm Sorry, I Haven't A Clue were asked to perform the feat. If you think a man in a lion costume is mundane fare then he is as nothing compared to the dire Arthur Caiger. Some traditions deserve to be discarded.

For me, the 4th May 1957 had got off to an unusual start. That very morning the postman delivered a package from Villa Park returning the away match programmes I had sent as evidence that I had attended 25 of the 26 away matches that season. It came with the sardonic note that "this was not enough to qualify for a Final ticket". Fortunately I had got one as a season ticket holder but even this only entitled me to the cheapest terrace ticket. Be warned.

I had the cheapest terrace ticket for the 1957 Final, which condemned me to a long-distance view of the action. But at least I was going to get to Wembley in style. Travel by car was an option available to very few in those days and coaches were still called charabancs. British Railways produced a claret and blue brochure describing the 19 special trains they were running to London for the Final. Proper trains, between 12 and 16 coaches long. Three of them included dining coaches and I was going on the most exclusive of them, from Snow Hill to the steps of Wembley Stadium.

The fare for all the trips was 23/3d (£1.17p) but for precisely £1 more it was possible to have a four-course lunch on the outward journey and a four-course dinner on the return. Perhaps I sensed then it was going to be a once in a lifetime chance to indulge myself on a Villa excursion. My Civil Service salary was £3/18/- (£3.90) per week.

The Barn Social Club on Brookvale Road had booked an entire dining coach to themselves on the previous Cup trains and I was not going to miss out on this special day. I was especially privileged because I was the only 'under age' drinker allowed to go with them. Long story.

No replica shirts in those days. I wore my best blazer and flannels - I was dining out, after all - plus the essential scarf, hat and rosette. And I carried the obligatory rattle. Most were plain wood but I had lovingly painted mine in Villa colours.

The train arrived at Wembley Hill station at 1.30 and from there it was a few yards into the stadium. I do not even remember encountering any United supporters although I did buy the souvenir Manchester Evening News, "flown in by air", to go with the morning edition Blue Mail and Sports Argus.

Admission was what now seems a derisory 3/6d but this was almost double the cost of standing at the Witton End. The price included tax. Over the intervening years I have often quoted the fact that Villa played in the last FA Cup Final at which spectators were charged Entertainment Tax.

There was never any doubt that the Villa were going to win. After all, just as they were leaving Birmingham, hadn't the team received a telegram from a certain FA Cup saying how much he looked forward to being with them again on Saturday? Nobody in Manchester had the wit to send one to their team!

Volumes have been written about the game and some of us often re-live it every time we see Peter McParland stroll across the North Stand car park before home matches.

The all-important question on the lips of Villa supporters was: would mascot Andrew Pugh be allowed to go on the pitch at the end? Would he even get to meet the Queen? She was a regular at the Final in those days before she decided that even duty has its price. I, and my friends, were totally jealous of Andrew. Here was this diminutive eight year-old leading out the team every week. We were already too old.

Whoever heard of a team having a teenage mascot?

Suffice to say that Andrew got his hands on the Cup - something very few Villa supporters were able to do, except at a cricket match against the Albion. It never occurred to anyone then to make money out of displaying it.

The return train left Wembley at 5.44pm and it was not the first to depart. Chaos would have resulted if United had equalised in those fraught last few minutes, but in truth nobody expected the Cup Final to go to extra-time in those days of the W formation. Every man behind the ball belonged to the rugby codes.

The train was timetabled to take three hours to get back to Birmingham, allowing plenty of time for wining and dining. Except that most people present would have preferred to be celebrating at the Social Club. Even when we did get back there it was not long to go before last orders. Soberly and reverently we returned to Villa Park next day for the march past.

Pat Saward and I were back at Wembley four days later. He, to play for the Republic of Ireland in a World Cup qualifier. Me to add to the exchequer in what was the last ever football match with Entertainment Tax thrown in. And I did get a better view of Stanley Matthews than Pat did.

My father had waited 33 years to see Villa at Wembley again. It never occurred to me that I would have to wait another 43 years. Not for my father the occasional visit in a consolation cup match in the intervening years. For me such visits to Wembley have never really been a consolation. Not helped either, by having been to six other FA Cup finals and seen six other teams take home THE Cup.

John Russell - a Villa fan who has few equals

I was 15-years-old when I came over from Waterford, Ireland in 1956 as I'd got an apprenticeship at Bellis & Morcon. I had always followed the Villa as my Uncle Larry lived in Birmingham and sent over to Ireland every week the overseas Daily Mirror – the week's editions in magazine form – and the Sports Argus. I was devoted to the Villa long before I came to Birmingham, and started following them after moving over. My brother John joined me in October 1956 and lived with me at our Uncle's house.

We watched them through the Cup run, culminating in the semi-final at Molineux. The tickets for the game went on sale at Villa Park on St Patrick's Day, 17th March 1957. We got to Witton Lane about 10pm on the Saturday to start queuing. There were about 500 people in front of us and it rained all night; the ticket office finally opened about 10am.

There was a sting in the tail at Molineux because Doc Pace was injured and Billy Myerscough came in. Pace never regained his place and I think he was bitter and never forgave; when he left to go to Sheffield United, I thought he made us pay every time we played them.

We drew and the replay was on the Wednesday afternoon at St Andrews. As we were working, we couldn't get the afternoon off. We beat the Baggies to go on to the Final - that for us personally was great, but the issue of the tickets was so small that it was mainly just season ticket holders. My Uncle Larry who first started me on the trail with Aston Villa was the only season ticket holder amongst us.

He said he'd watch the game on television and he gave us the ticket between us. We travelled to London and I met another uncle of mine – Michael and he took us up to Wembley, where we tossed a coin to see who would go in to watch the match. My brother John won the toss and he went in to see the Villa win the FA Cup. We travelled back into London and watched the match at the Old Forces Club and then went back to Wembley to pick John back up. The sting for me was that I'd been in Birmingham since 1956, followed the Villa all my life, as a pools promoter, a shareholder, a season ticket holder, while my brother John went back to Ireland in August 1957 and he's never come back to England since. Yet he has seen Villa win the FA Cup and I've been here for most of my life and I haven't, which is a bitter pill for me to swallow.

For me personally, that day was a painful one. I bought a pair of shoes from somewhere in New Street, Birmingham, never having bought a pair of shoes for myself in my life. The pair I chose were a half a size too small and after walking around London all day I took them off when we got on the train – and my feet swelled up like balloons. I couldn't get the shoes back on and I travelled back from New Street station on the number seven bus to Perry Common in my stockinged feet. That's my story of the FA Cup Final!

Patrick Flynn, Walsall

I remember the Bristol City match. John Atyeo scored one of the finest goals I've seen for many, many a long time. I was right behind the goal at the Witton End; he hit a daisy cutter from the edge of the penalty area and honest to Christ, it didn't lift three inches. Fabulous goal.

We stayed up all night on St Patrick's night for a ticket; we started at half-ten and at about three o' clock in the morning the heavens opened, but we got our tickets. Both Patrick and I went to Molineux and it looked like West Brom were going to beat us but the lads got the equaliser. A most unusual thing happened in the replay. Now I was at the replay and Pat wasn't; the Villa were leading 1-0 and a long ball came down into the Villa goalmouth and it went past Nigel Sims; it was just 12 inches from the goal and it hit a bump and it just trickled the other side of the post. I've never seen anything like it – it should have gone in. Villa were lucky to win the replay but they did have the Cup spirit and they really got stuck into it.

I was at Wembley as Pat told you and believe it or believe it not, after all this time I can name the two teams. You know a strange thing? I still have the old crepe rosette they used to wear at matches. My uncle was an avid Villa fan and applied for a ticket, he got one for 15/-. He tossed up between it and I won so Pat went to the pictures with my uncle, he had a Villa scarf on. When he came out, he asked someone who'd won and your man stood back and he said, "You're asking me who won the match and you've a Villa scarf?"

I was there myself just behind the Queen and it was a tremendous occasion in so far as that it seemed to pass so quickly, given the enormity of the Final.

John Flynn, Waterford

I was a callow schoolboy when Aston Villa lifted the Cup on that memorable day. Unfortunately my father was not interested in football so I never witnessed the game 'live' or on the old 12-inch TV set, in fact my memory of the day is being sent on an errand. As I was returning from the shops I well remember someone shouting to another person than McParland had scored.

My uncle was an avid fan and went to the Final. The following season he took me out of school on a dull day in January to travel to Molineux, home of Wolverhampton Wanderers, to see a third round FA Cup replay between the holders my Aston Villa and Stoke City, both previous games having been drawn (no penalties' in those magic days). The game took place on a Monday afternoon at 2pm.

So I witnessed the last 90 minutes we could ever claim the Cup was ours, disappointingly losing 2-0. The footnote of that rather solemn day was I did see a little bit of history being made, as a certain Stan Crowther would go into folk lore being the only player to play for two clubs in the same season in the FA Cup, later playing for Manchester United (post Munich) including the Final. It was his second consecutive Wembley, having played against United in 1957, then for them in 1958, when they lost 2-0 to Bolton Wanderers.

Mike d'Abreu, Redditch

I remember talking about the third round draw because my father was a very, very big Villa fan and I followed in his footsteps. We were both of the opinion it wasn't a good draw, but Luton Town - we should knock them out of the way quite easily. That was our opinion, as it turned out it wasn't easy but Villa did what was necessary. Of the replay I remember that it was very, very crowded and we all seemed to be jammed in a very tight area. There was the added incentive of it being a cup-tie, it gave you a little spark knowing that if you won the game you're further along the path to the Final, and that brings with it a lot of enthusiasm and expectancy. Johnny Dixon scored a classic poacher's goal, he came in between two defenders – he was a class player.

I think most of the problems were getting out of the ground afterwards. We were all really pleased about the result but the police were not very co-operative. They treated us all as hooligans, even the people generally walking out through the exits were getting bumped and pushed. It wasn't very pleasant. We had in the backs of our minds that we had won, so it wasn't too bad; it would have been different if we had lost.

Since 1957 things have changed so much. People haven't got the same attitudes; the Cup is not the priority any longer. At one time it used to be THE thing, if you were a big fan you went with your team, you supported them whatever was happening but nowadays you've only got to lose one match and everybody wants the manager out.

All of the players from that era were of the same ilk; they had time for people. If you stopped and spoke to them they would quite cheerfully pass the time of day, you could have a conversation with them – they were good. It's amazing how it has changed. I started working down the Villa in 1952 and the only reason I started down there was my father. He was the chief turnstile supervisor and had to go down early on the Saturday and go all the way round the ground and read the numbers off the turnstiles before they opened up, but it was too early for me to go with him. At the top of our road lived a footballer, Bob Iverson, and he used to come down and knock on the front door, "You ready to go John?" We'd walk up into Perry Barr to catch the outer circle to Witton. Players would turn up with their boots to catch the bus. If we got there early Bob would take me around to Mush Callaghan's house.

As I got older – possibly 12 or 14 - I would go down to Villa Park with my father. I didn't have the best of starts to my Villa career; we went up to the offices and my father left me on the landing while he popped into the office. Being young I had a nose about and saw a fire extinguisher, I somehow sat on it and the thing went off! I ran into the office yelling, "Dad, dad." He came out along with the officials, there was bloody spray all over the place. I started working at Villa at 18, on the gate, allowing people to transfer from the Witton End to the Trinity enclosure for 1/- a time. I worked up to being a turnstile supervisor. When my dad left they presented him with a season ticket for life and promoted me to his job.

I didn't go to the following round up at Middlesbrough but my friends went and they all said it had been a difficult game.

My father went to the semi-final, he didn't have a season ticket but was allowed two tickets for the games through his job.

We bought tickets for the Final a week or so beforehand. On the day of the match, father and me went with a friend of mine, Ray Dugmore in his car. We travelled down a bit earlier to have a wander around and the atmosphere was brilliant.

We got in the stadium about three quarters of an hour before kick-off. We had terrace tickets and the three of us stood behind the goal at the opposite end to where the players came out. We were concerned because United were a good team. We didn't expect Villa to get whipped like the papers said but we thought we might get beat. My friend Ray kept saying after we had gone one-up, "Mr Partridge, how long is there to go, how long is left? In the end dad got fed up and said, "Ray, I'll put my arm here so you can see my watch and DON'T ASK ME AGAIN!" Ray was getting himself in a right state. The famous incident between McParland and Wood happened at the goal we were behind and it was just a collision. So many people said McParland did it intentionally but there was no way, the ball was in between them and they both just went for it; neither of them was prepared to pull out. It just happened and unfortunately for Ray, he got the worst of it.

At that time you were allowed to shoulder charge. I think a lot of Villa fans anticipated that we were going to win when Wood had to go off. It was a shame it happened that way – but it did. Getting to half-time with no score we were happy with the way things were going. Ray Dugmore was happier than most – we were half-way there.

When the first goal went in it was absolutely brilliant and it was a really good goal. At the time I couldn't see the Villa getting anymore; I thought they would hold on with the one and the longer the game went on the more I felt inclined it would stay that way. When the second one went in we were over the moon. We thought this really is it! When Taylor pulled a goal back it got a bit tight – I must admit, it wasn't only Ray at that time - it was me as well. But dad kept saying, "Don't worry, they'll hang on, don't worry about it, they'll win."

We hung around and watched them lift the Cup – unbelievable. Villa's players came around the side of the pitch parading the trophy. We stayed in the ground for nearly an hour watching the players; they would stop in certain areas for interviews and pictures. We came out and spent the same amount of time just savouring the occasion. I must admit the Manchester fans were really good to us; it was the press who caused the trouble. The longest time was getting out of the car park but once away from there we got back quite well. I spent the rest of the night describing the day's events to anyone who would listen – including Blues fans.

John Partridge, Villa Park, Chief Turnstile Supervisor

I went to most of the games. Kenilworth Road, Luton Town's ground was nothing very good at all; me and a mate from work went down. It was a dull, grey day and there was a band playing on the pitch, we remarked that the band wouldn't have been able to read their music had it not been for Luton's poor floodlights. We did enough to get the replay back at Villa Park. Now if there was a match in the week, work (Walton & Brown's) would give you a pass out provided you went in afterwards and put the hours in you had lost.

We had a big crowd for the replay considering it was in the week and they brought a few up and we went through comfortably enough. We went up to Ayresome Park by train; the railways put on specials. What I remember most about Middlesborough and what stuck in my mind was the state of the pitch. I had the shock of my life at how good the playing surface was. There was no mud, the pitch was really grassy and flat – it was beautiful. We were told it was a result of the sea air blowing in; it must have been all the salt in the air.

That was a great game. Pace had a good match and Johnny Dixon, who scored our third was a superb player who could score clever goals; he was a beautiful finisher. It was a cracking afternoon actually but it was such a long way to travel. After getting the good result and playing some decent stuff, knowing that we had a few lads who could find the net, I thought we might be able to go all the way – it was such a good performance.

We were in good spirits after the game. Sitting on the train coming home, who should walk down through our compartment but Jimmy Dugdale. Obviously the team were somewhere further up the train and he came down to see some friends. We all gave him a bit of a cheer. He was a cracking centre-half, and you wouldn't see that happen very often today!

All I remember of the Bristol game was their striker John Atyeo and Jackie Sewell's diving header. I do recall us all giving both sides a standing ovation as they left the pitch because City had been a hard team to break down.

Burnley was never a very happy hunting ground for Villa in those days. They had some good players including the Irish lad McIlroy, who was the one that could make things happen for them, but we played well that day and got a good draw.

I remember seeing Billy Baxter. He'd got a Villa shirt and was leading a group of fans through the town on the way to the ground. We were expected to lose by a lot of the pundits but we got them back to Villa Park. Again me and my mate had to crawl to the gaffer and we had to go in after the game and put in a couple of hours to make up for going to the replay. Our foreman was a Villa season ticket holder but being in charge meant he couldn't just dash off.

We were standing in the Trinity Road enclosure for the replay and I remember the Villa winger McParland giving their full-back the run-around. The defender was trying to wind Peter up but Packy just smiled at him and walked away. It was a cracking game again, and a hell of a crowd for a midweek game. I recall the referee changing tops at half-time.

In the semi-final we played the Albion at Molineux, and I remember going to that game. It was a tight game and they led twice. It wasn't a great game; it was a very tense affair. I was distraught at missing the replay at Birmingham – the only one I missed. We were at work and I couldn't get off, but someone, somewhere had a little radio in and the gaffer kept coming, giving us the news - Villa had made the Final.

I had started taken my eldest lad to the games by then. He was nine and I was unsure what to do but my wife said he was too young and it would be best to leave it.

I got my ticket for the Final by saving the match stubs from the Cup games and went along and queued for hours from early in the morning. Some queued overnight but I wasn't that much of a nutter! The tickets were like gold; if you had a couple of them and wanted to sell them, you'd have made a few bob.

I got a reserved train from New Street which went all the way to Wembley Stadium. That was great because you didn't have to know your way round London. It was a great atmosphere travelling down, you could have a drink or a beer and there was a bloke in with us who had an accordion. Everyone was really buoyant on the train, even though we were facing Manchester United. The way we'd been playing suggested to a lot of fans that we were in with a bit of a shout.

At one end of Wembley there was a huge Radio Times advert and I stood almost under that, right high up. It was a terrific view, even if the players looked like little midgets. The atmosphere built up before the game with the guards or an army band marching up and down the pitch then out came the teams and the game got under way.

It was quite a good game and we were holding our own but in certain areas they had the edge over us, no two ways about it. They had a wing-half from Dudley, Duncan Edwards, who was a superb player. You wouldn't have thought he was a kid; he was more like the bloody captain on the field.

A cross come over and the goalkeeper gathered the ball and Peter, who was a big strong lad, and Wood who never really looked that physical, went down. Danny Blanchflower's younger brother Jackie went in goal. Wood eventually came back on the pitch but he couldn't do much. Now to me it was unfair on the Villa that a lot of the glory or credit is taken away from them because of the incident with the goalkeeper. It was a fair charge and the referee didn't give a foul. I've seen Villa goalkeepers get hammered into the back of the net way back under those rules.

Some of us from our end, which was the opposite end to where the goals went in, thought Billy Myerscough had scored, but it was Peter Mac. And then came the end – and, of course celebrations. But I don't think there were too many from up the north that regarded the Villa as having won fairly and that to me was totally, totally wrong. Anyway, it was a cracking day; we waited for the presentation and all that then finally came out. The organisation in those days was superb. You came out and you'd got your ticket for your special train; you weren't far away from the station, then on to the train and away. We were back home by eight. The missus had gone out; my brother-in-law lived with us then – he was he was an Albion fan by the way – but he was a nice bloke. Well, they'd gone up the road so I came in and got myself cleaned up a little bit and off I went with them. I had a cracking night.

The Cup win was a great, great time and a huge boost for the club. Eric Houghton had got them going in the right direction.

After that the Munich air disaster and they were allowed to go and buy players and we let them have Stan Crowther. To me, we gave up one of our prize assets. Obviously we got money for him but it didn't do the team any good.

Bert Field, Smethwick

I was at school at Four Oaks and mother would come and pick me up every day. But the day Villa played West Bromwich in the semi-final replay she had been sitting in the park listening to it on the car radio. She felt she needed to be on her own at that time; hence she was late picking me up. Mother, Eric and I went to the match. My father's parents and my cousins came from Lincolnshire direct. I actually stood with my grandparents, mother, younger brother and Neil at the match. My grandfather was on my left; I was about 13 at the time. The one recollection I have is when they sing Abide with Me before the Cup Final. I remember looking to my left and seeing the tears streaming down my grandfather's face and I haven't been able to listen to Abide with Me without recalling that memory.

I remember my mother when Manchester United scored; she had to go out and couldn't watch the rest of the match. I don't know if my younger brother went to the banquet on the night, but I did, though I can't remember much about it to be honest. We stayed overnight at the Grosvenor House and then we travelled back the next day. Father had to accompany the official party and we made our way back under our own steam. We weren't part of the celebrations in Birmingham and went straight home to Maple Road, Sutton Coldfield. My older brother Neil went back to school.

It's not relevant to this, but one of the stories I love that father told was the fact that when he joined the Villa when he was about 16 or 17, and he got into the first team, he was in digs at Washwood Heath which was quite close to the Birmingham City ground. They were due to play Birmingham so the trainer said, "You may as well make your own way to the ground as you're so close." So father got the tram and there was a big traffic hold up due to the match. This chap sitting next to him said, " Are you going to the match mate? When father said he was, the chap said, "If we get off here, I know a short cut, we can go across the allotments." So they got off the tram and ran over the allotments and got to the ground. This guy asked, "Are you going on the Spion kop mate? Father replied, "No I'm going to the dressing room!"

I also remember going round to Mush Callaghan's house with father, the Villa playing kit used to get washed there.

Gill Cooper (Eric Houghton's daughter)

In 1957, I watched Villa beat Manchester United in the Cup Final at Wembley and was accompanied by a very good school friend, Malcolm Smith. We watched enthralled as Peter McParland floored the United keeper Ray Wood and went on to score both Villa goals.

A few years later, Malcolm emigrated to Canberra in Australia and for a while we lost touch. I only met up with him twice in 40 years when he visited the UK.

With the advent of Internet and Emails, we resumed contact and in August 2011 I flew out to spend sometime with him, and we also managed to fly over to New Zealand and take in some of the Rugby World Cup. However, with the advent of Internet and Emails, we resumed contact and in August 2011 I flew out to spend sometime with him, and we also managed to fly over to New Zealand and take in some of the Rugby World Cup.

In my role as one of the Villa Park tour guides, I was privileged in April 2011 to interview Peter McParland when he joined us on of our very successful 'Tours with a Legend' and he obviously recalled that very special event.

Peter has been asked the same questions about the final on hundreds of occasions but never hesitates to recount the excitement of the 2-1 win against the Busby Babes who were the leading club of that era.

So, 54 years after THE Cup win, I managed to meet up again with my match companion once again but also spent some quality time with the man who was very influential in winning that trophy. 2011 was indeed a very special year.

Malcolm has now visited Villa Park and enjoyed a stadium tour and really enjoyed being photographed on the hallowed turf!

Pete Haden

Hooked on Elvis!
I was 12 and from a non-footballing family when I decided to support Aston Villa in solidarity with a friend who was seriously ill (and to whom I owe an enormous debt).

My dad was a coach driver and on Monday 7th January 1957 he took fans to the Villa v Luton Town third round FA Cup replay. The teams had drawn 2-2 at Luton on the previous Saturday and replays were always held the following week. As this was before floodlights the game kicked off at 2pm. It was a school holiday so along I went for my first match.

I had imagined that Villa Park was like the local park so I was amazed when we entered at the top of the (old, open) Holte End and this enormous stadium stretched out beneath me. Villa won 2-0 and I was hooked. I went home in raptures, excitingly recounting the experience to Mom, including that they had a player called Elvis – in fact Peter Aldis, an excellent player but not one to make the girls swoon with a hip swivel. This started a passion that has lasted a lifetime and taken me to places as varied as Moscow, Madrid and Middlesbrough. By coincidence, 50 years later to the minute I was at Old Trafford as Villa kicked off their third round at 2pm for TV.

Anne Edwards

I've been a supporter of Aston Villa all my life and I am 78 now. In 1957 I was doing my second year of National Service in the R.A.F. and I was based at Linton-on-Ouse in Yorkshire.

One day, on the main notice board in the mess there was a notice up saying anyone interested in a Cup Final ticket to put their name down and one lucky winner would be drawn, so I added my name. For all there were only a dozen or so names down I never thought anymore of it because I'm not the type to ever win anything. I think Villa were two games away from the Final – but they were still in it.

I remember rushing back from work listening to the result on the radio in the billet finding out we had beaten Burnley. My name came out of the hat apparently, I didn't know but I had a message to go to the Chief Station Warrant Officer, who was in charge of the camp. He informed me I had won the Cup Final ticket, I said, "That's amazing."

The officer then said he would like to buy it off me. Now if you can imagine you are talking to the chief man in charge of the entire camp, and me an ordinary little SAC (senior air craftsman) one of the lowest ranks as such. "I'm sorry," I said "but I've been a supporter of Aston Villa all my life – they're still in the Cup and heading towards the Final. If I've won I'd like the ticket." I was quivering in my boots a bit. He said "Okay, I accept that of course but then I could make sure you're on duty and couldn't get time off for it!" "Well that's up to you but a 36 hour pass is most normal," I replied. He didn't argue with that and that's how I came to get a ticket.

I was over the moon; Villa weren't going through a very good patch for most of my time supporting them. Although they were always in the First Division, if they were lucky they'd be in top six; if they were unlucky they'd be in the bottom six, and that's how it was in those days.

I was attached to a squadron who were on standby to go out to the Suez crisis so the camp was basically empty; I was left behind as I was an electrical engineer on the planes, waiting to be de-mobbed.

Off to the match I went leaving the base on Friday evening, staying at home in Knowle. I went early to New Street station on the Saturday morning because I was unsure of what would happen at the other end. I had to take the tube to Wembley – I just followed the crowd. On arriving people were selling rosettes, I had never had one before so I bought one. I kept it for years because it was part of my life.

My ticket was for a section behind the goal and the terracing was quite deep with very few people in at that time, I sat down and read through the match programme. As it started filling I realised there were very few colours, I later found that the area was basically for all the neutrals. Tickets for this section came from local football teams or armed forces etc, everyone was of the same ilk. They all remained impartial until Ray Wood was injured, after that they all became Manchester followers. I was the exception.

When Wood went back on the pitch, it unbalanced the Villa because he went out on the wing and was a clumsy sort of player and totally unorthodox. There was a stage where I thought they might come back at us now because never in my wildest moments did I think Villa were going to win the match. Lots of the game is a blur, but we won. At the final whistle tears were streaming down my face and I could hardly speak, it was an occasion I thought would never happen.

On the way down I had thought, 'I hope they don't lose too heavily' because Manchester United in those days were a top team – we never thought we'd ever beat them. Villa's winning wasn't so much about the brilliance of their football - I think it was down to the fitness that they achieved at that stage - it made all the difference and I was on Cloud Nine I just couldn't believe it. The source of getting the ticket made it even more fantastic.

When Taylor had scored it was heart-wrenching and I thought United would come back because we weren't playing against 10 men now. When Wood had been playing outfield the Villa seemed a bit put out by it all, it appeared they didn't want to tackle him and that caused Villa further problems. In my mind I started thinking Villa weren't supposed to win but it all came good in the end. It was one of those magic moments, your memory might fade but the fact that you were there was something. I was walking on air. It was a marvellous day.

I stayed at home on the Saturday night and travelled back to Linton on the Sunday. As for the Warrant Officer, I never encountered any problems!

Ernie Tarver, Banbury

I've been going down the Villa for 77 years, and for 58 of those years I was accompanied by Gladys, my wife, who passed away two-and-a half-years ago. We attended every match in the 1957 Cup run.

Villa were expected to beat Luton in the third round – it seemed more or less a foregone conclusion; but the Manchester United game is very vivid. We hadn't got any chance at all against them in the Final; you have to remember they were the top, top team of the time. Even though Gladys and I were season ticket holders we got our Wembley tickets from Amos Moss (the ex-Villa player and son of legend Frank Moss). I worked for the council and I regularly had to go to Amos's house on the Water Orton road. His next door neighbour was Joe Rutherford, the former Villa goalkeeper. In later years Amos and I worked for the same company.

Gladys and I went down to Wembley for the Cup Final by car. In those days I only had old cars, old bangers really, and we used to travel all over the country following Villa. Coming back from Arsenal once the car ground to a halt on the M1 – the wheel arch had collapsed and was sitting on the tyre. As I got out it lifted so I told my wife to sit in the back in the passenger seat, I also sat in the passenger side. I'm 6ft 4in and I drove the car all the way back to Birmingham from Daventry sitting in the passenger seat! If any of the cars broke down we decided we would flog them at the nearest scrap place and come back on the train. It only happened once.

Because we were driving down to the Final in my 1936 Austin Seven we set off from our home in Shard End at 4am - just in case we had any problems. We parked just off High Street, Wembley and went off on the tube to the market in Shepherd's Bush where we had a meal in a restaurant. Gladys then wanted to go and see Covent Garden and while we were there I paid 15/- (75p) for a claret and blue university-type scarf for her. We got it from Moss Brothers and it is signed now by Peter McParland, who I call Peter the Great; he's a good friend. I still have the scarf and it's immaculate. After buying it we were skint, but that wasn't important!

The atmosphere outside Wembley was fantastic. The Villa fans were amazing and you would have thought there were thousands more of us than United as we were cheering, singing and flagwaving – even though we didn't really expect to win. Like me, Gladys thought we would get beaten but we weren't too bothered; we were Villa fans and we were revelling in the experience of it all. We made our way into the stadium and sat along the side, although it was so exciting that you didn't really care where you sat.

I have spoken with Peter McParland about the collision and to be honest I think Ray Wood thought, "Here he comes – I'll stop him" But the keeper came off worse. Peter was my favourite player, though I did like Jimmy Dugdale too. I was driving past Villa Park one day in a Vanden Plas and Jimmy was coming out after training.

I gave him a lift as I was going up to Erdington and he lived near Spaghetti Junction. Even with Wood going off we didn't think it would make a lot of difference. It wasn't so much that he was a brilliant goalie; I just didn't think we had the firepower to get past their defenders.

Duncan Edwards was one of the finest players I ever saw. He had everything. But I thought the threat for the Villa would come from the wings. Once we got to half-time I thought we might be in with a bit of a chance, it would only need one goal - even an own goal and when that first goal went in – oh my god – it was absolutely unbelievable. The Villa supporters couldn't believe it. When the second went in, well, what can I say? It brings it all back to me; it was fantastic. When Tommy Taylor pulled one back late on I started to worry a bit, I thought 'oh blimey, they only need another one and then it'll be off up to Goodison Park for the replay.' I didn't want that.

When the final whistle blew, it was pandemonium; it was out of this world. Gladys and I felt like staying there until midnight, we didn't want to leave Wembley after such a fantastic result. There were tears in my eyes, the wife was crying – we just couldn't believe it. It was very special sharing these moments with my wife, she knew all the rules – including offside! We finally left about 9.30pm and got home to Shard End in one piece; our little Austin was immaculate.

Ivor Price, Erdington

In 1948, as a child, I had been squashed into the Witton Lane end behind the goal, to watch Aston Villa play a third round FA Cup game against Manchester United. After a breathtaking match, Villa lost 6-4. There was even a Dickie Dorsett penalty down our end, which nearly broke the net.

Eleven years later the teams were to meet again in the FA Cup, but this was at Wembley the so-called home of football and it was the Final. The end result was to bring the FA Cup back to Birmingham for the first time in 37 years. It was an historic victory, beating the wonderfully talented Manchester United team managed by Matt Busby. It was a team that carried such gifted footballers as Duncan Edwards, David Pegg, Eddie Colman, Roger Byrne and Tommy Taylor who were all later tragically killed in Munich when their aeroplane failed to leave the runway and crashed.

In spite of the multi-talented opposition team, full of stars, Villa had one man who brightened up the Universe. His name - Peter McParland. On that day in May he became a hero and villain. Following a collision between McParland and Ray Wood, the Manchester United goalkeeper could not be substituted, so Jackie Blanchflower, a centre-half and a younger brother of the former Aston Villa hero Danny, took his place in goal. But it was to be the day of Peter McParland as he scored two brilliant goals to win the FA Cup for Villa.

I watched the game on a black and white television set at home. Barry Smith, a close friend and Villa supporter, was one of eight people squashed into the front room, and when Villa scored their second and winning goal Barry leapt up shouting. His head hit the art deco lampshade, which came crashing down! But no-one minded; we had won the FA Cup and Peter McParland was our hero.

Stephen Morris, Aspiran, France

My father introduced me to the Villa and I watched my first game aged about six, when it was 6d for a child and 1/6d for adults. There were no trams where we lived at Vauxhall and he walked my brother Edmund and me there and back.

There were a lot of teams pretty similar at the time of the draw and you couldn't really forecast a result. I wasn't able to go to Luton but I went to the replay – I remember Jackie Sewell with his teeth out, covered in mud because in those days the sliding tackle was all the rage.

I went up went up to the Middlesbrough game with my brother and a few mates on a football special through LMS (London Midland and Scottish railways). It took us about six hours to get up there on the train. I was still in the Army at the time based at

Catterick (40 miles away) and went on a 48 hour pass, I had to go all the way back home to collect my ticket. My National Service duty with the Army didn't end until 17th February 1957. Even though we played well and got the result, I never imagined we'd get to Wembley.

The pitch for the Bristol City game was in a terrible state. Jackie Sewell had been moaning to the groundsman Bert Bond because he'd put some manure on when he'd reseeded it; it hadn't rotted down and Jackie, when he was sliding for the ball, was getting covered in the stuff and stinking!

I always stood in the Holte End because there was a hell of a lot of old characters. It was a great atmosphere; you could get huge crowds in there.

Burnley were our bogey side. We thought that was the end of the Cup; we'd always beaten them at our place and they would do the same up there. I didn't go up to Turf Moor. My dad took me along to the Albion, who were playing Arsenal in the Cup. We saw the board go up with the latest score and Villa were one goal down; we later found out that Aldis had put through his own net. My dad said, "Typical – they're there again." In the end they got out of it and we had to play them down Villa Park and if I remember there was a bit of confusion; it had poured down with rain all morning. I was working down the market and one of the customers, Mr Clark, who lived at Kingstanding and owned a fruit shop, said to me and the salesman, "Just go down to Villa Park and mention my name." He was a shareholder or something and we went down and got fixed up. When we went in about buying the two tickets for the Holte End the woman said, "If I was you I'd go along to the Witton End and have a look at the state of the pitch."

It had at least an inch of water standing on the top and there was a chance the game might be called off. Eventually they shifted some of the water; they must have used some big forks on it. What happened was that the groundsman used to borrow machinery from Aston Park and in return some of the players would go and shift snow off the pathways so people could walk through the park. Anyway the game was played even though the pitch was poor.

Villa borrowed Birmingham's red strip. The ref made a mistake because Burnley played in all-black and the referees of that time wore black coats; you could see the Villa players getting mixed up because it made it look like Burnley had 12 players on the pitch. The ref came out for the second-half with just a white shirt showing. It was a tough match and Burnley had some good players but we beat them.

I went to the semi-final at Molineux, I was at the end where you had to walk through the factory. I can't remember the name but it was the big end that held the most people. We were all on tenterhooks because Albion had a fantastic side, but we managed to sneak a draw. I went to the replay at Birmingham's ground straight from work at the Smithfield market – we started at 5am and finished in the afternoon.

The Villa supporters' entrance was the Tilton Road end. It was choc-a-bloc and we couldn't get through to get down on the terracing. I watched from where they had the Pathe news stand to record the match - I stood on a piece of scaffolding offcut and every now and then I had to get down and change feet. It was painful standing on a bit of round tube, then climbing back up to peer over the corrugated partition. It was a good job I'd been in the army and was fit.

Not very fortunate for the Albion was the Ronnie Allen accident because he was always a danger for them. I was at the end where Billy Myerscough scored the only goal and where the ball was diverted off Stan's heel in the second-half. I also remember the ball bouncing along the crossbar; it was all excitement. We had rattles and boards which we would paint claret and blue. Those rattles could make a din.

We bought the Birmingham Mail and the Evening Despatch to see what the ticket criteria were for the Final as neither Edmund nor I had season tickets. We wrote to Villa and sent them our vouchers and train tickets to prove we had been here and there and what have you. Weeks went by and we had heard nothing so we got in touch with the Villa and said we hadn't received any notification of whether we qualified. They sent us a letter to say we hadn't sent enough vouchers in – so we were sweating.

As it happens my uncle owned a crisp business in Saltley and he had greyhounds at Perry Barr and one of his best mates was Harry Parkes; another friend of his was Jimmy Eason who was a scout. Through Harry, my uncle managed to get me a 3/6d ticket for the Final and Edmund ended up with a more expensive ticket for the seats and his was over a £1. He sold that at face value outside the ground and got a 3/6d ticket to come in with me.

I've still got the ticket for the Final. I also have the photographs we had taken at New Street station of me and my brother and his mate. What happened was in those days the Evening Despatch and the Birmingham Mail had a cartoonist there, Norman Edwards, and in the week he'd do a cartoon about the match from the Saturday. I wrote and asked him if he'd draw me a big Villa Villan - the usual pointed hat, cloak and moustache. Eventually I had a letter off him saying, 'this is just a one off.' My brother went and collected it from the offices in Corporation Street and brought it home. It was big and I put it onto a piece of hardboard and stuck it on a broom stile that I painted claret and blue.

My mom made a big rosette, we cut the picture out of the Mail and she got some crepe paper – claret and blue – covered it and my brother wore it on his chest. We went to the driver of the steam train and asked him if we could put it on the front of the engine. When we arrived in London we had to get the tube out to Wembley, the rosette was still on the front of the train so Edmund took it and put it on his coat. We looked around London and found ourselves at Trafalgar Square. Edmund started blowing a trumpet a mate of his had got off one of the trains as he worked on the railways. The noise was deafening – and the pigeons all took off!

Finding a pub, we had something to eat before making our way to Wembley. The atmosphere was fantastic; on paper we had no chance to beat Manchester United. Right from the third round really because in those days we weren't a glamorous side at all – just good grafters. We had a drink and went into the stadium as the brass band was playing. The fellow with the white coat was there conducting the fans in the community singing. Little Andrew Pugh, the mascot, was reputed to be the first supporter/mascot to ever run around the Wembley pitch-side. What a cracking view we had. We were three-quarters of the way back at the opposite end to the tunnel.

The game had hardly started when the collision between Wood and McParland occurred. In those days you could literally do that. Wood set himself up because Mac charged him hoping he'd probably drop the ball. Of course then Blanchflower went in goal because there were no subs so they had a man less but even then they were all good players. I think the blow made the United lot put a bit more extra effort in, with a 'you ain't gonna beat us' type of attitude. Except, as it happens, we did beat them.

When our first went in it was a bonus because every section of their team was well covered and they'd had that spell in Europe, so we still expected Manchester to come back. Only when our second went in did I think we had a real chance. Taylor pulled a goal back at our end and with seven minutes or so left, and playing a team of their quality we knew it was going to feel like a lifetime. The only time I felt safe was when the final whistle went. It was a lovely feeling, except that Edmund started blowing his horn and it was so noisy.

What a great achievement. Villa weren't playing immaculate football and had only finished 10th, but we had won the Cup. As we left the ground you can imagine how busy it was with a crowd of 100,000. Edmund blew that horn again and everyone just moved aside for us to walk through. They thought it was a car!

Roy Fifield, Stetchford

I was born in Rowley Regis and was living there with my parents at the time (I'm now 75). My father was a cousin of Tommy Weston, left-back in the 1913 and 1920 FA Cup Finals. Tommy Smart, Weston's full-back partner in the 1920 Final, also lived locally. He was another great character. He often used to show me his winner's (1920) and loser's (1924) medals. Tommy said when he was given his loser's medal he told the rest of the team he didn't want a winner's medal as he already had one of those. He used to cycle from Blackheath to Villa Park (about eight or nine miles away) to train every day and wouldn't dream of playing a match without two pints of beer and two-penny worth of chips inside him.

I have been following Villa since the war years. I could give you many memories of matches but instead I can offer several off-field stories.

Seventh Heaven: Aston Villa's Victorious '57 Cup Campaign

When Villa last won the FA Cup in 1957 I was lucky to see every match including replays.

I have several memories from after the games. Villa drew at Luton in the third round and after the game the team travelled back to Birmingham on the same train as the fans. They rarely went by coach then. The train was packed and my friend and I were standing in the corridor when an attractive lady went to use the toilet but immediately came back saying the lock wouldn't work. Several minutes later she returned with Jimmy Dugdale and re-entered the toilet while Jim stood guard outside and told us what he would do to anyone who tried to enter while his wife was in there!

At Middlesbrough in the fourth round the team returned to Brum, again on the same train as the supporters. Johnny Dixon had not been well but still played and scored the winner with a brilliant goal. We were waiting on the platform for the train when the team arrived at the station. Some fans immediately made for Johnny and hoisted him on to their shoulders and carried him around the platform until the train arrived.

After the Final my friend and I decided to let the crowds make their way from the stadium and leave when the crush had finished. We decided to wait outside the players' entrance until the team came out to travel to their hotel for the celebrations. Wilfred Pickles, a famous radio personality of the time, passed us and said he was delighted that the Villa had won. Then a small door opened in the dressing room and out came Con Martin. We had noticed that when the team were parading the trophy around the stadium that Stan Lynn had seen Con in the crowd and insisted that he join them on the pitch. Con had left Villa at the end of the 1955-56 season after eight years great service to become player/manager of Waterford. We asked Con if he wished he had been playing and he stayed and chatted with us for a while and said he wished he could start his career all over again with Villa, who were the greatest club in the world.

We went to London's West End to celebrate. We had booked a day excursion from New Street to Euston and could return by any train that day. At about 7pm we were able to buy copies of the Birmingham Mail evening sports paper, which had a headline something, like "McParland puts Villa in seventh heaven."

They had been rushed from Birmingham to the West End for Villa supporters to buy. I was so thrilled with the result that I cut the headline from the paper, pinned it to my coat and walked around London proudly showing it to all and sundry.

One other memory. After the fourth round away win at Middlesborough the train returned too late for us to get the last Midland Red bus home to Rowley Regis so we had to get the Birmingham Corporation all night service number nine to Quinton. It was another three-mile walk from the terminus in Ridgeacre Road to our homes. In those days the pubs closed at 10pm and there were very few people around late at night.

While we were still a mile from home a policeman stopped us because he thought we were up to no good. There were plenty of bobbies on the beat then. Anyway, this copper would not believe our reason for being out so late until we produced the match programme. It probably saved us from a night in a police cell. The programme also became useful later. When Villa were allocating tickets for the Final, ticket stubs from the two all ticket games had to be sent when applying to Villa Park and it was going to be luck of the draw as to who got tickets.

Because we were able to send parts of the away tie programmes for Luton, Middlesborough and Burnley we were allocated tickets. Those programmes proved to be very useful indeed.

Frank Allen Droitwich, Worcestershire

I was 10 when Villa won the Cup. The abiding memory that I have of it was my mate's dad who was madly keen on the Villa – had a Cup Final ticket. He went down on the train to Wembley and was so convinced that they were going to win the Cup that he laid on champagne for the journey back. He and his friends had a load of champagne afterwards; mind, he said they were going to drink it anyway! Not many fans held the same belief; it was more a case of turn up and see what happened.

I hadn't watched the Villa by this time but I was a fan and followed the Cup run with schoolboy enthusiasm. I recall the Burnley game away when we got a draw. We played in pale blue shirts and Peter Aldis scored an own goal. Getting them back to Villa Park, I knew we would beat them.

Being that age and having just got interested in football, Villa's players were gods as far as I was concerned and they were going to win everything.

When they played the semi-final, obviously I didn't have a ticket but I went down with my mate to watch the Villa reserves against Manchester United and we won 2-1. In those days they had the little A, B, C boards and they would give you the Villa first team score every 15 minutes, so that was a good day. Nobody watched the reserve game, everyone was watching for the semi-final score coming through, but because they only put the score up every quarter of an hour, the latest we got was the 75 minute score when Villa were trailing 2-1 and we left Villa Park thinking we had lost. I presume the final score would have been put up five or six minutes after the final whistle but by then everyone would have left. I got the result shortly after, as we always stopped at Snow Hill station to get the Sports Argus.

I was at school on the afternoon of the replay so I don't remember much about that. And because we lived out at Shirley I wasn't able to go to any of the functions that the players had organised. I presume I was deemed too young to get involved in that kind of thing and never got to find out about anything until afterwards.

Johnny Dixon was my favourite player. I loved him, he was a brilliant player. I remember Villa going down a couple of years after the Cup Final and Joe Mercer dropped Johnny, and I was really upset about that, Id' have loved to have seen Johnny

Dixon bring them back up to the First Division again. I remember his last game because it was Charlie Aitken's first. He was a good servant, a Villa man through and through.

My dad Bill is a big Villa fan and we had lots of conversations about them getting to the Final. We had only recently moved to Shirley form Balsall Heath and it coincided with the match, we got ourselves a new television and virtually the first thing we watched – mom, dad and me - was the Cup Final. I expected Villa to win, the optimism of a kid really, you like to think your favourite team will win everything. I certainly remember Peter McParland's bullet header; that was amazing. He was nowhere to be seen then all of a sudden the ball was in the net. Even when Taylor pulled one back I didn't fancy United to come back. I never thought they had a chance really – it was a bit of a nervous few minutes, though. It was brilliant. We all celebrated and then my mate came round and we celebrated with him as well. I remember waking up the next day and thinking, "We'll be champions of the world soon."

John Harvey, Shirley

I was 24 at the time and I went to the Luton game at home, both the semi-final and re-play at Molineux and St Andrew's and also the Final. At the time of the third round draw with Luton away I felt we had an even chance of getting a draw or winning it, and I remember Dixon and McParland getting the goals in the draw. In the home game there wasn't a very big gate because it was played on a Monday afternoon.

In the next round we had Middlesbrough, who had a decent team. But Villa at that time were playing very well; it was in the days of five forwards and we had some good uns. The one guy who played very well didn't play in the Final – Derek Pace, he scored against Boro and later lost his place to Bill Myerscough. He was a very good forward who never had a fair rub of the green at Villa, especially when he lost out in the semi-final.

For the Bristol City match we had a big, big crowd there and Pace and Sewell got the goals. Then we met Burnley in the sixth round, and they were a superb side at the time. I didn't get up to the first game, where Peter Mac saved us, but I went to the replay where I seem to recall Dixon and McParland scored for us, and we played in Blues' second strip. There was another big crowd that day.

He was a fantastic player, McParland, the way he could head a ball and the way he could get down that left wing.

We had gates of 50,000-plus for both the semis and I remember the replay against Albion. They were all over the Villa; in fact they were in both games. I've got a picture of us going down on the train. Myerscough got us the goal but Albion hit the woodwork and all sorts, but it just seemed like it was Villa's day. I think it was written that it was our year. Derek Pace was a fantastic servant to the club and most people were sorry he was dropped, he probably didn't deserve it, but then again Myerscough justified his place by scoring the goal I suppose, and he played in the Final.

I honestly don't recall how I came by my Cup Final ticket. I know it posed no problems getting one as there weren't that many season ticket holders. We didn't have season tickets because only rich people could afford it in those days. Me and a friend, Clifford Orp, went down from New Street on the train on the Saturday morning just before lunchtime. We often used to go down to London on football excursions. We used to go from Snow Hill mostly and the fare was £1. We would get the midnight train back and get into Snow Hill at 4am.

We were playing the best team in the country at the time – the Busby Babes, and we should have got beaten but it just seemed to be written that we were going to win the Cup.

I remember the incident with Ray Wood, which certainly influenced the game. The United goalkeeper came back and played on the left wing because there were no substitutes and Jackie Blanchflower went in goal. Obviously that dictated a lot of the game. Peter McParland would never have got way with it today. Of course, we scored those two goals and the last 20 minutes or so it was one-way traffic towards our goal. I thought the match was never going to end. I don't know how far from the end it was when Taylor scored but we just held our breath; I just kept thinking 'blow the whistle'.

When you looked at what their team was it was fantastic – Duncan Edwards, Eddie Colman, Johnny Berry. Mind you, Villa also had a good side. Johnny Dixon was the inspiration and you'd also got Peter McParland, Les Smith and Pat Saward. There was Stan Crowther, who went to United after the Munich crash the following year.

The strongest emotion after the final whistle was sheer relief after all that tension. It was fantastic to see Johnny with the Cup on Jackie Sewell's and Peter Aldis's shoulders. But we couldn't hang around for long as we had to catch the train home.

Ron Hibbs, Castle Bromwich

I was 12 at the time of the Final. I had a sister but she wasn't interested in the football. It was my father who got me hooked. He came down to Birmingham after the war for a job and was a keen football fan. He wanted to choose a local side and picked the Villa. He always used to say that where he worked, Albion was slightly nearer but he'd re-membered the Villa from when he was in Newcastle. The Villa had played up there and there was an instant affection towards them. He became very keen and became a season ticket holder fairly quickly and went with two other chaps in the old Witton Lane stand right in the back row. Sometimes I'd get in for 'nowt' as my father knew secretary Fred Archer's assistant.

We were bought up in a very sporting household, when I was at school I got friendly with a chap I'm still very friendly with, and he was an Albion supporter. I think that sort of triggers an interest but winning the Final was amazing; you somehow felt you were supporting something special.

My father went to all the home games during the Cup run. I didn't go to any apart from the Final. He had taken me for a few years, but not to all that many games because he tended to sneak me in rather than buy me my own ticket, which would have meant me sitting somewhere else.

The one game when I really remember a feeling that something was afoot was winning against Burnley, because they were a very good team. My father went to the quarter-final and the replay and I remember him coming home quite cheerful. Then my Albion friend went to the semi-final and to this day he still can't believe the Baggies didn't win.

Father and I went to the Final. My mother was ill in hospital so my sister came as well and we stayed with father's aunt who lived in a flat on London's Edgware Road. We drove down from Northfield in father's car the night before the game. It was term time and I attended a private school where Saturday mornings were part of the school week, so we must have had permission for me to be absent.

The thing I remember almost more than anything else about the whole day was we were walking along the Thames embankment and seeing Cleopatra's Needle. It's got the name of the man who was involved in re-erecting it - John Dixon CE (chief engineer), but my dad claimed it stood for Cup Expert! In fact I went back when I went to the 2000 Final and had another look at it.

Father had a cine camera, so he took it to Wembley and filmed some of the Final. I have watched it since, but it's pretty limited, very short really compared to the total game. I think it's more of the band playing at the beginning as much as anything. Cine cameras were quite a rarity and rather expensive but father was a surgeon so he could afford one. In fact we used to go to the games and he used to say to the copper on duty where the parking was behind Witton Lane, "My name's Smith, I'm a surgeon at Dudley Road Hospital and I have to go back to work and operate this evening after the match, can you find me a good spot?" On one occasion the chap on duty said, "Yes sir, I know you Mr Smith. You mended my duodenal ulcer!"

I can't really remember too much about the Final. We went along to the game fully expecting to see Villa lose. I know we were at the side of the stadium and I recall United having 10 men for quite a lot of the game although I've got the feeling that this confused the issue for Villa. When you think what happened to the Manchester United team the following year, really it was extraordinary. It was the last major game for the Busby Babes.

My father had backed Aston Villa to win the Cup and won £30 after putting £1 on them at odds of 30/1 before the third round. That was quite a lot of money in 1957 but I think he blew it that night!

I went back to the flat in the evening and my sister was there along with someone to look after us. Dad disappeared for the evening, I think he hit the town and spent the £30 and didn't come back until we'd gone to bed. There was a certain amount of excitement about the whole affair.

The point about that Cup Final more than anything else was that it really cemented my liking, which became an obsession or fixation, with Aston Villa.

Clive Smith, St Johns, Worcester

I've been to one FA Cup final in my life – in 2000 – and it was obviously hugely disappointing because Villa lost. But I still absolutely loved the atmosphere, so what it must have been like to be down there all those years ago? That would've been wonderful.

I was 10 at the time of the 1957 Final. My dad was a mad, mad Villa supporter, which is where I got it from. He'd started taking me down to the matches when I was eight so I'd been going to Villa Park for a couple of years. I was certainly aware of the Villa's Cup run – it was a big thing. I can remember it being a long drawn-out route as there were a few draws in there. It was a long campaign, played in any sort of weather. I can't recall now having been at any matches, though it's possible I was as I used to go along with my dad. When we reached the semi-final onwards there was lots of excitement because two other Midlands sides were also through. One of my uncles was an Albion fan. I don't know if it's my mind playing tricks but I always thought there was more of a rivalry between Villa and Albion than Villa and Birmingham. Maybe it was just a family thing?

We counted the days down after the semi, the Final couldn't come quickly enough. Mom made a huge cake rectangular sponge cake with green icing and white lines, which in 1957 was pretty exotic. She made a couple of goals and she got the names of the teams piped on it as well - that's where my addiction to cake started! We didn't have a television but dad had a workmate from Lichfield which was just down the road from where we lived and his family had a TV, so we all decamped down there. I can't remember what the tele was like but I wouldn't think it was very big, and certainly not colour.

The cake went up to Lichfield and took pride of place in front of the TV before being devoured at the end of the match. It's amazing how little things like that stick in your mind.

My dad took me into Birmingham to see the Cup brought back; there were an awful lot of people – really, really big crowds. There was a lot of cheering and I had my little scarf on and my rosette, I've still got that rosette somewhere. On a kid of my age that made a terrific impact.

I went to the '57 commemorative dinner at the Metropole in 1997, having been invited by Sports Projects, the company that used to produce the Villa programme. Jackie Blanchflower was the guest speaker and was there as guest of honour from Manchester United. I remember a colour version of the 1957 Cup Final being played in the background. I've tried but I've never been able to get hold of a copy. The three guys on the same table as me were Jackie Sewell, Leslie Smith and Peter Aldis. It was an unforgettable night.

Norman Hood, Market Drayton, Shropshire

- Norman kindly supplied the fine caricatures for this book.

Thanks and Acknowledgements

I would like to take this opportunity to thank the following family, friends and associates who through their support have made Seventh Heaven possible. My thanks in no particular order;

To my longer suffering wife Debra and children. To my nephew Jay Abbott, for the website design and management, and assisting with the re-design of the eye-catching cover.

To Peter Brennan, Editor, owner and the driving force behind The Villa Times magazine for his expertise and the editing and setting out of this publication in readiness for printing. Stan Crowther for submitting the extended foreword and the use of his photo albums; Peter McParland, Villa's two-goal hero in the 1957 Final for being available whenever I needed to phone him and recounting all the memorable stories; Nigel & Marjorie Sims and Jackie Sewell for their contributions and memories.

To Jon Farrelly and Mick Tilt, both very good friends who willingly gave me their time and unlimited use of treasured items from their personal memorabilia collections, including football programmes and former Villa players albums and scrapbooks: without these two lads, this book would have remained a pipe-dream!

I extend my continued thanks to Paul Faulkner, Aston Villa Football Club's chief executive. He's a man with a very busy schedule but somehow always finds the time to respond to my requests.

Lee Preece and Laura Brett, Aston Villa Football Club Archives.

Villa's programme editor Rob Bishop - who is responsible for numerous books about the club - for his help and time trawling over and proof reading the finished article.

John Greenfield and Alan Williams of Villa's merchandising department, who have provided invaluable assistance.

Norman Hood - once again he has supplied an amazing one-off caricature for this publication - this is becoming a bit of a habit!

Andy 'Turnstile' Ullah, Martin 'Mozza' Moss, Mark Clarey, Ade & Hedda Nevitt and Richard Leach for their continued support.

Simon Goodyear, author – of most notably 'From Mine to Milan' The Gerry Hitchens Story - who gives invaluable advice when asked.

A special mention to Lisa Regan and all at Jellyfish Solutions for the phenomenal help and support with both In Safe Hands and now Seventh Heaven - as far as printers go I think they are unbeatable.

A big thank you to the following people who took the time to share their memories of Aston Villa's Victorious '57 Cup Campaign for inclusion in the Recollections and Memories section of Seventh Heaven, Neil Houghton and his sister Gill, John Russell, brothers Patrick and John Flynn, Mike d' Abreu, John Partridge, Bert Field, Anne Edwards, Clive Smith, Norman Hood, Ron Hibbs, Pete Haden, Ivor Price, Roy Fifield, John Harvey, Ernie Tarver, Stephen Morris and Frank Allen.

I would like to take this opportunity to thank everyone who pre-ordered Seventh Heaven; it gives me immense satisfaction to see the same names included in this publication's Roll of Honour, which reiterates how well received my previous book In Safe Hands has been. A big thank-you for your loyalty - it is very much appreciated!

I hope that I have remembered and acknowledged you all. My sincere apologies if I have overlooked anyone.

Last but certainly not least – a very, very big thank-you to the family of Aston Villa's 1957 captain Johnny Dixon. His wife Brenda and children Andrew and Helen were only too willing – regardless of how upsetting it all was to them personally – to share their sad memories of Johnny's suffering through Alzheimer's. They went to great length to help me and gave me as much of their time as I required. The family were unanimous in allowing me through a small part of this book to highlight the drastic life changing effects that Alzheimer's has - not only the victim but also the entire family.

Very best wishes
Colin J. Abbott

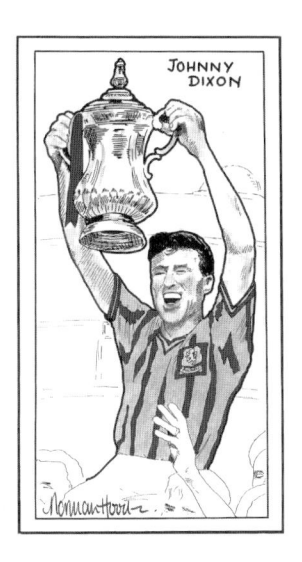

Johnny Dixon

"When Johnny's memory and character changed beyond recognition due to Alzheimer's, his doctor urged us that Johnny should really be in residential care, not only for his benefit but that of ourselves too. He was placed in a residential home in Lichfield – to say it wasn't suitable is an understatement. On taking him there on his first day, we had hardly made it back through the front door when a call came from the home. Johnny, they informed us, had disappeared. We were frantic and joined in the search. The Police later picked him up, he was found wandering, walking from Lichfield back towards Sutton Coldfield. It was extremely sad for us all, my daughter Helen still cries about it to this day. The home didn't want us to see him, they said he was resting but we insisted. When we got to him he was unrecognisable, his hair was dishevelled, he was drugged up to the point he didn't know who we were.

We couldn't have him removed before he was assessed and it turned out he was locked in his room by night - he bloodied his knuckles one night trying to get out – and then locked out of his room by day. He was forced to sit in front of the television with a group of old women, day in, and day out and appeared permanently drugged up. It was a dreadful place. As soon as it was possible we had removed and placed in a far more suitable accommodation in Tamworth. - **Brenda Dixon**

In a conversation Brenda Dixon said how it would be great if the Football Association owned and ran their own care homes especially for retired players who have Alzheimer's. Daughter Helen also backs up this train of thought. There are certainly plenty of them who suffer from it. They could have an area in secure grounds where they can go out onto a football pitch, somewhere they can meet like-minded gentlemen and talk together. Instead of nurse's uniforms, put the staff in tracksuits. She said, "There's nothing worse than a nurse trying to bath a proud old gent like Johnny, he absolutely hated it – he was a very proud man. Now put them in the hands of what they think is the football trainer and that's another matter."

Ten years ago my Dad was diagnosed with Alzheimer's and passed away in January 2009. Seeing at first hand how this cruel disease slowly robbed us of our loving Dad and my Mom of her husband, has left us with deep wounds making the good days prior to Alzheimer's sometimes hazy. The final two years were the hardest because unlike most conditions Alzheimer's makes it difficult to treat or look after your loved one because simple tasks such as giving them a bath, cleaning teeth or trying to cut hair, turns into a major operation which on occasion has taken days to achieve, by talking and finding the right moment. In later stages of the condition sufferers neither want nor accept help from anyone, family or otherwise.

My Mom worked very hard with Dad and she deserves all of our family's thanks for her hard work, patience and understanding. For 24 hours a day, 365 days of the year, Alzheimer's dictated my mom's life too.

I never want to see someone else I love go through this terrible suffering. I wrote my poem Alzheimer's 1 in 3 to sum up my feelings. We all need to be aware of the destructive power of the disease and with help, support, raising awareness and working together we can hopefully help to create a brighter future for generations to come and eradicate Alzheimer's completely.

Thank you for reading. **Helen**

Alzheimer's 1 in 3

Alzheimer's is an unhappy word to me
It took away my Dad's dignity
It took away the Dad I loved and knew so well
And left us with just the shell

A shell we no longer knew
Never knowing what he was going to say
Or what he was going to do

What a horrible way to go
Not knowing who was friend and who was foe
Not knowing who you are or what you've achieved
Not even knowing who to believe

What panic and frustration must go through their minds?
Yes Alzheimer's is truly unkind

Bit by bit, and day by day
It slowly took my beloved Dad away
For no longer is my Dad with me
For my Dad was the 1 in 3
Helen Freeman (nee Dixon)

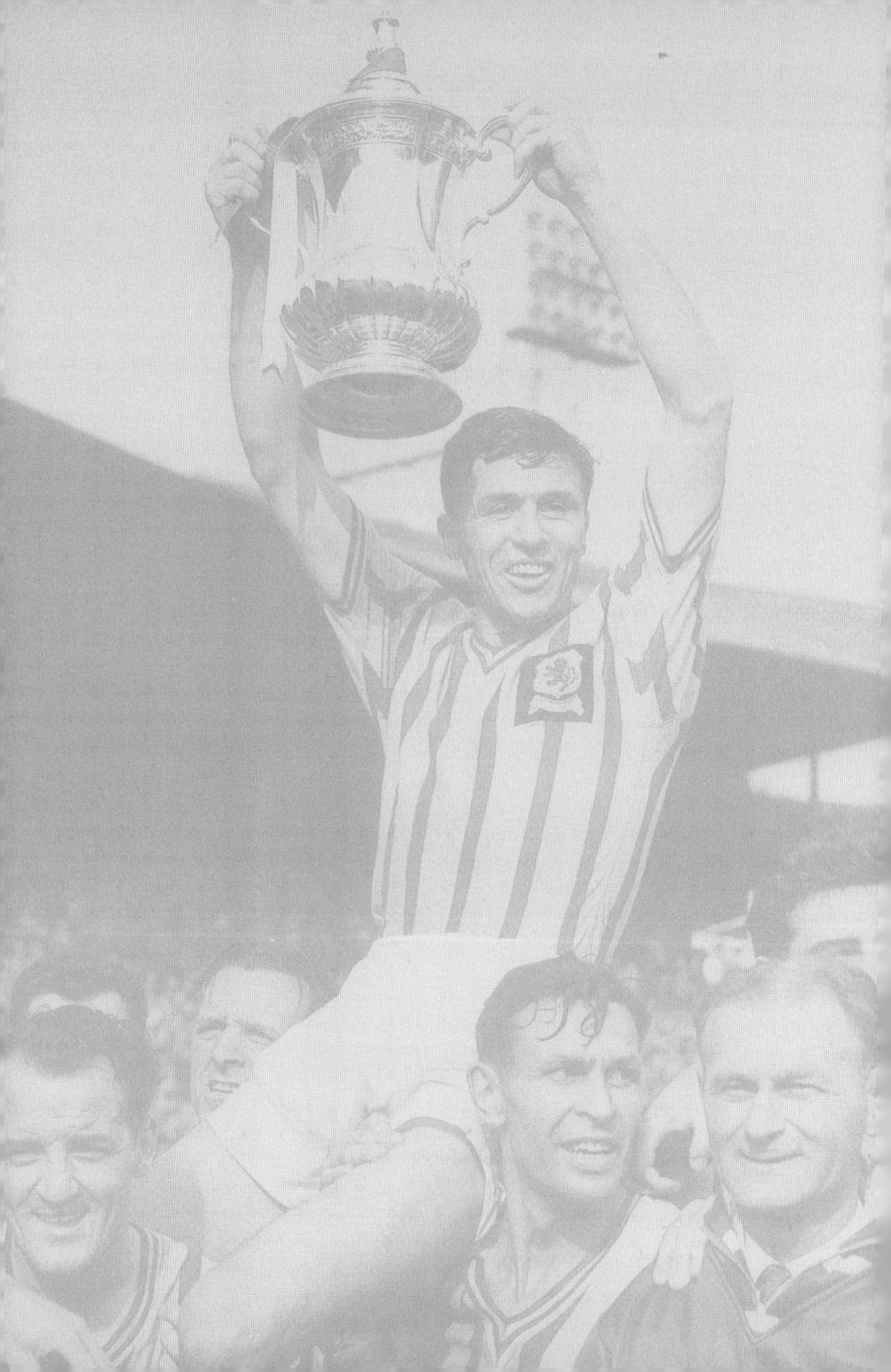

Bibliography

Books

Personal Scrapbooks and Albums of 1957 Players; owned by good friends, Jon Farrelly & Mick Tilt

Official Aston Villa Boardroom Minutes book

Personal diary of Eric Houghton; property of daughter Gill Cooper

Aston Villa, The Complete Record; Rob Bishop & Frank Holt

The Villa News & Record; Official Journal of the Aston Villa Football Club Limited

Aston Villa's Cup History; Norman Edwards

Aston Villa, The First 100 Years; Peter Morris

In Safe Hands, Nigel Sims' Football Memories; Colin J. Abbott & Debra A. Abbott

The Official History of the FA Cup; Byron Butler

Going for Goal, My Life in Football by Aston Villa's flying Irishmen; Peter McParland

Jackie Sewell; Keith Dixon

Claret and Blue Official Aston Villa magazine

The Complete Encyclopaedia of Aston Villa Football Club; Tony Matthews

Aston Villa, A History From 1905; Historic Newspapers

Who's Who of Aston Villa Tony Matthews

English Football League & F.A. Premier League Tables 1888 – 2009; Michael Robinson

Villa in the blood; Bernard Bale

Aston Villa, Head to Head; Peter Waring

Heroes and Villains, Aston Villa Fanzine; Dave Woodhall

Websites

Aston Villa news taken from www.astonvilla-mad.co.uk

Aston Villa History John Lerwill www.lerwill-life.org.uk

Heroes and Villains www.heroesandvillains.co.uk

Aston Villa, The Complete Record, was the sole source for attendances regarding Aston Villa matches!

Some of the information contained in this publication is hearsay from interviews conducted with former footballers.

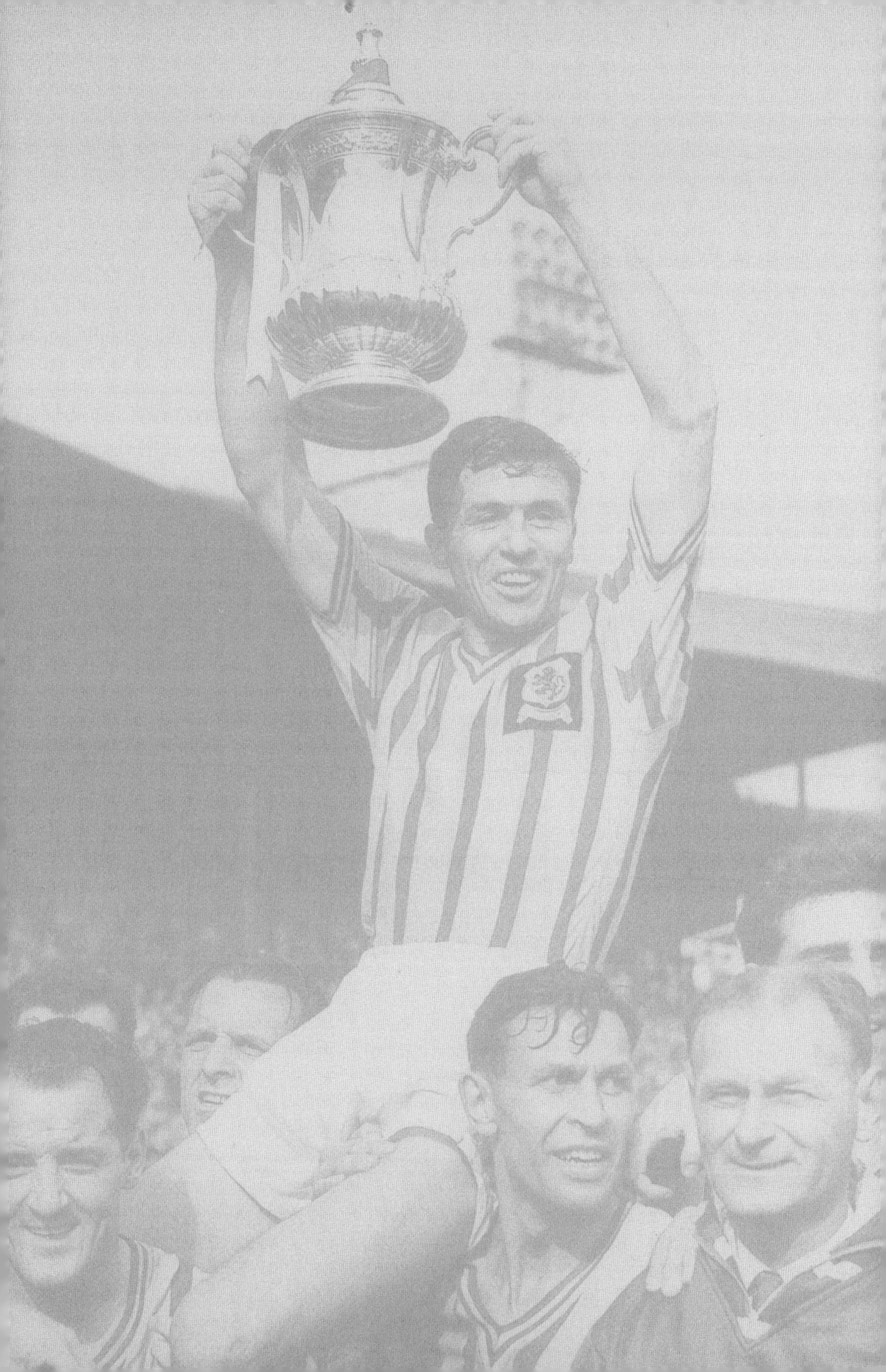

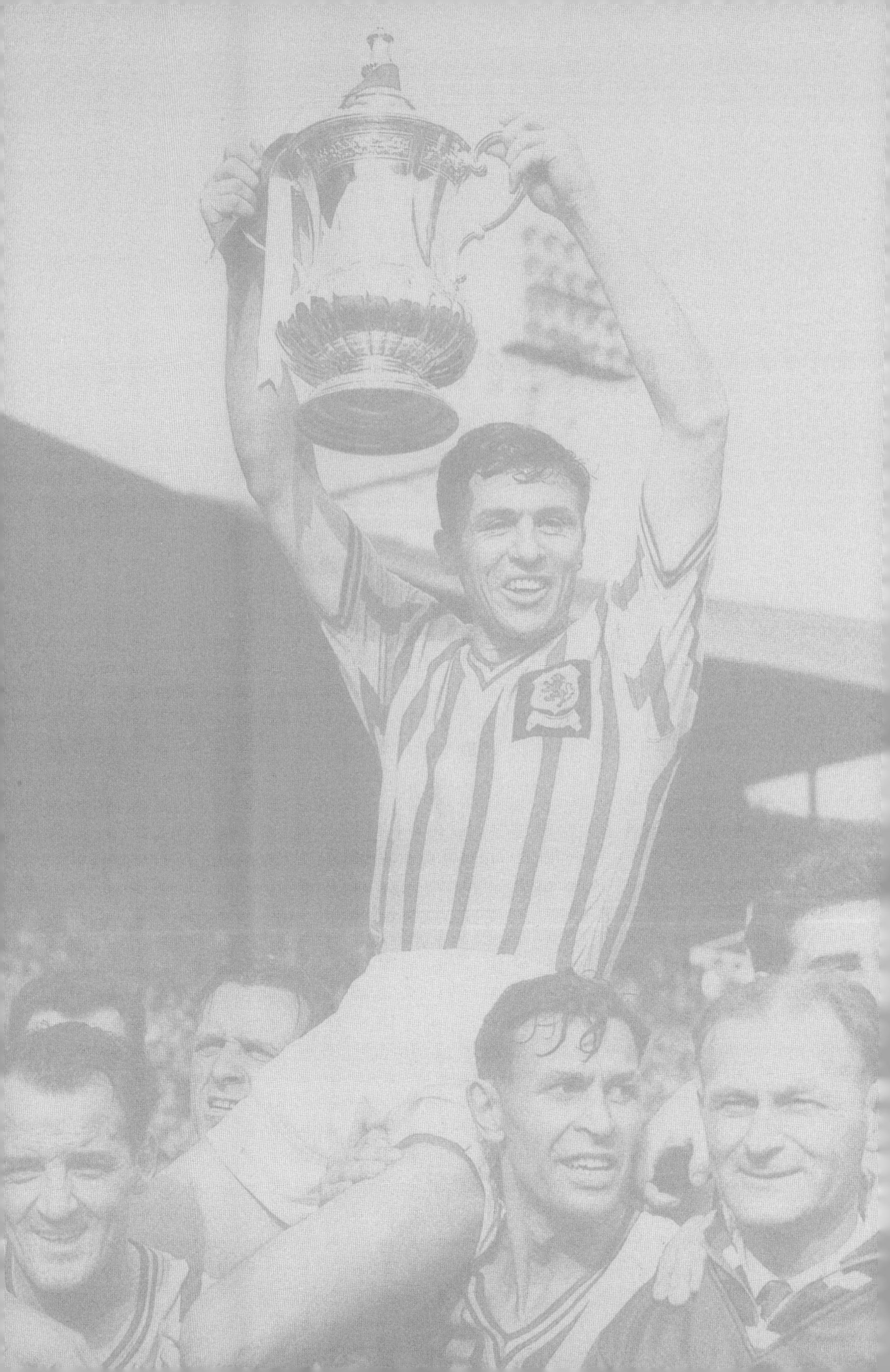

Roll of Honour
Presentation Copies

Aston Villa F.C.
Aston Villa archives
Sue & Mick Tilt
Jon Farrelly
Norman Hood (Cartoons)
Rob Bishop

Stan Crowther
Nigel & Marjorie Sims
Peter McParland
Jackie Sewell
Brenda Dixon
Paul Faulkner

In Memoriam Eric Houghton
In Memoriam Billy Moore
In Memoriam Stan Lynn
In Memoriam Peter Aldis
In Memoriam Jimmy Dugdale
In Memoriam Pat Saward
In Memoriam Leslie Smith
In Memoriam Billy Myercough
In Memoriam Johnny Dixon
In Memoriam Derek 'Doc' Pace
Colin J. Abbott
Peter Brennan
Andy 'Turnstile' Ullah
Martin 'aka Mozza' Moss
Mark Alan Clarey
Neil Houghton

Gill Cooper (nee Houghton)
Richard J. Bourne
Keith Morris~
Charles Thomas Morris~
28-12-1916 ~~08-03-1962~
In Memory of a Loving Father
Kyle 'ABZ' Abbott
Sammy Mackie
Richard Leach
John Greenfield
Lee Preece
Alan Williams
John Russell
Billy Dumbrell
Chris Berns
Rob McGrath
Peter J. Ross (Belbroughton)
Ade & Hedda Nevett
David Hodges (Southam)
Robert Gough (Daventry)
Neville Evans
Nigel Stevenson
Alan Gee
Ron Brunton
Tracy & Hayley
Simon Goodyear
Laura Brett
David John Coley
John Coley
Clive Waldron
Peter Stanisstreet
Paul A. Weston
P. J. Haynes
Eileen Haynes
B. McMullan

Steve (Rennie) Renshaw
Nigel Renshaw
Peter Donohoe
Nigel Paskin
Andrea Paskin
Andrew Owen
Karl, Sue & Alfie Court
Andrew Dixon
Robert Dixon
Helen Freeman
Graham Boulton
John Billinger
Barbara Billinger
Will Hughes
Mark Harris
Ted Smith
Roy Fifield
Ivor Price
In Memoriam Gladys Price
Alan Goodall
Mark Jones
Tom Goodall
Benjamin Watts
Philip Gray (Cheltenham)
Cedric Onions
Steve Knott
Harry Moore
Patrick Flynn
John Flynn
John Partridge
Andy Bigham
Ernie Tarver
Andy Thurman
Duncan Kemp
Emma Pearson

Harry Dewell
Martin Dewell
Kathy Harrison
John Harvey
Pam Bridgewater
Dave Bridgewater
Pete Haden
Anne Edwards
Jill Downes
Katie Baragwanath
Shirley Bladon
Jason Quek Chin Keong
Malcolm John Grant
Phil (Pepperami) Grant
Aston Stephen Grant
Stephen Morris
Frank Allen
Val Allen
Mike d' Abreu
In Memory of Uncle's~
Bert & Harry
Bert Field
Ted Timmins
Robin Wilkes
Ben Richards
Zuzanna Richards
Charlie, Matilda & Oscar Richards
Stephen Morris
Barry Smith
Dan Warner
Ron Hibbs
Robert R. Abbott
Roy Cresswell
John Rudge
Clive Smith

Arthur Bent (born 4th May 1951)
K J. Knowles
Brian C. Seadon
John Knight
Terry Knight
Christopher J. Turner
Ray Pearson
Chris Bicker
Graydon Daley
Bradley Lyndon
Tilly Janie Marjorie
Trevor Wilks
Roger Wilks
David Birt
John Birt
In memory of Jack Birt
Bryan Eldridge
Loz Hawkes
Mike Joiner
John Harrison
Malc Jones
Barrie Rhodes
Philip Fellows
Grace Fellows
David B. Collins
Nick Danks
Mark Goodwin
David Goodwin
Eddie Ratcliffe
Ross Leach (Staines)
David Wright
Graydon Daley, Bradley Lyndon and Tilly Janie Marjorie
In Memoriam of Sarah-Jane (Janie) Goodall
Dedicated to the memory of my younger brother~
Paul Stephen Abbott
1968-2008

great gift ideas from the CARTOONSTORE

check out our website now - www.cartoonstore.co.uk

INCREDIBLE CARTOON PORTRAITS

PRODUCED TO YOUR INSTRUCTIONS FROM PHOTOGRAPHS

Give someone a present they'll NEVER forget

Prices start at just £45 for an original cartoon

SPORTS - COMEDY - TV & FILM - MUSIC

Thousands of exclusive sporting and celebrity cartoons, available from just £2.50

Want more information?
d to check an idea with us?
ing or mail for immediate personal attention.
No pressure!!

AMAZE YOUR FRIENDS

SEND US A PHOTOGRAPH OF SOMEONE AND WE WILL PRODUCE A QUALITY PROFESSIONAL CARTOON, THEN ADD YOUR CHOICE OF STARS IN THE BACKGROUND.

A TOTALLY UNIQUE GIFT.
SEE OUR WEBSITE FOR DETAILS

make someones day!

ASTON VILLA superstars
MALONEY - YOUNG - CAREW - KELLY - AGBONLAHOR - MELLBERG - PETROV

Send us a photo - we'll put them in the kit - then put them in the picture!

1630 638828 - sales@cartoonstore.co.uk
www.cartoonstore.co.uk

Colin J. Abbott
Debra A. Abbott

In Safe Hands

Nigel Sims' Football Memories

Foreword by
Charlie Aitken

In aid of **acorns** *Care for the child, support for the family*

In Safe Hands, By Colin J Abbott

The book 'In Safe Hands' charts the early Derbyshire childhood life of Nigel Sims and then onto his professional football career that lasted just short of two decades. Regularly described by a later generation, as Aston Villa's best post-war 'keeper, he started on the groundstaff at Wolverhampton Wanderers as a youngster, then rose to stardom - being part of the victorious Aston Villa FA Cup side of 1957 whose seventh win was an outright record. Charlie Aitken an ex-teammate of Nigel's kindly submitted the foreword for the book and Sir Doug Ellis has also penned a few lines. Former Villa players, Wylie, Burrows, Deakin and MacEwan also added thoughts and memories. The purpose for the book was to raise funds to enable Nigel Sims to have the surgery he requires, the injuries being a direct result of his time playing professional football. It would also be a tool to raise funds for Aston Villa's charity partner Acorns Childrens Hospice to whom my wife and I have personal links.

Book costs £16.95 and is available from all official Aston Villa stores, via abz publications on the amazon website, follow our link at www.nigelsims.co.uk or contact the author directly at cjohnabb@hotmail.com

Testimonies

A most interesting read - brilliantly put together telling the story of a great Villa legend and hero.
MICK TILT

Takes me back to when i was eight or nine. Absolutely, wonderfully well written. Nigel was my boyhood hero and my dad used to tell me off for watching Nigel and not the game.
GRAHAM BOULTON

The book is from an interesting era about a very, very interesting person against a backdrop of a proper Football Club - an institution. Superbly well written with wonderful content.
RON BRUNTON

I think its fantastic really and I never thought about writing a book until I met you. A beautiful book written by Colin and his wife Debra, I am very proud.
NIGEL SIMS

www.abzpublications.co.uk